Religion and Spirituality
in Korean America

The Asian American Experience

Series Editor
Roger Daniels, Series Editor

A list of books in the series appears at the end of this book.

Religion and Spirituality in Korean America

Edited by
David K. Yoo
and
Ruth H. Chung

UNIVERSITY OF ILLINOIS PRESS

Urbana and Chicago

Library of Congress Cataloging-in-Publication Data

Religion and spirituality in Korean America / edited by
David Yoo and Ruth H. Chung.
p. cm. — (The Asian American experience)
Includes bibliographical references (p.) and index.
ISBN-13 978-0-252-03233-2 (cloth : alk. paper)
ISBN-10 0-252-03233-0
ISBN-13 978-0-252-07474-5 (pbk. : alk. paper)
ISBN-10 0-252-07474-2
1. Korean Americans—Religion.   2. Korean Americans—Religious life.
I. Yoo, David.   II. Chung, Ruth H.
BL2525.R4614   2008
200.89'957073—dc22   2007030882

In Honor of Our Parents,

Elders Chin Hyong and Dong Myong Yoo

and

The Reverend Dr. Suk Woo and Mrs. Grace Injoo Chung

Who have given lifelong service to Korean American churches

Contents

Foreword

Roger Daniels

The historian Jay P. Dolan, writing about Irish and German Catholics in mid-nineteenth-century New York, described the immigrant church as a "fortress" into which immigrant and second-generation Catholics could retreat and find comfort, if not protection, from a hostile Protestant world. As the essays gathered under the rubric *Religion and Spirituality in Korean America,* edited by David K. Yoo and Ruth H. Chung, attest, Korean immigrants and their descendants in America, who now number more than a million, have a similarly intense relationship with their churches to a degree highly unusual among contemporary American ethnic groups.

Guided by the editors' astute introduction, which provides a pocket history of Korean Americans for those who come to the book without a grasp of the group's past, readers will find essays that focus on individual denominations—Protestant, Catholic, and Buddhist—and others that compare them. Other chapters treat generational differences, gender, religious life on college campuses, and the particular significance of adoption among Koreans. The authors, largely younger scholars, represent a variety of academic disciplines and styles so that the overall effect is of an interdisciplinary nature.

While conducting a graduate seminar a few years ago, I asked the participants to comment on the virtues and deficiencies of a volume that analyzed American life during World War II. The last student to speak, one who had recently arrived from China, answered with a question. "How is it," he asked, "that the history of a Christian country has no section in it about religion?" It was an acute criticism and one that could be made about many other historical works. While few contemporary ethnic groups have the intense concentration on religion that the *Religion and Spirituality in Korean America* essays explore, reading them not only enriches our knowledge about Korean Americans but also makes us aware of how little that dimension is explored in so much of the literature about American ethnic groups.

Acknowledgments

It has been a long journey from the initial idea for this book to its publication, and we are thankful for the chance to acknowledge the support and encouragement we have received along the way. We would like to first recognize the contributors whose work is represented in this volume for their dedication as scholars and for their commitment to better understand and document Korean American communities in the United States. Although the collective portrait we have offered of Korean American religion and spirituality is partial and fragmentary, it nevertheless constitutes a wellspring of research, reflection, and experience. We also deeply appreciate the patience and goodwill shown to us by the contributors throughout the process.

The Louisville Institute provided a seed grant that enabled us to meet in person to launch the project. Dr. Sang Hyun Lee of Princeton Seminary and the Asian American Program that he directs graciously hosted us for the gathering. During that long weekend, we not only worked but also laughed and forged a sense of community. The Reverend Kevin Park looked out for us during our stay, and Ms. Linda Tuthill of Claremont McKenna College ably oversaw many of the logistics needed to bring us all together. Ruth Chung would like to acknowledge the award of a faculty grant from the Center for Religion and Civic Culture at the University of Southern California that aided the research and writing of her contributions to the project. Similarly, David Yoo acknowledges a faculty fellowship from the John Randolph Haynes and Dora Haynes Foundation that provided important support for his chapter. We would also like to recognize staff and colleagues at our respective institutions: the Department of History at Claremont McKenna College, the Intercollegiate Department of Asian American Studies at the Claremont Colleges, and Counseling Psychology, Rossier School of Education, at the University of Southern

California. We are also thankful for the research assistance from Laura Zapi-ain and Melissa Itsara of Claremont McKenna College.

In many ways, this collection grows out of conversations with a num-ber of colleagues with whom we study the role of religion in Asian American communities. While we cannot name every person or professional setting, we would like to underscore the important place of the Asian Pacific American Religions Research Initiative (APARRI) that in recent years has been linked to the Institute for Leadership Development and Study of Pacific and Asian North American Religion (PANA Institute) at the Pacific School of Religion. Fumi-taka Matusoka, the executive director of PANA, and staff members such as Chris Chua and Debbie Lee have provided important forums for projects such as this one. Of the many people associated with APARRI and related organi-zations, we would like to acknowledge colleagues who have helped us think through this project and from whom we have benefited through conversations or written comments. Many, many thanks to Jane Iwamura, Paul Spickard, Tim Tseng, Russell Jeung, David Kyuman Kim, Tony Alumkal, Lori Pierce, Caro-lyn Chen, Pyong Gap Min, Peter Cha, and the late Steffi San Buenaventura. At the University of Illinois Press, we have been fortunate to work with series editor Roger Daniels and with editor Laurie Matheson and her staff.

Years ago we thought about working on a project together, and this collection is the result. It is fitting that this collection is about a subject that has been such an important influence in our lives. Our siblings and their fami-lies have been an important source of support for many years, and we thank them for their many kindnesses. Our two boys, Jonathan and Joshua, have been too young to know much about the "book report" that we have been working on, but they have made their own contributions by being who they are. They are our pride and joy, and our hope is that one day they will be able to read and to learn from this collection. Finally, we dedicate this volume to our parents, who have given so much to us for so long and who have sacrificed and continue to work on behalf of Korean American faith communities.

Introduction

David K. Yoo and Ruth H. Chung

Although it could be said of many subjects, the study of religion and spirituality by nature borders on the absurd. How does one grasp the ungraspable, make known the unknowable, and speak of mysteries that defy words? Perhaps the place to start is to acknowledge the limits of any inquiry. These essays only begin to address the complexity of religion and spirituality found in the individuals, families, organizations, and other entities that collectively constitute Korean America. If these studies are offered in a spirit of humility, then it is also the case that each of the contributors seeks to shed light on an area of experience that rests near the center of this particular community.

It is our contention that the study of religion and spirituality cannot be confined to the sites that have most commonly been associated with the topic. While formal religious traditions and institutions are certainly important to the body of work in this collection, Korean American religion and spirituality can also be found in the process of migration, on college and university campuses, and within a variety of human relationships. Moreover, the subject matters reflected in these chapters are permeable, spilling over and complicating, as it were, boundaries or categories such as religion, culture, and society. Readers will also note in these essays an emphasis on the multiple and plural in recognition of the ways in which religion and spirituality in Korean America are situated simultaneously in varied contexts such as locality, race, and generation.[1]

The collection builds upon and joins several recent edited volumes that focus on the role of religion among Asian and Pacific Islander communities. These projects have brought a sense of critical mass and movement to the topic that previously was reflected in scattered publications across a number of academic disciplines.[2] Some of the work on immigrant populations and religions in the United States since the passage of the 1965 Immigration Act has included Asian

American groups and provided important outlets for research.[3] Focused on a particular group, this volume draws upon a number of publications on Korean Americans, including several studies that have examined particular aspects of religion such as its relation to family structures and women's experiences.[4] While the remainder of the introduction will provide a brief overview of Korean America, spell out some key themes and contributions, and discuss specific choices entailed in this collection, it should be stated that the volume is largely concerned with issues in the post-1965 era. Korean Americans have been in the United States since 1903, but the most recent wave of immigration has accounted for the large demographic upswing of this group. In terms of religious orientation, the essays are primarily about Protestant Christianity. While there is some coverage of Roman Catholicism and Buddhism, the emphasis on Protestant Christianity reflects the disproportionate influence of this tradition among Korean Americans. Before turning to the collection itself, we first provide a quick sketch of Korean America with a specific interest in the place of religion.[5]

BRIEF OVERVIEW OF KOREAN AMERICA

The U.S. Census for 2000 lists the Korean American population at 1.1 million.[6] Korean Americans have been in the United States for more than a century, and their history can be characterized by three waves of immigration and settlement: labor, picture brides, and independence (1903–1945); the postwar period (1945–1965); and the post-1965 period (1965–present). In every wave, religion, as it has manifested itself through institutions, ideas, and practices, has been a critical framework by which Korean Americans have given shape to their times. Religion has provided its adherents with vital social services, racial-ethnic spaces, and a means of faith and meaning. Recent studies point to the vitality of religion, evident in the more than 3,000 Korean American Protestant Christian churches nationwide.[7] There are a reported 154 Korean American Catholic parishes, and 89 Buddhist temples serve Koreans in the United States.[8] While figures vary, survey data suggests that nearly 80 percent of Korean Americans are affiliated with Protestant ethnic churches, 11 percent are Roman Catholics, 5 percent are Buddhists, and 4 percent are other or no religion.[9] Koreans in the United States—past and present—have been deeply influenced by the dominance, diversity, and at times divisiveness of religious experience.

Labor, Picture Brides, and Independence (1903–1945)

The first wave of Koreans, numbering approximately eighty-five hundred, entered the United States beginning in 1903 largely as a labor force for sugar cane plantations in Hawaii. Religion played an important role from the very start, as recruiters for American companies in Korea called upon Protestant missionaries in Korea to persuade those in their care to make the journey to the islands. As a result, Protestant Christians were among the first Korean Americans to venture to the United States, and approximately 40 percent of the early community claimed to be Christian.[10] Congregations on plantations, in Honolulu as well as on the mainland, quickly became the gathering place for Korean Americans and served as clearinghouses of information and social services. Churches also provided spaces, under the umbrella of religion, to explore a wide range of issues, including their status as racial-ethnic minorities in the United States and their role in the independence movement to free Korea from Japanese colonial rule. Key immigrant-expatriate leaders such as Ahn Chang-ho, Pak Yong-Man, and Syngman Rhee all were influenced by the reform-minded ideas based in the Christian institutions (schools, hospitals, churches) that had helped shaped their worldviews. Moreover, Korean Americans looked to religion for a sense of meaning amid the often harsh realities of life and labor that they encountered. At the same time, religion could also be the source of division, as churches and religious organizations could not but be enmeshed in the politics of community formation. For better and worse, religion—represented in the mix of the theological, cultural, political, and social—infused the lives of the majority of Korean Americans.

Postwar Period (1945–1965)

The second wave of migration, marked by the end of World War II, Japanese colonialism, and the Korean War (1950–1953), included Korean wives of American servicemen and their children, adoptees, and professional workers and students. Ties to the United States via the military, educational institutions, and church-related institutions provided select Koreans a means of starting new lives in America.

While the early gender ratio of males to females for immigrants was 10:1, during the postwar period the ratio was 1:3.5. The answer "housewife" was given as the majority answer for surveys that included the category of occupation.[11] Approximately seven thousand military wives entered during this period, often facing isolated circumstances on U.S. military bases. Many of these women brought their relatives to the United States during the post-1965 period.[12] Another group to enter during this period, also connected to the military and war, were the approximate seven thousand children adopted by American families largely through the Holt Adoption Agency. Many of these adoptees were of Amerasian racial background (46 percent Korean and European American and 13 percent Korean and African American). They embodied the legacy of the U.S. occupation of Korea, the Korean War, and the U.S.–South Korean military complex.[13] The final group, about six thousand persons, consisted of Korean students enrolled at U.S. universities and colleges. Students and their families were the most visible part of this wave within Korean American communities and religious institutions, as military brides and adoptees were often marginalized within the Korean American as well as other communities of which they were a part. The presence of students and their families in existing religious institutions would serve as a precursor of things to come in the post-1965 period. With the original first-generation immigrants aging and passing and with the second generation coming of age into full adulthood, the arrival of Korean immigrants after 1965 meant new growth and change, breaking with the restrictive immigration laws that had closed the door for decades.

Post-1965 Period (1965–Present)

The passage of new immigration legislation by the United States in 1965 removed restrictive and discriminatory measures that had been firmly in place for close to five decades. Korean immigrants, along with others from Asia, entered the United States in increasingly larger numbers, and at the peak in the mid-1980s, figures topped thirty thousand persons per year. This influx transformed smaller historic Korean American communities in urban settings such as Los Angeles and New York, and these newer immigrants and their families make up the majority of the million or so Korean Americans in the country today. The boom in the population has been accompanied by a substantial increase in the number of immigrant churches, temples, and other religious organizations. This largely Protestant phenomenon in part reflects the growth and spread of Protestant Christianity in Korea, but it is also clear that many men and women have affiliated with churches after their arrival in the United States.

Religion continues to be the heart of this racial-ethnic community, informing the daily lives of men and women in the midst of the pressures of economic survival and sociocultural adjustments set into motion by the migration and settlement process. Institutions range from small house-based groups to megachurches that rival any religious organization in the country in terms of membership, programming, and resources. Religion has continued to play a critical social service function for Korean Americans, creating webs of relationships that attend to a host of needs. Religious and racial-ethnic space, moreover, has been intertwined for Korean Americans, just as it has been for so many other immigrant groups throughout our nation's history. Religious institutions have offered psychic and physical space within which individuals and communities affirmed traditions and customs from the home country, even while wrestling with the changes and conflict engendered by new settings. As a source of faith and meaning and as a locus of ritual and spiritual practice, religion has been and continues to be a powerful and enduring influence in the lives of the diversity that is Korean America, from attending services in churches and temples to the less institutional and more popular forms of devotion and ritual activities.

Perhaps the defining moment of the post-1965 period has been the 1992 Los Angeles riots. The ways that this event and its related issues have been refracted through the religious landscape of Korean America—from joint services with African American congregations to community assistance programs to apathy, denial, and neglect—suggest that while religion constitutes the core of this community, its nature is by no means uniform. The rise of second-generation English-speaking Korean American, Pan-Asian American, and multiracial and multiethnic institutions signals the dawning of a new era. Some of the issues raised here will be discussed further in the sections ahead.

KEY THEMES

In an effort to provide a road map for the collection, the next section of the introduction will focus on key themes that run through the various individual chapters. While no single, neatly identified thread runs throughout the text, three themes serve as one possible way to frame the issues that the individual essays address even while recognizing that such categories do not necessarily do justice to the breadth of material contained therein. Race, diaspora, and improvisation are offered as a way to frame the collection and to suggest how our essays contribute to the study of religion and spirituality in the United States. Invoking terms such as "race" and "diaspora" potentially open up long-standing and contested debates and discussions about definitions, theorizing, and the like. The aim in using such words is not so much to engage in those debates and discussions but rather to briefly highlight how such concepts in light of the work presented here provide a chance to think critically and creatively about the study of American religion and spirituality.

Race

Studies of American religion have been influenced heavily by a model of immigration and assimilation in which the standard narrative structure is such that people from all over the world have come to these shores and brought with them their religious traditions and practices. Religion has served as an important means by which these groups have fashioned a sense of community based on shared languages and customs. Because of the lack of an established religion and the constitutional guarantee protecting the freedom of religion, many groups have found religious spaces important to their transition to life in the United States. While it is the case that most groups have encountered initial hostility and even persecution, over time the Protestant dominance has given way to a more inclusive Judeo-Christian framework in which Catholicism and Judaism have become American religions. The narrative rings true in certain cases, and yet the exceptions to the rule force us to reconsider the pattern. One major exception is the presence and persistence of race. Native Americans obviously do not fit within a traditional immigrant framework, nor do African Americans. Latinos in conquered territory also complicate the story and disturb the unidirectional westward movement usually invoked. The various Asian American groups who have immigrated to the United States most closely resemble the pattern of European migration and settlement but vary in significant ways, even for those groups, such as Korean Americans, who are largely Christian. Part of what this volume attests to is that it is not coincidental that these four groups, despite real differences between them, have been marked by race in ways that set them apart, religiously and otherwise. Indeed, the very process of inclusion of European groups into an American white identity has been predicated upon the exclusion and othering of these so-called problem people.[14] The constructions of race over time, well documented by numerous scholars, represent a complicated trajectory for the nation as a whole as well as for its various parts. Nevertheless, it is safe to say that race has remained a critical and yet largely segregated dimension of the study of religion in the United States.[15]

Race underscores a deep ambivalence for Korean Americans in their relation to the nation and, more specifically, to the process of becoming Americans. All immigrants and their children who have come to the United States have wrestled with such issues, but the factor of race for Korean Americans has entailed a perpetual foreignness that has been a feature of Asian immigration to the United States. Given the fact that the majority of Korean Americans are Protestant Christians, a natural assumption is that religion has served the greater acceptance of this group, but we would argue that the case of African American Christianity is more instructive. Race has proved to be more salient than religion for Korean Americans, supporting the Reverend Dr. Martin Luther King Jr.'s oft-cited statement that eleven o'clock on Sunday morning is the most segregated hour in America. Time has done little to dispel King's words, as a recent study reports that about 7 percent of Protestant churches and 15 percent of Catholic parishes in the United States are multiracial (in which no single racial group is 80 percent or more of an institution).[16] The story of Korean Americans reminds us that the hospitality rendered in images such as the Statue of Liberty have been more the ideal than the reality, especially for those for whom racialization has endured.

Race as a specific category of analysis is relatively muted in the essays that follow, but it informs every chapter. If the experiences of Korean Americans cannot and should not be reduced to race, then at the same time, race impinges on nearly every dimension of those experiences because of the ways that race is so deeply embedded into the fabric of American life. Howard Winant's study of race and democracy since World War II makes even a stronger case for the centrality of race when he says that "race must be grasped as a fundamental condition of individual and collective identity, a permanent, although tremendously flexible, dimension of global social structure."[17] In terms of the essays that follow, race forms what might be considered a consciousness that reflects the ways it operates within the spaces of religion and spirituality and how those spaces are also connected to the social structures, cultural forms, and imaginations that inhabit Korean America. David Kyuman Kim's ruminations about the inscriptions of race (and diaspora) suggest how Koreans Americans give shape to their moral, political, and existential commitments and actions as individuals and communities and how questions of identity are about finding meaningful ways of being in the world.[18]

Korean Americans are part of a legacy of race that has marked and set some groups apart from others, but their experiences also attest to the fact that all peoples in the United States are racialized in one way or another. The racial legacy of the United States, moreover, has been tied to religion from the very beginning and has continued in its variations over the course of our nation's history. The demonization and racialized discourse regarding Islam since September 11, 2001, is only the most recent example. In underscoring the importance of race, we also expressly reject the notion that race is somehow only or largely relevant to certain groups and instead argue that there is a pressing need to view all of American religion and spirituality through the complicated lens of race. Placing this category in the center helps us to more accurately understand the phenomena itself.

Diaspora

As with the theme of race, the concept of diaspora informs the volume in signaling the relationships that individuals and communities have to nation-states. Robin Cohen's mapping of the term into the typologies of victim, labor, trade, imperial, and cultural diasporas is suggestive of the ways in which the term has developed over time in different parts of the world as well as its internal complexities and variety. Cohen's point about how groups encountering hostility and resentment may turn to diaspora to speak to issues of alienation and detachment is especially relevant in the case of Korean Americans.[19] Jana Evans Braziel and Anita Mannur offer further perspective on diaspora by saying that "where diaspora addresses the migrations and displacements of subjects, transnationalism also includes the movements of information through cybernetics, as well as traffic in goods, products, and capital across geopolitical terrains through multinational corporations." The two concepts are closely linked, but the emphasis within diaspora on the fundamentally human phenomenon versus the more impersonal forces embedded in transnationalism is a helpful shorthand for thinking about the concept of religion and spirituality in Korean America.[20] For some Korean Americans, especially Christians, the religious dimension of diaspora rooted in the Jewish experience and exilic motif (seen for instance in Psalm 137) has been a powerful symbol for understanding their migratory experiences.

Whether through the sending of Roman Catholic priests to Korean American parishes or in the movement of missionaries between Korea and the United States as well as other parts of the world, various chapters incorporate the theme of diaspora. The genealogy of the term is less important for our purposes than the idea that many Korean Americans, especially immigrants, give meaning to their identities—religious, racial-ethnic, and so on—that include but also transcend the nation-state. This is certainly not unique to Korean Americans, especially in recent decades when ease of travel and global networks of communication and technology (including popular culture), shrink the physical and psychic distances between different parts of the world. And religion and spirituality are by no means a new dimension of diaspora, but in many ways they are a prime example and even a defining feature of these terms, as in the case of the Jewish diaspora and the origins of this term.

Religion and spirituality in Korean America necessarily invoke the ties between Korea and the United States. An important part of the tangle in those relations involved the arrival of U.S. Protestant missionaries in Korea in the late nineteenth century. The connections formed—involving churches, schools, and hospitals as well as religious worldviews—were linked to notions of American civilization and progress, representing part of the ideological and material mix of a Korea in upheaval during the late Chosun (1392–1910) and Japanese colonial (1910–1945) periods. The presence of the United States in the division of Korea, the Korean War, and its continuing role in the Republic of Korea (South Korea) place the development of Korean American religion and spirituality into a broader and much lengthier frame than post-1965 immigration might suggest. The growth and development of Korean Christianity, for instance, has had bearings upon the trajectories that Korean American Christianity has taken, not only in terms of immigrants from Christian backgrounds but also in styles of leadership, denominational structures, pastoral development, and joint ventures between Korean American and Korean Christians in the sending of missionaries. The migration and settlement of Koreans in the United States, especially Protestant Christians, represents a dynamic exchange of peoples, capital, ideas, and institutions that have had profound and lasting implications for all involved. At stake have been (and continue to be) issues of power, neocolonialism, and human rights, to mention only a few.[21]

To the extent that Koreans in the United States form part of a global diaspora, the notion of home takes on significance as immigrants and successive generations negotiate their location within nation-states and other forms of community. As racialized people in the United States, some Korean Americans have found meaning in situating themselves as part of an overseas Korean community, even as Korea itself undergoes change. The search for home for others includes their religious identities, and diaspora comes into play for traditions such as Buddhism and Christianity (Catholic and Protestant) since there have been close relationships between religious communities in the United States and Korea and, by extension, to other parts of the world that have been settled by Koreans. Like all migratory peoples, Koreans in the United States have relied on various strategies to carve out spaces for themselves and those close to them, ranging from vibrant ongoing relations with the homeland to an array of diasporic imaginings that collectively represent multiple variations on a theme.

And yet, the working out of homemaking in the diaspora, as it includes immigration to and life in the United States, has hardly been a uniform or neutral process. This fact was painfully made evident in the 1992 Los Angeles riots/uprisings, an event that many have characterized as a wake-up call for Korean America. The ugly racialized politics that unfolded left largely unexamined the structural issues that set up the violence and destruction. The spin of mainstream media and the absence of police and fire departments spoke volumes about privilege and for whom the motto "to protect and serve" was intended.[22] Amid the chaos, some people turned to their faith communities to try to make sense of what had happened, and while not without its shortcomings, efforts by Korean American and African American Christians to build coalitions and to foster greater dialogue offered a measure of hope amid the ashes.[23] In the search for meaning and in the search for home, many Korean Americans questioned their place in the United States, and this collection of essays reflects the role that diaspora has and continues to play in the study of religion and spirituality in the United States.

Improvisation

The third key theme, improvisation, is drawn from the world of jazz music and underscores the tremendous creativity that Korean Americans have exhibited in working out their spirituality and in the making of sacred spaces. Several of the authors in this volume illustrate how the post-1965 English-speaking Korean Americans have forged their own religiosity that borrows from the immigrant congregations that have been part of their upbringing but also from campus ministries, Pan-Asian, and multiracial and multiethnic religious settings. The results demonstrate the changes that are happening in our midst, with several models emerging from English-language congregations nested within immigrant churches as well as independent churches and other variations. Never-married women have fashioned their own sense of religion and spirituality that resists any singular notions of those categories in Korean America. How Buddhists face the dominance of Protestant Christianity among Korean Americans also suggests something of the creativity of women and men and communities. Improvisation is about the adaptability, flexibility, and continuing innovation of individuals, institutions, and communities as they live out and practice their religion and spirituality.

Such improvisation can also be conceptualized in terms of place or locale, and it is the case that the bulk of the essays are situated in large metropolitan areas in the United States. As Robert Orsi points out, urban spaces are often not thought of as religious spaces, but Korean American experiences, as those of so many others, demonstrate how misguided such a notion is.[24] Urban and suburban physical spaces have been themselves important sites and sources of the improvisation for Korean Americans. Southern California is home to the largest population of Korean Americans, and given the strong presence of evangelical Christianity in the region that cuts across racial-ethnic groups, it is not surprising to see interesting convergences of worldviews, peoples as well as innovative institutional configurations. College campuses, as one of the essays illustrates, are fertile spaces for this mixture. It is not simply the case that religion and spirituality take place in the metropole, as it does anywhere. Rather, something dynamic takes place in which the physical, psychic, and social intertwine, and this provides a unique grounding for religion and spirituality.[25]

If metropolitan areas serve as sites of Korean American religious improvisations, then this theme also has to do with the charting of change in contemporary American religion. In focusing on race, this volume joins the work of others in highlighting the persistence of racial markers, even while recognizing the fluid ways in which constructions of race continue to change. On the most basic level, the point is that race needs to be a central focus of the study of religion and spirituality in the United States because of the interpenetration of both spheres and the larger context of the nation. The theme of diaspora pushes the boundaries beyond the nation-state, reminding us not only of the ways that people, communities, and institutions occupy multiple spaces at the same time but also that experiences of groups such as Korean Americans call into question standard narratives of religion, migration, and settlement in the United States. The improvisational qualities represented in this collection speak to the continual refashioning of religion and spirituality to reflect changing circumstances and to find and make meaning within such contexts. All these themes suggest why religion and spirituality are such important, if understudied, dimensions of human experience, revealing how it is that spaces are made sacred within the ambivalences that characterize Korean America.

ABOUT THE ESSAYS

The first set of essays, grouped together under the heading "Traditions," examine Roman Catholic, Buddhist, and Protestant faith communities. Although the focus is upon Protestant Christianity among Korean Americans, the experiences of adherents of other traditions as well as the relationships between them form an important part of Korean American religion and spirituality. The lead article by Anselm Min on Korean American Catholicism provides a helpful overview of this largely neglected group, tying the experiences of those in the United States with the real and continuing ties to Catholicism in Korea. Readers will not likely be surprised that Korean Catholics have found a measure of solace and comfort from the hardships of migration and racism in their parishes. It might be less obvious, however, to find that the diasporic claims of Korean Catholicism on religious life in the United States have been as divisive as they have been ameliorative.

Sharon Suh's study of a Los Angeles–based Buddhist temple also sheds light on a little-known dimension of Korean America religion and spirituality. Her essay discusses the long shadow cast by Korean American Protestantism and the efforts by Buddhists to carve out their own religious sensibility, not only as adherents of a particular religious tradition but also as Koreans situated in the United States. Suh's in-depth interviews reveal interesting interpretations by members of the temple on their status as Americans and other topics such as their children's religious affiliations. Like many of the essays, Suh's research touches on the ambiguousness and ambivalence that mark Korean America and, in this instance, from the perspective of Korean American Buddhism.

In a study of Korean American Buddhists and Protestants, Okyun Kwon notes that immigration has often increased the overall religious participation of the immigrants. Kwon's research is based on surveys, interviews, and participant observation in the New York City metropolitan area. While several studies have focused on the functions and roles of religion among Korean Americans, Kwon examines the role of religious beliefs. Kwon concludes that Korean American Buddhists tend to be more focused on the self, with self-reliant religious practices such as home shrines. Protestants tend to focus more on obedience to the will and guidance of a supernatural power, with a more other-reliant form of spiritual practice.

The second section of the volume discusses lived religious experience loosely gathered as passages of one kind or another. Jae Ran Kim's essay examines the role of religion in the world of Korean adoption to the United States. As Kim points out, this passage while physical and psychological is also spiritual, especially since the agencies facilitating the adoptions have been faith-based organizations. Ironically, because the vast majority of adoptees have been placed with European American families, these women and men have rarely surfaced within the network of Korean American churches.

Sang Hyun Lee addresses the passage into the spiritual practice of worship. Lee explores how Korean Americans live in a world marked by ambiguity and how their experience of liminality is reflected in worship within the Christian context. Although the position of being in-between can be a source of pain and loss, Lee suggests that it can also serve as a source of positive transformation and creative action for Korean Americans. This essay suggests the improvisational possibilities for Korean Americans, even as questions of race and diaspora inform his exploration.

Jung Ha Kim's essay on never-married women asks how Korean American Christian women's experiences demonstrate both active participation in organized religious institutions and spiritual agency to recognize the sacred presence in their own everyday lives. In the process, Kim discovers how this particular subset of women operates as religious practitioners as well as theological innovators. The status of being never-married also illustrates the diversity of women's experiences and how multiple social locations can be occupied at the same time. Kim focuses on survey and oral history research to document how the consciousness of her subjects address the roles of race, ethnicity, gender, and marital status play in the construction of religion and spirituality.

Ruth H. Chung and Sung Hyun Um's essay also takes up the theme of marriage among Korean Americans. Based on survey data of immigrant, 1.5-generation, and second-generation couples, Chung and Um examine religiosity as a predictor of marital commitment and satisfaction. Their findings suggest that more frequent church attendance contributes to greater marital commitment. Such was not necessarily the case for marital satisfaction.

The essays in this last section of this collection, "From Generation to Generation," are all concerned with how 1.5-generation and second-generation

Korean Americans, who are largely English-speaking, are expressing their religion and spirituality. At the same time, many of the essays touch upon how Korean American religion and spirituality is intergenerational. While the last three essays focus on the younger generations, the presence of the immigrant generation is felt if not always seen. Sharon Kim tracks the creative and varied ways that second-generation ministries are unfolding in Southern California. She argues that these children of immigrants do not fit into the standard categories marked by assumptions of assimilation or by models strictly understood within the context of religious pluralism that stress ethnic maintenance. Kim's chapter is a solid example of the theme of improvisation, and her research is based upon extensive interviews and fieldwork conducted over many years. Her findings point to the interplay of race, ethnicity, generation, and religion.

Rebecca Kim moves her questions about the next generation to the college campus and asks why Korean American Christians in a university setting with multiple religious organizations have chosen to participate in ethnic-specific (Korean American) ones. The students in her study have grown up in largely European American majority suburbs and have had ample exposure to and familiarity with mainstream society and culture. High levels of education and acculturation would suggest lowering levels of racial-ethnic orientation, but Kim's research suggests otherwise. Shared culture and identity issues for many of these Korean Americans proved to be important factors in choosing how to live out their religious commitments, including notions of such spaces as their religious organizations providing a sense of home.

In the final essay, David Yoo takes a historical view of generational transition through a case study of a particular Korean American Christian congregation in Los Angeles. Celebrating its centennial in the spring of 2004, this historic church has been a site witness to and part of the entire scope of Korean American experience in Southern California. Original second-generation issues in this church date to the 1930s, and the experiences of the church in the post-1965 era are instructive in thinking about how change over time takes place. While some of the story of this congregation is familiar ground to religion in the United States, other aspects involving race and the current demographics of Asian America and Korea America also represent new twists.

A NOTE ON METHOD AND SUBJECTIVITY

While the authors in this volume have been trained in various disciplines of academic study, the volume is intended to bring together a variety of perspectives that provide multiple entry points into the topic at hand. Indeed, it is the interest in Korean American religion and spirituality, rather than any particular method or disciplinary approach, that has spawned the work presented here and brought this collection into being. At the same time, it is important to note that many of the authors in this study have conducted extensive fieldwork, including in-depth interviews, survey research, and participant observation. Along with the other contributions to the study of religion and spirituality in the United States, the data contained in these essays represent a valuable source of information and documentation.

In terms of locating ourselves in this study, it is the case that all of the contributors are of Korean ancestry. Some of us came to the United States for study,[26] others immigrated with their families as youths[27] or as an adoptee,[28] and some are U.S. born and raised.[29] While each of the authors might define what it means to be Korean American differently, it is the case that all of us, to varying levels, bring our own experiences into the process of studying religion and spirituality. Many of the authors in their chapters situate themselves in terms of religious affiliation (or nonaffiliation), and the range of experience on this front further informs insider and outsider issues. Although the contributors operate from a number of fields that have varying stances on the issue of objectivity, we, the editors, think it is a fair statement that all of the essays here reflect particular perspectives that contain our biases (conscious and unconscious) and that the aim of the volume is not to provide a definitive word on the subject but rather to contribute to an ongoing conversation.[30]

NOTES

1. The literature in spatial theory is expansive, but we have found Michael J. Dear and Steven Flusty, eds., *The Spaces of Postmodernity: Readings in Human Geography* (Oxford: Blackwell, 2002) helpful in thinking about how the concept of space can provide a vehicle for exploring religion and spirituality in Korean America. Also helpful are David Chidester and Edward T. Linenthal, eds., *American Sacred Space* (Bloomington: Indiana University Press, 1995), and Kate A. Berry and Martha Henderson, eds., *Geographical Identities in Ethnic America: Race, Space, and Place* (Reno: University of Nevada Press, 2002).

2. See Tony Carnes and Fenggang Yang, eds., *Asian American Religions: The Making and Remaking of Borders and Boundaries* (New York: New York University Press, 2004); Jane N. Iwamura and Paul Spickard, eds., *Revealing the Sacred in Asian Pacific America* (New York: Routledge, 2003); Pyong Gap Min and Jung Ha Kim, eds., *Religions in Asian America: Building Faith Communities* (Walnut Creek, CA: Altamira, 2002); David Yoo, ed., *New Spiritual Homes* (Honolulu: University of Hawaii Press, 1999). The temptation in listing these recent works is to overlook the fine work of earlier scholars who have laid the foundations for what might now be seen as a subfield in its own right. Space does not allow a listing here, but all of the

cited works above bear witness to the contributions of these scholars, and, of course, the work continues.

3. To cite only a couple of examples: R. Stephen Warner and Judith G. Wittner, eds., *Gatherings in Diaspora: Religious Communities and the New Immigration* (Philadelphia: Temple University Press, 1998), and Helen Rose Ebaugh and Janet Salzman Chafetz, eds., *Religion and the New Immigrants: Continuities and Adaptations in Immigrant Congregations* (Walnut Creek, CA: Altamira, 2000).

4. Several studies provide a helpful overview of contemporary Korean American experience. See *Amerasia Journal: What Does It Mean to Be Korean American Today?* 30(1) (2004), which represents the second of a two-part special issue; Mary Yu Danico, *The 1.5 Generation: Becoming Korean American in Hawaii* (Honolulu: University of Hawaii Press, 2004); Kyeyoung Park, *The Korean American Dream: Immigrants and Small Business in New York City* (Ithaca, NY: Cornell University Press, 1997); In-Jin Yoon, *On My Own: Korean Businesses and Race Relations in America* (Chicago: University of Chicago Press, 1997); Pyong Gap Min, *Caught in the Middle: Korean Merchants in America's Multiethnic Cities* (Berkeley: University of California Press, 1996). Several books have been published that focus on various aspects of religious life among Korean Americans, including Su Yon Pak, Unzu Lee, Jung Ha Kim, and Myung Ji Cho, *Singing the Lord's Song in a New Land: Korean American Practices of Faith* (Louisville, KY: Westminster John Knox Press, 2005); Sharon A. Suh, *Being Buddhist in a Christian World: Gender and Community in a Korean American Temple* (Seattle: University of Washington Press, 2004); Young Lee Hertig, *Cultural Tug of War: The Korean Immigrant Family and Church in Transition* (Nashville: Abingdon, 2001); Ho-Youn Kwon, Kwang Chung Kim, and R. Stephen Warner, eds., *Korean Americans and Their Religions: Pilgrims and Missionaries from a Different Shore* (University Park: Pennsylvania State University Press, 2001); Jung Ha Kim, *Bridge-makers and Cross-bearers: Korean-American Women and the Church* (Atlanta: Scholars Press, 1997); Victoria H. Kwon, *Entrepreneurship and Religion: Korean Immigrants in Houston, Texas* (New York: Garland, 1997); Ai Ra Kim, *Women Struggling for a New Life: The Role of Religion in the Cultural Passage from Korea to America* (Albany: State University of New York Press, 1996). Numerous book chapters and journal articles have also been published.

5. Because others have provided detailed information on Korean American immigration, we will only provide a minimal commentary and will point readers searching for more information to the following texts: Won Moo Hurh, *Korean Americans* (New York: Greenwood, 1998); Bong-youn Choy, *Koreans in America* (Chicago: Nelson-Hall, 1979); Wayne Patterson, *The Korean Frontier in America: Immigration to Hawaii, 1896–1910* (Honolulu: University of Hawaii Press, 1988); Wayne Patterson, *The Ilse: First Generation Korean Immigrants in Hawaii, 1903–1973* (Honolulu: University of Hawaii Press, 2000).

6. Census figures offer some guideline in terms of population, but it is likely that the figure is low because of underreporting and Koreans who entered the country unofficially.

7. Pei-te Lien and Tony Carnes, "The Religious Demography of Asian American Boundary Crossing," in Tony Carnes and Fenggang Yang, eds., *Asian American*

Religions: The Making and Remaking of Borders and Boundaries (New York: New York University Press, 2004), 48.

8. Ibid., 49, and Suh, *Being Buddhist in a Christian World,* 3–4.

9. Hurh, *Korean Americans,* 24; Lien and Carnes, "The Religious Demography of Asian American Boundary Crossing," 48–49.

10. Hurh, *Korean Americans,* 106.

11. Ibid., 38–39.

12. Jung Ha Kim, "Korean American Protestant Faith Communities in the United States," in Pyong Gap Min and Jung Ha Kim, eds., *Religions in Asian America: Building Faith Communities* (Walnut Creek, CA: Altamira, 2002), 194. See Ji-Yeon Yuh, *Beyond the Shadow of Camptown: Korean Military Brides in America* (New York: New York University Press, 2002).

13. Kim, "Korean American Protestant Faith Communities in the United States," 193.

14. See, for instance, George Lipsitz, *The Possessive Investment in Whiteness: How White People Profit from Identity Politics* (Philadelphia: Temple University Press, 1998); David Roediger, *The Wages of Whiteness: Race and the Making of the American Working Class* (London: Verso, 1991); Tomas Almaguer, *Racial Fault Lines: The Historical Origins of White Supremacy in California* (Berkeley: University of California Press, 1994); Matthew Frye Jacobsen, *Whiteness of a Different Color* (Cambridge: Harvard University Press, 1998).

15. Among the many fine works, see Alexander Saxton, *The Rise and Fall of the White Republic: Class Politics and Mass Culture in Nineteenth-Century America* (New York: Verso, 1991); Gary Gerstle, *The American Crucible: Race and Nation in the Twentieth Century* (Princeton, NJ: Princeton University Press, 2001); Howard Winant, *The World Is a Ghetto: Race and Democracy since World War II* (New York: Basic Books, 2001); Philomena Essed and David Theo Goldberg, eds., *Race Critical Theories* (Oxford, UK: Blackwell Publishers, 2002). The works by Winant and the collection edited by Essed and Goldberg issue a call for race to move beyond national borders, a call especially appropriate for race studies in the United States.

16. The Congregations Project website is http://www.congregations.info/index .html, and the statistics are drawn from its quick facts page.

17. Winant, *The World Is a Ghetto,* 3. He makes a persuasive case for the study of race in global terms, but his case for the centrality of race can and has been made for the United States.

18. David Kyuman Kim, "Enchanting Diaporas, Asian Americans, and the Passionate Attachment of Race," in Jane N. Iwamura and Paul Spickard, eds., *Revealing the Sacred in Asian Pacific America* (New York: Routledge, 2003), 334–37.

19. Robin Cohen, *Global Diasporas: An Introduction* (Seattle: University of Washington Press, 1997), ix–xi.

20. Jana Evans Braziel and Anita Mannur, eds., *Theorizing Diaspora: A Reader* (Oxford: Blackwell, 2003), 7–8. See also Kandice Chuh and Karen Shimakawa, eds., *Orientations: Mapping Studies in the Asian Diaspora* (Durham, NC: Duke University Press, 2001).

21. For a good overview of Protestant Christianity in Korea, see Chung-Shin Park, *Protestantism and Politics in Korea* (Seattle: University of Washington Press, 2003). For a broader treatment of religion in Korea, see James Huntley Grayson, *Korea: A Religious History* (New York: Routledge Curzon, 2002), and Lewis R. Lancaster and Richard K. Payne, eds., *Religion and Society in Contemporary Korea* (Berkeley: Institute of East Asian Studies, University of California, Berkeley, 1997). For general histories of Korea, see Ki-baik Lee, *A New History of Korea,* translated by Edward W. Wagner (Cambridge: Harvard University Press, 1984), and Bruce Cumings, *Korea's Place in the Sun: A Modern History* (New York: Norton, 1997).

22. There have been a number of works that focus on these events and black-Korean relations, including Robert Gooding-Williams, ed., *Reading Rodney King, Reading Urban Uprising* (New York: Routledge, 1993); Nancy Abelmann and John Lie, *Blue Dreams: Korean Americans and the Los Angeles Riots* (Cambridge: Harvard University Press, 1995); Eui-Young Yu, ed., *Black-Korean Encounter: Toward Understanding and Alliance* (Los Angeles: Institute for Asian American and Pacific Asian Studies, California State University, Los Angeles, 1994); Kwang Chung Kim, ed., *Koreans in the Hood: Conflict with African Americans* (Baltimore: Johns Hopkins University Press, 1999); Claire Jean Kim, *Bitter Fruit: The Politics of Black-Korean Conflict in New York City* (New Haven, CT: Yale University Press, 2000); Patrick D. Joyce, *No Fire Next Time: Black-Korean Conflicts and the Future of America's Cities* (Ithaca, NY: Cornell University Press, 2003).

23. Ignacio Castuera, ed., *Dreams on Fire/Embers of Hope: From the Pulpits of Los Angeles after the Riots* (St. Louis: Chalice, 1992). The book notes that all royalties from the book go to a reconciliation fund administered by the Interreligious Council of Southern California.

24. "Introduction: Crossing the City Line," in Robert A. Orsi, ed., *Gods of the City: Religion and the American Urban Landscape* (Bloomington: Indiana University Press, 1999), 42.

25. I borrow these ideas from Orsi, "Introduction," 41–45. See also Lowell W. Livezey, ed., *Public Religion and Urban Transformation: Faith in the City* (New York: New York University Press, 2000).

26. Okyun Kwon, Sang Hyun Lee, Anselm Min, and Sung Hyun Um.

27. Ruth H. Chung, Jung Ha Kim, Rebecca Kim, and Sharon Kim.

28. Jae Ran Kim.

29. Sharon A. Suh and David K. Yoo.

30. We are indebted to the work of scholars who have gone before us, and much of that work is reflected in the notes throughout the book and in the bibliography.

Section I

TRADITIONS

Mention of religion often brings to mind particular traditions, formalized through organizational structures, governing bodies, and established creedal boundaries. However, religious traditions are constantly in flux, a situation compounded in the case of Korean Americans through immigration into and adaptation to the religiously pluralistic United States. Anselm Min provides a helpful overview of a neglected tradition within Christianity, Korean American Catholicism. Readers will not likely be surprised that Korean Catholics have found a measure of solace and comfort from the hardships of migration and racism in their parishes. It might be less obvious, however, to find that the diasporic claims of Korean Catholicism on religious life in the United States have been as divisive as they have been ameliorative.

Sharon Suh's study of a Los Angeles–based Buddhist temple also sheds light on a little-known dimension of Korean America religion and spirituality. Her chapter discusses the long shadow cast by Korean American Protestantism and the efforts by Buddhists to carve out their own religious sensibility not only as adherents of a particular religious tradition but also as Koreans situated in the United States. Okyun Kwon's study of Korean American Buddhists and Protestants argues that immigration has often increased the overall religious participation of the migrants. Kwon examines in particular the role of religious beliefs.

Chapter One

Korean American Catholic Communities

A Pastoral Reflection

Anselm Kyongsuk Min

The first Korean Catholic community in North America was founded by Korean Catholic students studying at the University of Southern California in January 1969 with the Reverend Jong Soon Lee as their chaplain at what is now St. Agnes Church in the heart of Koreatown, Los Angeles. Among the founding members was Mr. Young Hoon Kang, who later went on to become prime minister of South Korea. The students had been meeting for the periodic celebration of the mass since August 1968, culminating in the founding of a community several months later with the approval of the Los Angeles archdiocese.[1]

From this modest beginning in 1968, Korean American Catholics have developed into a group numbering, as of December 31, 2006, 90,250 Catholics organized into 102 communities and 70 mission stations and served by 118 priests, 11 of them non-Korean, and 66 nuns. Some of these communities are parishes in the full canonical sense, but most of them operate as special ethnic pastoral centers of the respective dioceses to which they belong. Many of these communities, especially the ones located in big cities such as Los Angeles, New York City, Toronto, Vancouver, Philadelphia, and Washington, D.C., have grown into large communities, each with more than a thousand faithful. The Queens community, with over 5,000 members, is the largest.[2]

In telling the story of these communities, I would like to begin with a brief history of Catholicism in Korea, a necessary background for an understanding of Korean Catholic communities in North America; move on to the history and characteristics of these communities; discuss some of the pastoral problems facing these communities for some time; and end with a reflection on the most fundamental of pastoral problems, the problem of overcoming the still widely prevalent preconciliar mentality (i.e., the spiritual orientation of

Catholicism prior to the reforms of the 1962–1965 Second Vatican Council), as expressed in clerical authoritarianism and passivity of the laity, and the transition from a preconciliar, monocultural to a postconciliar, multicultural church in North America. Because I am a theologian, my discussion is primarily pastoral, even though it presupposes and contains much historical and sociological material.

A BRIEF HISTORY OF KOREAN CATHOLICISM

Although Korea's first contact with Catholicism goes back to the late sixteenth century (1593–1595), when Fr. Gregorius de Cespedes, a Portugese Jesuit, came to Korea as chaplain of the invading Japanese army, the Korean Catholic Church traces its formal beginning to the baptism in 1784 of Peter Sunghoon Lee, a scholar and diplomat, in Beijing, China, and the formation of the first Catholic community, without the assistance of the clergy, with fellow scholars he baptized in the same year. Members of the early community were mostly from the upper class, many of them some of the first-rate intellectuals of the day. Korean scholars had already been exposed to aspects of Western thought, including Catholicism, since the early seventeenth century through the works of Jesuit missionaries in China such as Matteo Ricci and Adam Schall. For all its promising beginning, however, Catholicism soon came under severe persecution, suffering four major persecutions in 1801, 1839, 1846, and 1866 and producing some ten thousand martyrs, until it received freedom of religion in the Korean-French Treaty of 1886. The causes of this century-long persecution included the conflict between Confucianism and Catholicism; Catholicism's suspected collusion with Western colonial powers, especially France; its underlying challenge to the political status quo; and the power struggles among different factions of the ruling class. The Church during this period was a transplant of the post-Tridentine French Catholicism in its theology and spirituality with a strong streak of triumphalism and exclusivism toward non-Catholic religions, dualism of body and soul, and absolute loyalty to the papacy and hierarchy.

Korea soon fell victim to the bloody rivalry among the imperialist powers of the late nineteenth century (Japan, China, Russia, and the United States of America), coming under the formal occupation of Japan in 1910 and remaining under its colonial rule, often unparalleled for its brutality, until 1945 when World War II ended. For the Church that had just survived a century of persecution, this was a period of quiet growth, spreading its roots among the people and mostly concentrating on individual conversion and the establishment of parishes. During this period, as during the century of persecution, the Church was a church of foreign missionaries including, this time, not only the members of the French Foreign Mission Society, who were the only missionaries during the preceding century, but also the French Sisters of St. Paul of Chartres, American Maryknollers, Irish Columbans, and German Benedictines, both nuns and priests. Two indigenous religious orders were also founded at this time: the Congregation of the Blessed Martyrs of Korea and the Sisters of Our Lady of Perpetual Help. The theology and spirituality of the Church was dominated by the teachings of Vatican I that carried the post-Tridentine tendencies mentioned earlier to their logical culmination. The Church generally collaborated with the Japanese colonial government and suppressed any nationalist politics of protest and independence among Korean Catholics. It also laid the foundation of the later more Korean, more indigenous church by multiplying apostolic vicariates in Seoul, Taegu, Wonsan, Jonjoo, and Choonchun, founding seminaries, convents, and schools and ordaining the first Korean bishop, Paul Keenam Ro, in 1942.

The period since 1945 to the present has been a most turbulent time in Korean history. It has seen unprecedented changes in all areas of life as well as immense human suffering, spiritual confusion, political oppression, and ambiguous economic growth followed by a new outburst of national hope and confidence. Since the end of World War II, Korea has experienced liberation from Japan (1945); the territorial, military, and ideological division of the country into the Soviet-dominated North and the U.S.-dominated South; the three bloody years of the Korean War (1950–1953); the Student Revolution of 1960; the military coup of 1961; the exhilarating years of the Second Vatican Council (1962–1965); the Vietnam War (1964–1975), the reign of terror and economic growth under three successive military dictatorships (1961–1992); steps toward genuine democracy during two successive civilian administrations (1993–); and small but significant steps toward national reunification.

In the face of these enormous challenges and in part encouraged by them, the Church in South Korea has continued its remarkable growth in membership, from only about 100,000 in 1930 to about 150,000 in 1950 to more than 1 million in 1974, more than 2 million in 1985, more than 3 million in 1992, and more than 4.7 million—9.6 percent of the entire population of 49.6 million—at the end of 2006. As of December 31, 2006, there were 12 dioceses, 3 archdioceses, 1,476 parishes, 9,770 nuns, 1,444 male religious, 32 bishops, 3,874 priests, 2,087 catechists, and 1,380 seminarians as well as 7 seminaries, 66 secondary schools, 13 colleges and universities, 22 major hospitals, 1 major daily, 2 weeklies, 11 monthlies, 5 publishing houses, and 1 television station run by the Church. (It must also be pointed out that only about 20 percent of Catholics attend mass every Sunday.)[3] The Korean hierarchy was established in 1962, and in 2006 all the diocesan ordinaries, except 1

Maryknoller, are Koreans, including 2 cardinals. As of 2006, there were 106 women's and 46 men's religious congregations working in a variety of apostolates from orphanages to schools to hospitals to retreat houses.[4] Pope John Paul II's canonization of 103 martyrs killed in the great persecutions of the nineteenth century during his first Korean visit in May 1984, the holding of the World Eucharistic Congress in Korea in 1989, and the pope's second visit to attend that congress were highly symbolic of the national self-confidence and institutional maturity of the Korean Church. In terms of number, personnel, organization, finance, and activity, the Church in Korea is perhaps as well established as any national church in the world.

The Church has also been building and consolidating its Christian presence in Korean society at large through its many schools, hospitals, and media outlets. Since the 1970s it has been raising its prophetic voice in the area of social justice and human rights, notably through the activism—public statements, prayer meetings, hunger strikes, etc.—of the Association of Korean Catholic priests for Justice organized in 1974 in response to the unprecedented imprisonment of a bishop for his outspoken criticism of General Park Chung Hee's military regime. Cardinal Stephen Kim Sou-Hwan and Archbishop Victorinus Youn of Kwangju—both retired now—were the leading prophetic voices not only among Christians but also in Korean society at large during the two decades of political oppression. The compound of the Myongdong Cathedral, the seat of the archbishop of Seoul, has been known for decades as the sanctuary of democracy where students, workers, politicians, human rights activists, and practically any dissatisfied segment of society can gather to air their grievances without fear of police arrest. Its courageous witness to justice and peace has made the Catholic Church one of the most respected and trusted institutions in Korea as a whole. The proportion of Catholics in the professions, law, medicine, college faculty, electoral politics, and military command is twice as large as that in the general population.

In recent years, especially since the 1980s, the Church has also been turning its attention outward to missionary work and problems of human suffering overseas. There are three communities of priests and nuns established for the express purpose of training overseas missionaries. As of December 31, 2006, there were 634 missionaries working in all continents of the world.[5] The Church has also been contributing generously to the relief of disaster victims overseas. Spreading throughout the Church is an awareness that it is now time for the Korean Church, so long at the receiving end of foreign aid since the time of the Korean War, to start reciprocating and giving to others.

Like the rest of Korean society, the Church too is caught in the throes of rapid changes brought about by sudden economic prosperity and the problems they create. The tension between rich and poor, rampant materialism, increasing bourgeoisification, and enervation of the evangelical spirit of poverty and prophetic witness remain challenges to all in the Church. Like churches in many nations, the Church in Korea faces the pastoral problems of widespread abortion, broken families, the impersonality of the superlarge urban parish, care for the urban poor and oppressed, and the special needs of rural areas increasingly abandoned for the cities. The Church also face the pastoral and theological challenges of a whole series of unresolved contradictions, between traditional feudalism and the new capitalist individualism; between the dominant, largely preconciliar or pre–Vatican II mentality and the challenge of conciliar and postconciliar reforms; between the inherited, still largely dominant Western spirituality and liturgy and the demands of inculturation; between entrenched clerical authoritarianism and the increasing self-consciousness of educated laity; and between endemic sexism and growing women's movements.

The devotional life of Korean Catholics is quite traditional. In addition to Christmas and Easter, the feasts of the Assumption and All Saints are special favorites, the first because of their special devotion to Our Lady, the second because of their special reverence for deceased ancestors. The feasts of St. Joseph, Little Flower Therese, and the recently canonized Korean martyrs are some of the most popular feasts. A movement has been afoot to have more of the nineteenth-century martyrs canonized. Among the popular devotions are the rosary and the stations of the cross. The Legion of Mary has been perhaps the most active group among Korean Catholics since 1954, the year it was introduced into Korea. These traditional forms of piety and devotion have been joined, since the 1970s, by new imported forms such as the charismatic movement, the cursillo movement, marriage encounter, and Bible study.[6]

CHARACTERISTICS OF KOREAN AMERICAN CATHOLIC COMMUNITIES

The history of Korean Catholic communities in North America goes back to the late 1960s and the early 1970s, when large-scale immigration from Korea began. The story of a small community in Charlotte, North Carolina, should be most instructive in this regard. In this mostly white city, around 1974 Koreans discovered other Koreans by running into one another in supermarkets. Catholics among them also discovered other Catholics by chance encounters and hearsay. They were mostly immigrants on labor contracts with some American businesses and factories, occasionally tae kwon do masters, medical doctors, and college professors. Catholics met among themselves because they had so much to share. They were joined by non-Catholic friends who also needed company and fellowship in a strange land. Since 1978, they started gathering for common prayer, discussion, and fellowship. Finally, in 1980, ten families organized themselves into a community under the leadership of a layperson, a college professor with theological and seminary training. With the permission of the bishop, the community located an American parish and invited a Korean priest, a Benedictine monk stationed in Atlanta, for a monthly mass, instruction, and the administration of sacraments as necessary. In the meantime, the community also invited an Euro-American priest to celebrate the weekly Sunday Mass for the community where the scripture readings and many of the prayers were done in Korean. The lay leader gave catechetical instructions for converts, and the Korean priest baptized them on Christmas and Easter. The community also organized regular prayer meetings, devotional exercises, public lectures, and other activities. In the mid-1980s, Korean priests studying in Rome were invited for a three-month summer ministry to the community. The Sunday liturgy is now celebrated entirely in Korean, with Korean hymns sung by a trained choir.

In the late 1980s, at the request of the bishop of Charlotte, a diocesan bishop in Korea sent a priest to the community to serve as a resident pastor. By now the community has grown to thirty families and raised money to buy a house to serve as rectory and built a 5,000-square foot chapel. With the coming of a resident pastor, the community has all the requisites of a small parish. In addition to the regular celebration of the Sunday liturgy and the administration of sacraments such as baptism, reconciliation, and the sacrament of the sick all in Korean, there are regular catechetical instructions for converts and regular activities of groups such as the charismatic prayer group, the Legion of Mary, and area groups. Most importantly, a pastoral council is organized to advise the pastor about the issues facing the community. In the meantime, with new converts and the influx of new Catholics from elsewhere, the community has grown to seventy families and needs a large space for activities and fellowship. With most of the families in the middle class, funds are easily raised to build an addition to the existing chapel. On the occasion of the completion of the fellowship hall around 1998, as on the occasion of the completion of the chapel in 1992, the bishop was invited to bless the new space, as are members of the Korean community in Charlotte at large. The community enjoyed a big celebration with congratulations on its own growth and maturity. Thus, a small community of ten original families has now grown into a community of almost one hundred families with all the institutional maturity of a small parish.[7]

This story of a Charlotte, North Carolina, community is typical of most Korean Catholic communities in North America. Just as the beginning of Korean Catholicism was traced to lay leadership in 1784, so the beginnings of most communities in America are due to lay initiative and leadership. Catholic families come together for fellowship and prayer, first on a monthly and then on a weekly basis, inviting priests, Korean or American, whenever and wherever they are available, for the Sunday liturgy, gradually also organizing prayer, Bible study, and other activity groups and undertaking catechetical and charitable works as best they can. From these modest beginnings and thanks to the growing availability of Korean priests for overseas ministry, there have now emerged communities, especially in big cities, that are as well established as any middle-class American parish in terms of number, finances, organization, and activity.

In these communities the Eucharist is celebrated, sacraments are administered, the Gospel is preached, Sunday schools are taught, and increasingly numerous group activities take place. With increases in membership, many communities are busy raising funds for the construction or purchase of their own places of worship. Generous donations are collected for the poor, the missions, the needs of the mother dioceses in Korea, disaster victims, leprosariums, the physically challenged, and other worthy causes. Charismatic, cursillo, the Legion of Mary, and marriage encounter conferences regularly take place regionwide and often nationwide. With more and more religious orders such as Jesuits, Benedictine nuns, and Sisters of Our Lady of Perpetual Help getting involved in ministry to Korean American Catholics in recent years, opportunities have been growing for workshops on prayer, Ignatian retreats, Jesuit-sponsored Christian Life Communities, advanced biblical studies, and public lectures on important subjects. Since 1992, the North American Coalition of Korean Catholic Laity, an independent national lay network, has been sponsoring an annual conference for the continual updating of lay leaders in theology, biblical studies, and ecclesiastical affairs. In these communities there is a certain vitality of faith, an intense search for spirituality, an intimacy of sharing, a cohesiveness of community, and a sense of joy in being Catholic.

In addition to carrying out the normal activities of an ecclesial community, these communities have also been making signal contributions as immigrant communities of Catholic faith. They have helped new immigrant Koreans preserve their Catholic identity in a world so prone to destabilizing all identities. They have helped to maintain a strong sense of devotion and loyalty to the Church and the Catholic faith inherited from the homeland. The communities have also served well as havens and shelter from the slings and arrows of life in a strange culture, where immigrants can gather among their own kind, sharing their own joys and sorrows, in a language they don't have to strain to understand and in a manner they don't have to learn. To a minority under constant threat of assimilation and discrimination, these communities have been sources of identity, consolation, and hope. Likewise, they have also contributed examples of living ecclesial faith to the white Catholic community. They have shown a degree of loyalty to the Catholic faith, respect for the tradition, and love for Mary and the saints that was typical of preconciliar Catholic churches in the West and that have been considerably weakening in contemporary white Catholic churches. Bishop Mugavero of Brooklyn, before his death, is quoted as saying that "if you want to see an example of a vibrant faith community, go and visit a Korean community."[8]

SOME PASTORAL CHALLENGES

These Korean Catholic communities in North America have also had their share of growing pains and problems, some plaguing them from the beginning, others surfacing as they grow, some rooted in contingent particularities, others more deeply in the clash of two cultures, Korean and American, preconciliar and postconciliar. They can be grouped into four categories: pastoral, communal, cultural, and organizational.

Pastoral problems include those of youth education, healing of broken families, pastoral care for the elderly, reevangelization of those who quit coming to church or leave for other denominations, and lack of a positive evangelizing spirit. The problem of providing religious education to the younger generation has always been a problem but has become more acute, as a whole new generation of young people have now grown up in the United States who do not know Korean and who are more used to American culture. There is the problem of the paucity of appropriate catechetical material in Korean, then that of creating programs for youth, and, most critically, that of lack of personnel with professional training to conduct those programs. Most communities simply manage with volunteers who have plenty of enthusiasm but little professional training. Divorced and broken families are increasingly frequent among Korean immigrants, and Catholic families are no exception. There is, however, no national pastoral concern, apart from the marriage encounter movement, to deal with the issue of broken families and marriage annulments in Korean American communities. Ad hoc, unprofessional, spiritual counseling by pastors and friends is all that exists.

The generation of Koreans who came to the United States in their prime in the 1970s—during the first large wave of immigration to the United States— are now approaching retirement age with all its problems. Korean Catholic communities, again, are completely unprepared in terms of appropriate pastoral care. Likewise, a significant portion—estimated by some to be almost 20 percent—of the Korean Catholic population either simply quit coming to church or leave for one of the Protestant denominations each year. Members of the Legion of Mary visit those who do not come to church, but pastors rarely do. More significantly, Catholic communities in North America, like their counterparts in Korea but unlike Protestant communities, have no active program for outreach and evangelization to non-Catholics. They simply wait until non-Catholics come and ask for instruction in the faith. In all of these areas the Korean Catholic communities—and especially their leadership—are challenged to the utmost of their creativity and flexibility to create methods of pastoral care appropriate to a new situation, not merely to reproduce the old Korean ways.

Communal problems include chronic divisiveness, clerical autocracy, lack of democratic culture, and cultural isolation. Divisiveness has been endemic from the beginning. There are very few communities that have been free from this problem. Contentiousness, quarrels, conflicts (occasionally physical), and splits occur over issues of pastoral policies, clergy assignments, financial and sexual scandals of the clergy, building projects, and other community issues. Most often, pastors run the communities in a high-handed autocratic manner as they have always done back home, making decisions arbitrarily without appropriate consultation of the pastoral council. They want to stay longer than their original assignment. They involve themselves in financial and sexual scandals. These issues always split the community into those who are loyal to the pastor and those who protest those irregularities but are labeled as traitors. Sometimes the problems fester and the community remains split for years, without the Korean bishops, always on the side of the pastors, recalling them or doing anything to restore peace in the community.

Contributing to this contentiousness is the lack of democratic culture and cultural isolation. Brought up on authoritarian culture at home, the communities, both clergy and laity, lack democratic culture as a way of resolving communal disputes. Instead of dialogue with respect for others' opinions, discussion with respect for parliamentary procedures, analysis of issues with objectivity, and in general a rational approach to conflict resolution, pastors and different factions tend to personalize and exaggerate the issues with no respect for the other side. Likewise, culturally isolated from the larger society, they tend to seek prestige, recognition, and identity within their all-too-small communities, and every issue becomes an invitation for them to stake their honor and invest their passion, inevitably overblowing the issues that do arise.

Cultural problems involve isolation from the American Church at the parish and diocesan levels as well as from the larger American society. Until they find buildings for their exclusive use, they have to rent or share the facilities in most instances with a Euro-American parish. Even after they do, they still have to deal with the diocesan bishop and his staff. In either case, there have been problems galore. They cannot schedule their Sunday worship at a time convenient to them, always having to first accommodate the needs of the white community. The Korean pastors generally do not speak English and run into problems of communication with their American counterparts and the diocesan officials. The white communities are not always welcoming to ethnic minorities. Korean pastors do not always know the way things are done in American churches and refuse to attend clergy gatherings of the diocese. Communities largely remain isolated from the events and issues of the American Catholic Church. These are largely problems of cultural difference.

One recent incident, in June 2001, is quite illustrative. In a Western diocese the bishop decided to replace the current pastor of a Korean community with a new one. The new one belongs to the so-called 1.5 generation, that is, those who came to the United States at a relatively early age, went through school and college here, and speak perfect English as well as good Korean. The bishop wanted to have someone with whom he could communicate; he could not communicate with the old priest, who came here from Korea on a four-year assignment. The bishop committed two faux pas in this case. He reneged on a four-year contract, bringing the shame of dishonorable discharge in military language to the current pastor. He also had the naivete of inviting the current pastor to stay on as an associate of the new pastor, adding even more shame because the current pastor is almost twenty years older than the new one and has so many more years of pastoral experience, a perfect example of the breach of the Confucian rule of seniority.

The Korean Catholic communities were originally formed to meet the needs for mutual fellowship and religious identity in an alien culture. The tendency, therefore, is to do things in their own Korean ways, that is, in the way things were done back in Korea, such as periodic contributions to the church in addition to the Sunday collection, sitting down during the Gloria rather than standing, appointing rather than electing the membership of the pastoral council, etc. The Korean pastors, sent here from Korea without any preparation for overseas pastoral work, simply reproduce the ways and structures of the typical parish in Korea with all their authoritarianism, the only thing they have known, without ever thinking of adapting to the specific needs of an immigrant community in a foreign culture. They often think of the immigrant communities they are pastoring as overseas extensions of the Korean dioceses they come from. The Korean bishops themselves also tend to think of Korean communities in the United States as their own overseas bases.

The pressure, then, is to create a haven of sharing and intimacy for fellow Korean Catholics, a ghetto of their own in which they can be safe from the challenges and hostilities of the surrounding alien culture. The communities tend to withdraw into themselves and be so preoccupied with their own internal matters as to be cut off from the rest of the world, from the events in their own American dioceses, certainly from the problems of the universal church, and from the secular society in which they live. All the activities of the community—from prayer meetings to retreats and Bible studies—do not show much evidence of interest in problems of social justice, an issue on which the magisterium of the Church has issued so many excellent teaching documents over the years. Nor do they show much evidence of openness to the problems of multicultural society in which they live. Even while society at large is embroiled in issues of racism, sexism, interreligious dialogue, tensions of a multicultural society, and globalization, these communities show only transcendent indifference and unagonizing tranquility.

The last program, which is organizational in nature, involves lack of national coordination in pastoral matters. There has been no national coordinating agency that can study the above problems and challenges that are common to all the communities, stimulate a nationwide discussion of the issues and solutions, and oversee implementation of practical measures. The problems are serious enough, but what makes the situation worse is the lack of a national agency to recognize the problems as problems and take effective measures to respond to them. Communities are so isolated from one another that there is no awareness of common national problems and no common will to solve them together, not even a national debate and discussion of the issues. Each community is so conditioned to think only in terms of its own problems and its own solutions. No pastor is farsighted and courageous enough to take the initiative in bringing about national awareness and national coordination regarding pressing issues. Each Korean bishop who comes to the United States to look over his missionary priests thinks only in terms of the needs of his own diocese. So many Korean bishops come here on pastoral visits every year, but little ever changes. Those American bishops who have Korean communities within their jurisdiction feel reluctant to intervene because of linguistic and cultural barriers.

To be sure, there are a few national agencies, such as the Committee for Overseas Ministry within the National Conference of Korean Bishops and the Office of Pastoral Care for Migrants and Refugees within the National Conference of Catholic Bishops of the United States. These agencies can perhaps cooperate in stimulating a national awareness of common problems and searching for common solutions, but thus far nothing effective has come of them apart from the distribution of the annual Overseas Korean Catholic Directory, some agreement between the two episcopal conferences about the appointment of Korean pastors in the United States, and the recent appointment of a vicar general in America for the episcopal chair of the Committee for Overseas Ministry at home. Besides, the Office of Pastoral Care for Migrants and Refugees handles not only Korean but all Asian and Pacific Catholic affairs. The only other national coordinating agency, an agency that can be expected to be more effective because it is directly involved in ministry to the communities, is the North American Association of Korean Priests, which meets once a year. Since its beginning in the mid-1980s, however, it has produced no significant pastoral initiatives or responses to the problems, and it is a purely clerical association exclusive of the laity and does not represent their perspectives and concerns. Its annual meeting has been more an occasion for mutual fellowship than an opportunity to discuss real issues and solutions.[9]

The Birth of a New Church: The Challenge of Transition from a Preconciliar Monocultural to a Postconciliar Multicultural Church

Over and beyond these particular problems, however, there is a more fundamental problem facing these communities, a problem that underlies all other problems, a problem whose solution therefore is prerequisite to the solution of every other. It is the prevalence of the preconciliar mentality, a mentality acquired from the centuries of Catholic theology and spirituality prior to the reforms of the Second Vatican Council, and its twin expression, clerical authoritarianism and lay passivity, with an overriding need for the education of both clergy and laity in the reforms and reorientations of Vatican II and its aftermath and the rebirth of Korean communities as new postconciliar communities.[10]

Formed in preconciliar theology without the aggiornamento of Vatican II and without the stimulus of external contacts with the American Church, these communities simply reproduce the old forms of Korean Catholic life prior to Vatican II. Their beliefs still reflect those of the Tridentine church, a church formed in the teachings and spirit of the sixteenth-century Council of Trent: polemical, self-defensive, triumphalist, and closed to the world. In fact, the Catechism of the Council of Trent, with very little modification, is still in print and is used in some places. The manual of the Legion of Mary, perhaps the most active group in the communities, still refers to Mary as the mediatrix of all grace,[11] a title almost universally abandoned as dangerous by postconciliar theology. The same preconciliar condemnatory and polemical attitudes toward Protestantism and non-Christian religions persist both among the clergy and laity. Converts from Protestantism are routinely rebaptized.

The prevailing spirituality in the communities is the old dualistic spirituality that looks down upon the external, material world as evil and stresses the all importance of the salvation of the individual soul and inner spiritual life, indifferent to the problems of massive human suffering, oppression, and injustice in the world. Papal teachings on social justice and human liberation are actively suppressed. One of the reasons for the popularity of the charismatic movement is its emphasis on individual salvation, individual consolation, and individual healing, often on the basis of a superstitious, magical conception of divine grace; the charismatic movement simply reinforces the dualistic mentality of the preconciliar era.

The circumstances of the formation of these communities have strongly contributed to their predominantly preconciliar orientation. Most communities have come into existence under lay initiative, but most of the lay leaders came to the United States in the early 1970s, without the benefit of any formation in the theology of Vatican II. Most of the priests now pastoring these communities are also preconciliar in their education and mentality, a reflection of the still largely preconciliar theological ethos of the Korean Catholicism at home. Furthermore, as immigrant communities they tend to form ghettos of their own, intimate among members of their own communities but closed to the outside world. Having come into existence as independent, individual communities without national coordination, each community also tends to close itself off even from other Korean communities. The result is that without external stimulation from other Korean communities or from the American Church, there has been no felt need for the continuing theological education and updating of the clergy and laity in the reforms of Vatican II.

The preconciliar orientation of the Korean communities is most conspicuous in the relationship between clergy and laity, especially the authoritarianism of the clergy and the passivity of the laity. The clergy still exercise all the power, influence, and initiative in making pastoral decisions, with the laity expected to merely follow and obey. No attempt is made to raise the self-consciousness of the laity regarding their own dignity, responsibility, and rights in the church, still less to encourage and empower them to exercise their own proper charisms in fulfilling the mission of the Church.

This clerical authoritarianism is best shown in the way that pastoral councils are run. In most communities the chairperson and members of such councils are simply appointed by the pastor, not elected by the communities. The meetings of the councils are generally pro forma, rubber-stamping decisions already made by the pastor. No real attempt is made to consult the council before making an important pastoral decision, and no attempt is made to encourage a truly free and informed discussion in the council as a prerequisite for real consultation. There is a general and widespread frustration of the intention of Vatican II and the 1983 Code of Canon Law regarding the pastoral council as an institutional way of sharing power between clergy and laity as well as promoting unity in the community. Instead, it is used simply as an administrative organ executing the decisions already made by the pastor without real consultation and often as a way of rewarding his own cronies and punishing his critics by appointing the former to the council and excluding the latter from it, further dividing the community. Financial matters are also generally handled as the sole, exclusive responsibility of the pastor, with rarely a full and regular public disclosure of expenditures and revenues.

Few pastors are imbued with the teaching and spirit of Vatican II and are willing to help liberate the laity from their traditional, preconciliar passivity and subservience and empower them to take the initiative in exercising their own charisms in the Church and without. Not many pastors are truly willing to regard the laity as real partners in the mission of the Church and share both power and responsibility with them. Any lay criticism of the clergy is often regarded as verging on sacrilege. The reverence for the priesthood often approaches the idolatry of identifying the priest with Jesus himself. Most priests, including the ones ordained in the decades after Vatican II, are basically preconciliar and authoritarian in their ecclesiology, a trait reinforced by the still-dominant Confucian authoritarian ethos of traditional Korean culture.

The other side of clerical authoritarianism is the propensity of the laity to follow blind subservience to clerical authority and power. Laypeople have been conditioned to be passive and ignorant, always dependent on the clergy for orders and instructions and totally helpless when the clergy are not around. The laity compete for favors from the pastor, the symbol and center of power in the community, and struggle to get into his inner circle. The pastor in turn often does not mind dividing his congregation into loyalists and traitors according to the degree of their personal loyalty and ready obedience to himself. This, I am afraid, is the most prevalent cause for the scandal of division and feud so characteristic of Korean communities.[12]

This also argues for the urgency of reeducation of both clergy and laity, a reorientation of the prevailing preconciliar mentality of the communities toward the postconciliar, and a rebirth of these communities with a new ecclesial self-understanding and praxis. All the problems mentioned earlier will only remain problems unless reeducated clergy and laity become aware of them as problems in the first place and motivate themselves enough to do something about them. In this sense the prevalence of the preconciliar mentality and reeducation of clergy and laity remain central to all other issues.

An absolute priority in this regard must be given to the reeducation of the pastors in the theology and spirit of Vatican II. They should learn to regard their ministry precisely as diakonia and to respect and empower the laity as equal partners in the common mission of the Church. They should be open to new ideas, approaches, and cultures beyond those of traditional Korea; willing to learn and experiment with new pastoral methods beyond the Korean ones they have been taught at home; and farsighted and courageous enough to lead their communities out of their self-imposed ghettos, as would be only appropriate to pastoral leadership in a rapidly changing multicultural society.

Equally urgent is the need to reeducate the laity, especially the leaders, in the theology of Vatican II so as to make them more conscious of their own dignity, responsibility, and rights both in the Church and in the world. Almost all the lay leaders—chairs and members of the parish councils, catechists, members of the Legion of Mary, area captains, and leaders of prayer and other groups—have received no further theological education beyond the simple catechism they memorized decades ago. Furthermore, these are the ones who actually run the communities in their day-to-day operations and, in those communities without resident pastors, actually make all the important decisions as well. With the increasing shortage of priests, lay leaders will be shouldering more and more of the responsibilities of the clergy in the years to come. Given the increasing importance of lay leadership in the communities as well as the pitifully low state of their current theological formation, no need seems greater than that of the massive reeducation and updating of these leaders—thousands of them across the continent—in a sound theology of Vatican II. The reeducation of lay leaders should focus on those elements essential for pastoral leadership: basic dogma, basic moral theology, basic liturgy, basic canon law, etc. Clerical authoritarianism can be overcome only by an educated and self-conscious laity. Ghettoization can be overcome only by a leadership with a global political consciousness and a moral sensibility to the problems of human suffering in the world.

This need for updating, however, is not confined to the area of the basic theology of Vatican II and its openness to the problems of the world. It extends to all the areas of urgent pastoral care mentioned earlier—catechesis, youth ministry, ministry to broken and divorced families, direction of spiritual movements such as the charismatic, care for the elderly, the problem of lapsed Catholics, relations with other ethnic groups, and training in leadership as such—and countless other problems of pastoral care that emerge as society becomes more complex. As the need becomes more and more sophisticated, the remedy has become more and more professionalized. Pastoral care in these different areas increasingly requires professional preparation and training. Thus far, lay volunteers equipped with goodwill but not much else, certainly not much theological or professional training, have been shouldering the responsibility for these ministries. After some four decades since the beginning of Korean Catholic communities in the United States, the time has now come for the introduction of professionals or at least some degree of professional training into the various forms of ministry, as is currently the case in the American Church. The Korean American Catholic communities cannot afford to continue their unorganized, haphazard, and makeshift ways of pastoral care.

A practical measure to ensure the reeducation of clergy and laity and to study all matters of national pastoral concern would be to establish a national pastoral institute for the Korean communities. The tasks of such an institute can include collecting and distributing data and information relevant to pastoral care for the communities, beginning with basic pastoral statistics; undertaking research and conferences on pastoral problems of the communities, including those mentioned in this essay; publishing periodic newsletters; publishing a brief history of Korean Catholicism in North America, which becomes rather urgent today because many of the founding members of various communities are now passing away; promoting theological reflection on the Korean American experience so as to help produce Korean American Catholic theology;[13] devising and conducting orientation programs for newly arriving pastors; and producing appropriate catechetical material. However, unquestionably the most important task of such an institute would be sponsoring regular seminars and learning sessions for the continuing reeducation of the clergy and laity, especially lay leaders, which I consider to be the single most critical problem.

The preconciliar mentality served the Catholic communities well when they felt vulnerable and insecure as newly arriving minorities in an alien and discriminating culture. It provided secure Catholic identity as well as a haven of intimate fellowship from a heartless, alienating environment. In this sense the preconciliar mentality was the strength of these communities. Now that they have grown mature in terms of years as well as in human and financial resources and achievements, no longer helpless victims and powerless minorities, this very strength, when persisted in, also becomes their weakness and burden. As mature communities they have to break their endemic isolation from both the American Church and the world at large and learn to bear witness to their faith by making their share of contribution to the fulfillment of human needs and the healing of human suffering in the world.

Laypeople should awaken to their responsibilities and rights in the Church and the world. Both clergy and laity should open up their communities to the needs and challenges of the American Church and those of the Church Universal and learn to do their share in the mission of the Church as a whole. They should help the Church bear more effective witness to the reign of God in the world by heeding the cry of the oppressed, the alienated, and the marginalized. They should learn to use the rich theological resources of the Catholic tradition in solving the central problem of our time: how to live together with others who are different in religion, gender, ethnicity, national origin, and economic status or how to contribute to the solidarity of others. For Christians, the doctrine that all human beings, regardless of their contingent differences, are children of the same God, sisters and brothers in Christ, and members of his body in the reconciling and unifying power of the Holy Spirit should provide abundant motivation and hope for working toward the solidarity of the different that is so urgently needed today. Korean Catholics should take an active part in the tasks of this great transition from a monocultural to a multicultural society, and that means, first of all, overcoming the comforts of the preconciliar mentality and learning to face the challenges of the postconciliar world.[14]

The Korean American Catholic communities have not been immune from the problem of ambivalence characterizing all immigrant communities in their race relations with the white mainstream, in their diasporic existence physically separated from but emotionally still dependent on the ancestral culture of their homelands, and in the imperative of improvisation in adapting to the challenges of an ever-changing society. As the communities get larger and as American society itself becomes more multicultural, Korean American Catholic communities will be challenged even more to leave their self-isolation and find a way of cooperating with other ethnic groups—African Americans, Hispanics, and other Asian communities—both in their respective dioceses and in the larger American society. As they take deeper roots in the American diaspora, they will also be pressured to find a way of defining their ethnic and religious identity more reflectively and more clearly; they cannot just muddle through. As they increasingly face the radical challenges of American society itself now in the throes of globalization, the need to improvise and do so wisely will also grow. The task of achieving clarity in an essentially ambivalent situation will test all the pastoral resources of these communities. The question is whether they will be equipped with a pastoral leadership, both clerical and lay, ready to rise to the challenges. Much hope lies on the shoulders of a new generation of pastors and lay leaders.

Korean American Catholic communities are now part of the larger American Catholic communities and are fully caught up in the challenges and ambiguities of a class-divided, multicultural, and globalizing world, as is American society at large. Catholic communities in different parts of the world have been responding to these challenges in different ways, with churches in Europe and North America being more concerned with issues of secularism, churches in Latin America being more concerned with issues of poverty, and churches in Asia being more concerned with issues of poverty and religious pluralism. How the new papacy of Benedict XVI will steer global Catholicism through these challenges has been a matter of much public speculation. While his concern over the increasing secularism and materialism of Western society is well known, whether and how he understands the complexities of the rapidly globalizing world and seeks to respond to them is less well known. Korean American Catholic communities, like their counterparts in Korea, are theologically in tune with the general conservatism of the new papacy with its overriding concern for preserving Catholic identity, an important value in an indiscriminately relativizing world. How such an identity will also acquire complexity and openness to the challenges of the new world will be something that needs close observation and examination in the years ahead with regard to both the papacy of Benedict XVI and the Korean American Catholic communities.

NOTES

1. Jung, Sookhee. "Thirty Years of Korean American Catholicism," *Hankook Ilbo* (Los Angeles edition), December 31, 1999, A13.

2. The statistics in this paragraph are taken from "The Statistics of the Korean Catholic Church for 2006," compiled by the Catholic Bishops Conference of Korea, May 25, 2007, http://www.cbck.or.kr.

3. Ibid.

4. Ibid.

5. Ibid.

6. For a history of Korean Catholicism in English, see Jaesun Chung and Changmun Kim, eds., *Catholic Korea: Yesterday and Today* (Seoul: Catholic Korea Publishing Company, 1964). For readers of Korean, there are many histories of Korean Catholicism in Korean by historians such as Hongyol Ryu, Sukwoo Choi, Kyuhyun Moon, and Wonsoon Lee. For an analysis of the preconciliar theology and spirituality of Korean Catholicism, see my *The Spiritual Ethos of Korean Catholicism* (Seoul: Sogang Jesuit University Social Research Institute, 1971). A summary of this book constitutes the first two chapters of Anselm Kyongsuk Min, William E. Biernatzki, and Luke Jin-Chang Im, *Korean Catholicism in the 70's* (Maryknoll, NY: Orbis, 1975).

7. This story of a Charlotte, North Carolina, community is based on my own intimate involvement in that community from 1974 to 1992 and my continuing contacts with it since.

8. There are no systematic studies, Korean or English, of the history and development of Korean Catholicism in America. The four issues of the Korean-language annual journal of theology and opinion titled *Monminuibit* (Light of Nations, Lumen Gentium), which I edited for the North American Coalition of Korean Catholic Laity for 1993, 1994, 1995–1996, 1997–1998, contain many reflections on the situation of Korean Catholicism in America. The *U.S. Catholic Historian* 18(1) (winter 2000) issue, devoted entirely to Asian American Catholics, contains two articles on Korean American Catholics: Angelyn Dries, OSF, "Korean Catholics in the United States," 99–110, and Thomas J. Curry, "A Korean Catholic Experience: St. Philip Neri Parish in the Archdiocese of Boston," 111–25. The best sources of information on the activities of various communities are the two Catholic weeklies, *Pyonghwa Shinmun* and *Catholic Shinmun,* both in Korean.

9. This survey of issues facing the Korean Catholic communities in America is based on my own experiences, observations, and reflections complemented by conversations with numerous Catholics, both clerical and lay, throughout the country over

two decades. Many of these issues are discussed in the Korean-language journal mentioned in note 8 above.

10. For readers who are not familiar with postconciliar Catholicism or Catholicism as reshaped by the reforms of the Second Vatican Council, see Rene Latourelle, ed., *Vatican II: Assessment and Perspectives,* 3 vols. (Mahwah, NJ: Paulist Press, 1989).

11. *The Official Handbook of the Legion of Mary* (Seoul: Catholic Press, 1987), 16.

12. For readers of Korean, I provide a detailed discussion of the problem of clerical authoritarianism in Korean Catholicism in my *The Korean Church 2000: Beyond Authoritarianism and Ecclesiocentrism* (Waeguan, Korea: Benedict Press, 2000).

13. I make a first attempt at Korean American theology in "From Autobiography to Fellowship of Others: Reflections on Doing Ethnic Theology Today," in Peter Phan, ed., *Journeys at the Margin* (Collegeville, MN: Liturgical Press, 1999), 135–59.

14. My theological reflection on this multicultural reality of our time is found in a number of publications, including "From Autobiography to Fellowship of Others: Reflections on Doing Ethnic Theology Today," in Peter Phan, ed., *Journeys at the Margin* (Collegeville, MN: Liturgical Press, 1999), 135–59; "From Tribal Identity to Solidarity of Others: Theological Challenges of a Divided Korea," *Missiology* 27(3) (July 1999), 333–45; *The Solidarity of Others in a Divided World: A Postmodern Theology after Postmodernism* (New York: T & T Clark International, 2004).

Chapter Two

Asserting Buddhist Selves in a Christian Land

The Maintenance of Religious Identity among Korean Buddhists in America

Sharon A. Suh

The Christians think that Buddhists are devils and that you only have to believe in God to be saved! In Korea, Buddhism was the original teaching but now they [Christians] think of it as the devil. I used to follow my younger sisters to church when I first got here because I wanted to learn something about Christian beliefs. But now, even though I don't go to church anymore, my sisters still think I believe in Christianity. They don't know that I go to temple because I don't tell them. If they knew they would keep asking me why I didn't believe in God and they would keep on bothering me. But belief is my own choice, so I don't want to hear any protests. I don't say a word; I just go alone to temple diligently and think of the Buddha inside my heart.

Mrs. Oh

Mrs. Oh, a fifty-one-year-old Korean Buddhist immigrant, explains over tea the complex circumstances surrounding her religious worship after settling in Los Angeles.[1] Having moved to the United States in the winter of 1998, Mrs. Oh, like many new immigrants, followed her family members to a Korean Christian church despite the fact that she was a Buddhist. When asked why she decided to go to a church rather than seek out a temple, she explained that her sisters were ardent members of a Korean church in Koreatown and that in the United States it was easier to find a church dedicated to first-generation Korean immigrants. "But," she adds, "[even though] I went to church a few months with [my siblings] who said that believing in Jesus in one's heart was a good thing . . . he wouldn't enter into my heart. . . . Then I found Sa Chal temple and encountered the Buddha there."[2] Yet despite reencountering Buddhism in America, Mrs. Oh keeps this information from her family members and walks alone to Sa Chal temple every Sunday morning in the Koreatown district of Los Angeles to sing in the choir and worship among fellow Korean Buddhists.

That a woman finds it necessary to hide her Buddhist identity from her own sisters (themselves previous Buddhists back in Korea) illustrates the reality that many Korean Buddhists encounter on a daily basis: the ubiquity of church affiliation among Koreans living in America. For most Korean Buddhists, it is not uncommon for fellow Koreans to assume a priori that their religious identities are Christian, for most people assume that all Koreans are Christian, and many Buddhists, like Mrs. Oh, choose not to divulge their Buddhist identities. In this study, I examine Buddhist responses to the increasing Christianization of the Korean American community and focus the implications of maintaining a Buddhist identity despite the changing religious face of the majority of this ethnic group. In so doing, this study demonstrates the ways in which religion is a highly improvisational practice where identities are reshaped and recast in the context of new environment through temple participation. Korean American Buddhist identities are not articulated with any explicit emphasis on assimilation into American culture or even larger Buddhist communities outside the Korean ethnic group. Rather, Buddhists attend the temple to worship with fellow ethnic Koreans to invoke memories of the homeland, sustain community identity, and help alleviate some of the pressures of immigrant life.

Based on interviews conducted with fifty first-generation Korean American male and female members of Sa Chal temple in Los Angeles, I illustrate (1) how a Buddhist identity shapes an individual's response to the experience of religious marginalization within his or her own ethnic community, (2) how a Buddhist identity can lead to the development of high self-esteem despite this religious minority status, and (3) how Buddhist teachings have been interpreted by women and men at Sa Chal as a strategy of self-elevation in relation to their Korean American Christian counterparts. To begin this study, I turn first to the temple where members such as Mrs. Oh worship as Buddhists.

Housed in a former Jewish synagogue in the northern section of Los Angeles's Koreatown district, Sa Chal is the largest Korean Chogye order temple in the United States.[3] Currently, the temple offers weekly dharma services, lectures through its Buddhist college, memorial rites, and English courses. Additionally, social services are provided through its nonprofit Korean American Buddhist Community Service Center. Thus, like many immigrant religious institutions in the United States, Sa Chal provides a central venue for the development and experience of social cohesion and ethnic identification, particularly as mainstream American institutions cannot always fulfill culture-specific needs (e.g., alleviation of stress due to minority status, economic hardship, and racial conflict). Sa Chal temple was established on March 10, 1974, after a Buddhist priest was invited from Korea to serve as the first abbot.[4] Located in a small apartment complex on South Ardmore Avenue in Los Angeles, Sa Chal began to spread Chogye order lay Buddhism among Koreans living in America. Expressly opened to engage in missionary work in the United States, Sa Chal has served the Korean American community for more than twenty-five years. Since 1975, Sa Chal has enjoyed the unique position of having consistent leadership under Abbot Lee, as the temple operates independently of Chogye Order headquarters in Seoul. Because of Sa Chal's consistent leadership over twenty-five years, the temple has enjoyed a stable flow of worshipers and a consistent membership of approximately 720 registered families.

THE RELIGIOUS LANDSCAPE OF KOREAN AMERICA: THE GROWTH OF THE CHURCH

The rapid multiplication of Korean American Christian churches comes as no surprise to Buddhists at Sa Chal. Many Buddhists in fact complain that they are often urged to convert to Christianity while they shop at the Korean markets, do business with fellow Koreans, and meet with friends. Even their children are pressured to convert at their high schools and colleges, where Korean Christian church groups are becoming an increasingly powerful presence. One Sunday afternoon at Sa Chal, Michael, a fourteen-year-old member of the temple's youth group, complains to his friends about how "an old woman kept following me in a car and tried to give me flyers to come to her church!" Kristine, a college student, sympathizes and adds, "once I was in the Korean market and some grandmother tried to get me to go to her church, but I told her I was Buddhist. She then got really upset and told me that it was wrong for young people to believe in Buddhism!" Both students then roll their eyes in exasperation and sigh, "Christians just don't understand about free choice!" Lisa, a high school senior, concurs. "Yeah, my friends are always trying to get me to come to church. They tell me that I am going to go to hell because I don't believe in God." As an indication of the growing presence of Christian student groups on campuses, fewer and fewer Korean American students have been attending Sa Chal services over the years.[5]

Readily aware of the decreasing number of Buddhist youths attending temples, the abbot of Sa Chal has been working feverishly to attract more members to Sa Chal through an increased recruitment campaign in Korean-language newspapers local radio and televisions spots. Sa Chal is currently the largest Korean Buddhist temple of the Chogye Order of Son [Zen] Buddhism in the United States.[6] In residence are four Buddhist monks from Korea who remain at the temple year-round. One of the temple's main projects involves the dissemination of Buddhist teachings in the United States, an endeavor that has resulted in the recent establishment of a Los Angeles branch campus of the Eastern Mountain Buddhist College in Seoul. Administered through the main headquarters of the Chogye order, the college offers a two-year certificate course in Buddhist studies to lay members. In addition to attending lectures by visiting Chogye scholar monks from Korea, students also listen to taped lectures of the Korean monastic college professors, read textbooks published in Korea, and also attend weekly Friday night lectures in Sutra studies, Korean Buddhist history, Buddhist practice, and general Buddhist studies.[7] Here students are given a rigorous course of study that accommodates their work schedules and are taught the essentials of Buddhism as established by the main headquarters.

In addition to providing knowledge and specific understandings of Buddhism for practitioners, the school is also part of the temple's strategy to spread Korean Buddhism in the United States, which may be seen as a response to the increasing numbers of Koreans who continue to convert to Christianity. By training Korean lay members and offering certificate degrees in Buddhist studies, Sa Chal works to create its own staff of learned Buddhist missionaries in the United States to increase the number of Buddhists who attend temple. The explicit mission of the Buddhist college administrators is to provide a fundamental education in Buddhist theory, doctrine, and practice that the laity can then use to disseminate Buddhism to others.

While these programs have the specific goal of *pogyo*—the dissemination of Buddhism to the Korean and, recently, the non-Korean community—they also reflect the struggles that Buddhists encounter as they move from a historical position of relative religious majority in the homeland (28 percent of the entire population in Korea) to a marginal position in the United States.[8] Yet in the contemporary Korean context, Christianity has experienced phenomenal growth.[9] The figures for Korean Americans' participation in the church is significantly higher: an estimated 70–80 percent of all Korean Americans are affiliated with the Korean Christian church, yet 40 percent of that population is said to have converted to Christianity after immigrating.[10]

According to survey data collected from the 1999 Korean Directory of Los Angeles, there are 348 Korean-language churches throughout Los Angeles County; the Buddhist temples equaled a mere 19.[11] Perhaps even more staggering are the nationwide results that indicate a total of at least 2,800 Korean Christian churches serving the immigrant community.[12] This total number results in one ethnic Korean church for approximately every four hundred Koreans living in the United States; although not formally tabulated, the current population of

Koreans living in America is more than one million.[13] In contrast, a tabulation of the number of Korean Buddhist temples indicates 89 temples serving the total Buddhist population of the Korean American community in the United States.[14]

Given these staggering statistics, it is no wonder people have said that "when two Japanese meet, they set up a business firm; when two Chinese meet, they open up a Chinese restaurant; and when two Koreans meet, they establish a church."[15] There are many factors that explain the rise of Christianity among Korean Americans, factors that make Korean Americans one of the largest Christian groups among all Asian Americans, second only to the Filipinos.[16] For these immigrants, "to become a Christian in Korea meant to become Westernized or Americanized," which partially accounts for the larger number of Christians than non-Christians who first arrived in the United States.[17] In addition to the historically Christian background of many of the early immigrants who associated Christianity with modernity, there are a number of other factors leading to their phenomenal growth: social services, psychological comfort, opportunities to worship and socialize with fellow ethnics, and the religiously pluralistic nature of American society in which religious distinctiveness has played an important role in the preservation of cultural and ethnic identities.[18] Yet despite the increasingly large percentage of Korean Americans who self-identify as Christian, most adult Buddhists I encountered at Sa Chal express no interest in converting to Christianity.

THE BUDDHIST RESPONSE

In response to their smaller population in the United States, many members of Sa Chal indicated that the only way to effectively reach out to the younger generation of Buddhists is through the education of the parents, who would then bring their children to temple with them. Some parents maintain that the temple should be held responsible for passing the tradition onto students and providing English-speaking dharma instructors, who could then teach the children about Buddhism. Others at Sa Chal advocate that the only way to spread Buddhism throughout the Korean American community is to offer programs that appeal to men, for if more men were interested in Buddhist temples, membership would double. Yet a significant portion of the remaining members have come to terms with their newfound minority status within the Korean community by invoking Buddhist discourses on karma and Buddha Nature whereby individuals are held to be their own agents in determining their religious identities. In response to this issue, many parents thus argue that their children must make up their own minds about which religion to follow, for Buddhism is about karma and awakening the Buddha Nature (the potential for enlightenment inherent in all beings) in oneself. Therefore, children must not be forced to become Buddhists but rather will become Buddhists if they have the right karma.

Implicit in these statements is a strong distinction drawn between Christians, who are viewed as too aggressive and coercive in their efforts at proselytization, and Buddhists, who are praised for being more liberal and independent. Ironically, however, this emphasis on Buddhist karma and self-agency has had the unintended consequence of an increasing Christianization of many second-generation Buddhist children, who simply choose to socialize with their Korean American peers, most of whom are heavily involved in the church. Similarly, although threatened by the rise of Christianity, there are many Buddhists who envy the style of proselytization of the churches and the ministers' efforts to attend to the social, economic, and psychological needs of their congregants. In many ways, Buddhists at Sa Chal long for a monastic clergy that could provide the type of personal connection that they perceive to exist between minister and churchgoer. Furthermore, most Buddhists lament the fact that the majority of Korean Buddhist monks in Los Angeles cannot speak English, a major deterrent to reaching out to the younger-generation offspring of current worshipers at the temple.

Yet given the slight percentage of Buddhists in the Korean immigrant community and the large percentage of former Buddhists who convert and seem to enjoy a more economically successful life (according to my participants), what is it that makes individuals maintain their religious identities? In other words, why have Buddhists at Sa Chal sought to remain Buddhists even when their own children and siblings are turning to the Christian church? What does being a Buddhist in a Christian world mean for the person who consciously chooses not to convert? Does he or she equate being Buddhist with a stronger sense of self, open-mindedness, independence, and, by extension, Americanness despite or in reaction to his or her minority status? It is to these questions that I have sought answers and interpretations among members of Sa Chal, for these are some of the primary concerns and the stakes involved in the religious practices of contemporary lay Korean Buddhists in the United States. Not one of my participants at the temple appeared unaware of or unconcerned about these issues, since all of them have had a family member convert and have also felt the pressure to convert. In fact, most Buddhists at Sa Chal have had the experience of attending church either by going to a missionary school in Korea or by going to church in the United States with a friend or family member.

Of the fifty Buddhists interviewed in this study, most participants appeared rather flexible about passing down their religious traditions to their children. Although most parents preferred to see their children attend temple as devout

Buddhists, members' responses have centered on two main reasons for their flexible views. First, since karma plays a large role in Buddhism, most participants believe that their children will become Buddhist if and only if they have a certain past relationship based on karma. In other words, since Buddhism is about self-awakening, a Buddhist identity cannot be arbitrarily forced upon a person. Second, since Christian churches have become a hot spot for young adult socialization, most Buddhist mothers and fathers would rather see their children commingling with fellow Koreans who share similar values outside of religion than spending time with non-Koreans. Parents ease the anxiety they feel about their children's informal conversions by maintaining that they themselves have a more profound understanding of Buddhist doctrines, which necessitates their acting in a more liberal fashion. For these Buddhist parents, children must be allowed to act according to their own karma. Thus, when comparing themselves to Christians, Buddhists at Sa Chal pride themselves on their more democratic attitudes.

Conspicuously absent from regular Sunday worship services, the second generation has become a main concern among parents at Sa Chal, who nonetheless wish that their own children would be more inclined to attend temple. In fact, throughout my research and interviews, I have noted that only one of my participants had a child above the age of twelve who attended Sa Chal on a weekly basis. Most of the children in the temple youth groups are below the age of twelve and are therefore unable to take care of themselves while their mothers attend temple. Hence, most of these young kids can be found in the basement of the temple playing with other children while their parents worship upstairs in the main dharma hall. At the same time, while most parents I spoke with would prefer to have their own children become Buddhist and attend on a regular basis, most also claimed that it was up to the children to decide their own religious fates. In other words, while parents hoped that their children would practice Buddhism, the idea of forcing their children to become Buddhists was deemed highly unsavory and particularly un-Buddhist, for they believe that self-knowing Buddhists should know that they cannot determine the karma of another individual.

BUDDHISM AND THE RHETORIC OF INDIVIDUALITY

In the remainder of this study, I examine the ways in which members of Sa Chal experience and express their religious identification. The responses given below are the result of an analysis of qualitative data collected from June 1997 through June 1999 in Los Angeles. During that time, I engaged in participant observation and on-site participation with fifty members of Sa

Chal temple and compiled extensive field notes, surveys, and in-depth, open-ended interviews. The sample of individual members' responses I reference below derive from interviews conducted in both English and Korean with temple participants. Based on my research, I found that for many members of Sa Chal, individuality is seen as one of the key defining characteristics of being Buddhist.

Despite the hopes of many Buddhist parents that their own children would attend temple services, members of Sa Chal indicated that they believed that their children should choose their own religion. This choice for many Buddhists is, above all, the measure of what being a Buddhist is all about. Mrs. Jin, for example, a fifty-year-old mother of two, prides herself on having encouraged her sons to attend church so that when they decided for themselves what religion to practice, they would make an informed decision. "I even sent my kids to church. Why did I send them to church? I told them that they should try going to church and try to compare the merits of each faith. Since I have taken them to temple with me since they were young, they were not influenced by [Christianity]. Rather than telling them not to go to church, I told them that they should try to understand the Christian faith in God so that later on, if they chose to believe in Buddhism, their beliefs would be deep and strong because they have chosen for themselves."

It is this emphasis on informed choice about one's religious affiliation that emerged throughout my interviews with Korean Buddhists as a central point of distinction from fellow Koreans who attend Christian churches. I have also found throughout my study that Buddhist parents often make this distinction as a means of coping with their children's church attendance, which may appear to be a break from parental authority. Rather than conceding their authority over their children, many Buddhist parents claim that, in fact, the opposite is true, for their children who attend church are doing so because their parents encourage them to do so as a way to strengthen their children's faith in Buddhism.

Thus, although parents such as Mrs. Jin may be deeply involved in Buddhism, the notion of individual choice, interpreted as the central aspect of Buddhist practice and ideology, necessitates giving children the freedom to do as they wish. Related to this identification of Buddhism with individual choice is the interpretation of Christianity as a faith that demands overly strict adherence to a specific set of beliefs, the exact opposite of Buddhism. Since Buddhism is defined by Mrs. Jin as "having to control oneself so that nobody is going to tell you to come and go [to temple]." Buddhism "is not about evangelization [like the Christian churches are]" at all. Instead, for many Buddhists, religion is interpreted as self-motivated and guided by the individual who controls his or her own fate.

Yet parents such as Mrs. Jin are also well aware that Korean churches offer many services that are appealing to immigrants, such as social or business services and personal connections with fellow members that will particularly appeal to the youth. This outreach to immigrants and their children by churches is something that many Sa Chal members believe Korean monks have failed to achieve. Mrs. Jin explains:

> Right now if you have ten Korean Buddhist temples, they will have ten different youth groups, but the monks won't invest in them. If you go to church, even from nursery school age, kids listen to teachings about Jesus, and they remember this forever and they won't convert. But that doesn't work at the temple because the monks haven't really . . . invested in the youths' education. So that's why even in Korea, Buddhists keep leaving to Christianity. About 80 percent switch to Christianity or maybe even more than that. Why? At church, they do a lot of things to help immigrants. But Buddhism [is not like that]. When I first came to the U.S. and went to Sa Chal, we didn't know where anything was! Even though we went to the temple, the monks didn't ask us when we came to America where we lived, what we did, and what we needed, etc. If we didn't have a place to stay, they were supposed to help arrange it for us. If we didn't have a ride, they could have given us a ride! That's what they [monks] have to do, but they think they are too good for that! I heard that at the church when the minister sees people coming and going, he will greet them and tell them to have a good week.

This critique of the temples and comparison with Christianity indicates the resentment that many members may have toward the temple, which they claim does not play an active enough role in helping immigrants adjust to life in the United States. Because they contend that monks do not have much in terms of financial resources to offer in the way of services, they also believe that many Korean immigrants convert to Christianity because it provides an easier path to adjustment.

Mrs. Jin's comments also reflect an unintended consequence of Buddhism at Sa Chal. Since Buddhists do not consider themselves demanding people, they are unable to garner the support among the monks to actively bring people over to the temple. Since Buddhism is about karma and self-reliance, the general belief is that people should be individually motivated to practice. Many Buddhists in fact take pride in the flexibility that such an orientation provides, although they are also aware that such a hands-off policy has had and will continue to have a detrimental effect on the future survival of the religion.

Kwak Soo Young, a nursery school teacher in her early fifties, claims that while Buddhism is about free choice, she limits this association to religious practices alone. She too has no problem allowing her children to choose their own religion, yet when it comes time for choosing an appropriate spouse, she practically shouts, "Marry an American? No, never!" Despite this seemingly contradictory interpretation of Buddhist doctrines of karma and self-reliance, she explains, "ever since my children were young, I told them that getting married isn't just about two people, it's about the whole families as well." Fearing a language and culture gap between the families, she explains that "to the mother and father, it would be so hard because there will no longer be that tie with parents, and you will be further apart." So, to her children she often warned that "you have to think of how many other people are going to be uncomfortable about the decision that you make and not just think about yourself!" Buddhist doctrines of karma and free choice then have their proper application in choosing religious affiliation but not in choosing the proper mate. Here we find a distinct irony whereby Korean cultural values run counter to the individualism and independence that she values in being American, which indicates that there are some aspects of American culture that she chooses to ignore.

Thus, while many respondents maintain that their own children should choose which religious path they will follow, they also abdicate any self-responsibility for making Buddhists out of children. Ironically, while many Buddhists equate religious doctrines of karma with free choice whereby a person will choose a particular religion based on her of his karma, they criticize the Buddhist temples for not providing children with the proper incentives to become Buddhist.

BUDDHISM AS A NONINTRUSIVE RELIGION

Throughout my interviews at Sa Chal, I have found that comparisons are constantly drawn between Buddhist and Christian doctrines, with Buddhism usually being described by women as a more independent practice that relies on the self as the arbiter of experience. Included in these descriptions of Buddhism is the characterization of the religion as free and without intrusion in one's personal life. For example, for Dr. Lim, a forty-six-year-old woman who recently converted to Buddhism following her second marriage, Buddhism seems to provide less stress in her life because it has far fewer rules and regulations to follow. Dr. Lim, as a young girl growing up in Korea, was raised as a Buddhist through the influence of her grandmother. Yet like many Korean women, Dr. Lim converted to Christianity upon her first marriage, for her "first husband's family was a Christian family and, they told [her] that [they] had to go to church together." Dr. Lim admits that she had no problem switching religious affiliations since she had attended a Christian junior high and high school and the Christian-affiliated Ewha Women's University in Seoul.

When Dr. Lim married her second husband approximately six months before our interview, she renounced her membership at a local Korean Presbyterian church and began to attend Sa Chal's Buddhist services. The transition back to Buddhism was quite smooth for her, and she claims that since the temple's services have a choir, sermon, and songs, it does not seem that different from Christian services. Based on her experiences at both a Korean Christian church and a Buddhist temple, she indicates that she actually prefers Buddhism to Christianity because the former offers her much more flexibility to do as she wishes. She explains that "at church, all you have to do is believe in Jesus and you'll receive help, but here at the temple they don't have that [philosophy] of just believing in someone else. So it seems like the dharma is a little more liberal. It's not exclusive, and Buddhists don't believe that 'only my way is the right way.' There really are some easier things about [the temple]. At church, first of all, you always have to attend services. There are so many meetings, and they always tell you to go to them. If you don't go, then a phone call comes . . . and also they say that you *have* [to] proselytize. If you don't do it very well, then they sort of publicly recognize it. But if you go to the temple and say that you couldn't proselytize [to] other people, it's just not a big deal. But in church it's sort of a sin."

Dr. Lim's comments illustrate the widely held belief in the independence of Buddhism, which fosters the democratic value of freedom of religion. As a result, many claim that Buddhism is a liberal religion that does not intrude into one's personal life. As a side benefit, many temple members experience Buddhism as more suitable to their busy schedules since the temple does not expect too much commitment from them.

At the same time, with this lack of pressure comes a price for members who admit that the Korean Christian churches offer opportunities for socializing and making business connections that might in fact be more beneficial to their livelihood. While many Buddhists maintain that Christians are too afraid to rely on themselves to make it in America, like the Buddhists they also acknowledge that a spiritual connection through Christianity may create a bond of mutual trust and generosity that can be useful for economic success in America. Buddhist often cite this bond as the main factor in the increase of Christianity among Korean immigrants because it provides an opportunity to worship in Korean as well as a place for good business contacts, especially for someone who runs an ethnic-specific business.

Throughout my interviews with members of Sa Chal, this topic of Christianity and business success consistently emerged as one of the most common social distinctions drawn between Christians and Buddhists. Most men, for example, insisted that Koreans frequented churches over temples because at church, one could bring along business cards and expect to find both jobs and potential customers as well as a system of business facilitated by the ministers, held to be social brokers. Nonetheless, no man indicated that he wished that the Buddhist temple and the monks would perform similar functions or that the temple ought to provide business opportunities between members. Rather, most men indicated that the monks should spend less of their time involved in worldly affairs and more time involved in studying the sutras and Buddhist philosophy.

Throughout my research, I found that this critique of monks often stemmed from a desire for self-esteem through high status positions with an ethnic group that is unavailable to them outside the Korean American community. This yearning for status within the temple leads many of them to compare the temple with the many Christian churches that offer both ritual and administrative positions. Furthermore, since Buddhist men are highly conscious and, at times, envious of the economic and social benefits of belonging to the church, many have responded to this situation by highlighting what Buddhism has to offer that Christianity cannot: independence, self-reliance, and freedom (also noted by the women). These three benefits are held to be more important than business success and social prestige, for they are not contingent upon what Buddhists deem a submission to an outside agent other than oneself: compliance to authority figures such as God, Jesus, or ministers. Furthermore, they are held to be compatible with American democracy and values of independence. In fact, it is these benefits accrued from practicing Buddhism that are said to keep a man from becoming a Christian in spite of the obvious attractions of financial acumen and prestige among peers. Aware of their marginal statuses within the Korean American religious community, Buddhist men respond by placing higher value on self-knowledge and finding oneself oversubmitting to an authoritative figure.

Jae Woo Shin, for example, a twenty-eight-year-old graduate student, maintains that Buddhist meditation and worship focus on self-awakening as opposed to relying on an outside force such as God as the means for religious salvation. It is this difference of agency that appeals to him, for Buddhism teaches him to depend on and awaken himself. He visited a number of Protestant churches in Korea during his sojourn in the army and while living as a college student in Iowa. "I believe in Buddhism," he says, "because I don't believe in any God or other person. If I go to heaven when I awaken, then I go by my own self-effort. But the church believes in many things like that God will actually pick you up and save you." He goes on to explain that "because people can't find Buddhist temples, they usually go to church, and they often go for business reasons and not really for a belief in the church, in my opinion. Maybe 40 percent really believe in the church, and 40 percent are not even native speakers of English, and so they come to the church so that they can speak in Korean. If you have no company, you just go to church on Sunday, and many Korean people gather together, and he can have an easy time getting some business items and ideas. Or he can sell things because he can meet many people . . . because usually they can't speak English well. Their English is really poor, and so they go to church and learn business, [but] they don't believe in the church."

For many participants in this study, being Buddhist is a more difficult challenge in the United States, yet it ultimately symbolizes an individual's stronger character and independence, since he or she does not take the easy way out by joining a church.

BUDDHISM AND AGENCY

As part of the response to the discrimination experienced by many Buddhists in the larger Korean American community, Christianity is interpreted as the dependence on outside agents (God and the church), which are held to prohibit self-reliance. As Mrs. Chin, a woman who immigrated to the United States in 1992 and has since divorced from her Christian husband, puts it, "In Christianity, you ask for your well-being. In Buddhism, though, you are the subject and therefore you have to come to a realization of yourself and discover your well-being through the teachings. I find this to be more practical in daily living. In Christianity, you are not the subject; you leave everything up to the spirit [of God to decide]. This does not make sense to me, because if you need to go somewhere, you have to know the directions for getting to that destination." Like many Sa Chal members, Mrs. Chin equates those who have converted from Buddhism to Christianity with loneliness and weak-mindedness, thus illustrating the position that because Christians help people find jobs and visit their homes, the weak-minded are more likely to switch religions.

Christianity is also defined as being heavily coercive and exclusive, for, as Mrs. Chin explains, Christians "believe one should believe in one god, only their God, and if you don't believe then you can't go to heaven. Christianity tells people that if you don't follow the ways of God, then you will not go the right path." On the other hand, Buddhism "is a philosophy which shows a way of living that people can experience and choose for themselves." For Mrs. Chin and many other temple members, "people should experience and decide for themselves" which religion they choose to follow, again a very American value. In choosing for themselves, Buddhists at Sa Chal reflect a preference for the noncommittal aspect of Buddhist worship style. In a rather telling statement of Buddhist practice, Mrs. Chin comments that "I don't have a set practice. I practice whenever I am in need of it. It's like an alarm clock. I don't set a specific time in order to get up in time. If I need to wake up at a certain time, then I tell myself to wake up and my eyes open automatically at the right moment. Ever since I became aware of Buddhism, I no longer needed the alarm clock to tell me what to do." Buddhism is thus held in higher regard than Christianity, which demands faith and dependence on someone other than oneself. Even though Christianity might attract more Korean immigrants, it is the Buddhists who are said to be more successful at withstanding life's ups and downs, particularly the psychological struggles of immigrant life.

Perhaps the individuals most affected by the rise of Christianity within the Korean American community are those students who encounter Christianity on a daily basis. For many Buddhist youths at Sa Chal, Christianity plays an important role in their everyday interactions with their coethnic friends. Encouraged by their parents and comforted by the familiarity afforded in such friendships, Korean Buddhist kids are often challenged by their own Christian friends to attend churches. For many of these students, such challenges and invitations to come to church serve as a source of pressure because if they do attend church, they will participate in a religious practice counter to their parents. Yet if they do not attend churches and Christian activities, they may risk losing the friendships they have with fellow Koreans. It is a very difficult social position that the students find themselves in. Not only are they a perceived minority in the larger context of American culture, but they also have to defend their religious identities. Based on my interactions with Buddhist students, it appears that religion and choice are very much at the forefront of students' relations with other Korean Christian kids. The questions of the validity of Buddhism and the issues of conversion seem to emerge quite a bit in everyday life. Yet there are also those students who deeply pride themselves on being Buddhist despite their acknowledgment that Korean Christian churches often provide services and company that temples do not.

For example, James Jang, a twenty-one-year-old college student, maintains that being Buddhist is synonymous with being independent, a characteristic far more important than being a dependent, albeit comfortable, Christian. For James, being a Buddhist has never been a source of stress or embarrassment, for although he has numerous Korean Christian friends, his religious practice is something that he is drawn to for personal and not social reasons.

Nonetheless, James does envy the Korean Christian churches for providing young adults what the temple does not: a strong sense of community. Based on the few times he attended churches with his Korean friends, he comments:

> I don't know why but the Christians have a really good sense of community building. I think it sort of goes back to the question of whether or not a religion can provide some sort of social activities. As Buddhists, we are used to sitting

in a room, meditating and praying. But Christians are used to praying, singing, and going out to reach for other people. They go to a particular house weekly and practice a service there, and that provides an opportunity for other people to meet one another. For those people who [immigrated] to the United States who are really unfamiliar with the culture, tradition, and language, they kind of long to [keep] being Korean even before they even decide to make themselves United States citizens. So they go out looking for people who can understand them and who speak the same language, know the same culture and traditions. I think that's what created a whole different community of Christians. But as far as the Buddhists are concerned, I see a lot of individualism among Buddhists in Los Angeles.

The churches better fulfill an immigrant's need for comfort among fellow ethnics and opportunities to socialize as a group to escape the challenges of adjusting to life in a new country.

In the matter of business affairs and social support, James admits that being a Buddhist "is really hard." Speaking of his own parents' retail clothing business and their relative social isolation within the larger Korean community, he admits:

> I am pretty sure that if my dad were a Christian, he would do a much better job running his business. That's what I feel, but knowing my dad and how they act in front of other people, I think that they are doing a great job of making other people feel more comfortable looking at Buddhists. My parents tell other people they are Buddhists all the time; they don't hide it. I tell all these people that I am a Buddhist, and I am really proud of it. My family has a social life involving all these Buddhist activities like going to temple every week and meeting all these people that are involved in the temple. But I guess in a sense we limit ourselves within a boundary because if you are a Buddhist and want to meet all these Buddhists who live in Los Angeles, then you are bound to end at a certain point. There are only a limited number of Buddhists living in Los Angeles. There are so many people who are Christian or Catholic, so we don't have as large of a connection between Buddhists like Christians or Catholics [do]. My parents don't have that social life created by being involved with other Christians. So, in that way, it's really hard being a Buddhist in Los Angeles.

Yet as noted from his comments above, James remains extremely proud of his parents and himself for not hiding their religious identities no matter what the social and economic consequences may be. Here we find that Buddhism is held to be the tougher yet ultimately more rewarding path. Furthermore, he believes that while the Christians may have better community-building tactics, a stronger network of social support, and economic success, Christianity cannot provide the one critical element that makes being a Buddhist the better option: self-reliance. Speaking of the freedom of choice and the need to depend on oneself that he finds so attractive in Buddhist teachings, James adds:

> I think that being a Buddhist, you have to know actually who you are and about your innermost feelings. For example, Christians do what Jesus tells them to do: do this, do that, follow this way, then I will lead you to [salvation], and you will get a better life. But I think we Buddhists have to create our own way and find our own path. We have to create our own future and our own pathway that's going to lead us to our main goals. I guess it's really hard for any individual to create a pathway that's going to lead them straight to the nirvana stage. But that's what I really love about being a Buddhist, sitting in a really big dharma hall and sort of meditating and breathing in and out. While you sit there you think about what you did in the past and what you want to do in the future. And in that spot, you sort of create your own path.

Choosing one's own path thus becomes the most important aspect of religion, as opposed to following the tenets set out for an individual. Buddhists, like Americans, are held to do things for themselves and on their own.

When asked about his views on the conversions of Korean Buddhists to Christianity, James equated conversion with self-weakness and an inability to make one's own decisions. "I see myself as a really unique person, I don't like to do stuff that other people are doing. I don't like following other people. I see all these people who don't have much pride in themselves so when other people lead them into doing certain things, they actually commit themselves to doing that. But I am not like that. So, it's not likely that other people are going to pursue me to convert to change from Buddhism to Christian. I . . . am pretty sure that being a Christian is going to help you out in your career, because you have better connections and that Christian community where you can bond, but I never thought about converting."

Like many Buddhist men I have met at Sa Chal, James places ultimate importance in being responsible for his own actions and making decisions based on deliberation rather than on responding to a set of rules that are laid out for him a priori. Thus, even though the churches may have more members and more success, he finds that Christians are incapable of thinking for themselves. As he puts it, "I really love being Buddhist because you get to find out about yourself. I see all these people who think [they know] who they are . . . but I think they don't know [anything] about themselves!" Buddhists, he contends, do know something about themselves and how to depend on themselves. Thus, for this Korean American student, "being a true Buddhist, you create your own life," which he considers a much better option than relying on others to tell you how to live your life.

ANALYSIS AND CONCLUSIONS

In this study, I have shown how religious affiliation represents more than different spiritual orientations and practice. In particular, I indicated how views of the other (Christians) play a crucial role in understandings of the self in the negotiation of identities and the development of self-esteem for temple members. That is, members of the same ethnic group who share a different religion play the role of oppositional other than in the construction of a specifically Korean American Buddhist identity. This study also drew specific attention to the tension and irony in the association of Buddhism's injunctions of self-reliance and independence with the cardinal virtues of American culture itself: independence, self-rule, and democratic values. By contrasting their own beliefs and practices from Christians who are defined as weak willed, overly dependent, and coercive, Buddhists indirectly claim that despite the better economic success enjoyed by Christians in churches, such Christians are not as American as the Buddhists because their practices are too dependent on others for support. A Buddhist identity and the rhetoric of self-reliance are thus heavily tied to improving one's self-esteem both as an immigrant and as a Korean American living in a Christian world.

Yet at the same time, I have found that Buddhists see themselves as better Americans, while, paradoxically, Korean Christians are seen as too Westernized for having adopted Christianity. This paradox reflects tensions between the pros and cons of American values. Yet, to be Buddhist is to be independent from the majority, which for many participants in this study enhances self-esteem. Buddhists thus construct themselves simultaneously as more authentic Koreans and better Americans. Many members of Sa Chal justify the smaller numbers of Buddhists in the Korean immigrant community by maintaining that Buddhism is the more difficult yet ultimately more rewarding pathway precisely because it teaches and fosters independence, a cardinal American virtue deemed necessary for immigrant success.

For Sa Chal members, being American has a certain cachet in terms of the independence that Buddhism is held to encourage in the person, yet at the same time there are certain aspects of Buddhism that are more conducive to loyalty to one's homeland. Both aspects are necessary for these Buddhists who assert a new Korean American identity defined by neither one or the other but rather by both of the highest virtues attributed to each country: loyalty and independence. By combining these two forms of virtue, Sa Chal Buddhists pride themselves on being able to stand apart from the crowd and, at the same time, find solace in their smaller numbers. In this way, Buddhism offers a way of being at ease and gives a sense of pride to the Buddhist for having chosen a path that stands apart from the rest. Although aware that they are a religious minority in their own ethnic group, many Buddhists thus pride themselves on their ability to stand outside the majority and rely on themselves to forge ahead in the United States. Sa Chal members thus envision Buddhism's ideals to be the same as American values and demonstrate to themselves that despite hard times found in America, Buddhists have the psychological wherewithal and strength of mind to achieve success.

That asserting a Buddhist identity is directly related to the development of self-esteem can be seen in the claim made by many Buddhists that being Buddhist also means being better able to withstand the stress of living in American culture and a certain mental fortitude to endure and bear hardship on one's own. Hence, members of Sa Chal claim that even though they too had the difficult journey abroad, they did not have to rely on the social support networks offered in Christianity. Because they have to rely on themselves to find relief and not on the monks or the temple, Buddhists also maintain that they are more successful in their transition to life in America. Value is thus placed on being a true Korean who can be a better-adapted American and can truly understand the values of America's democratic spirit of independence. In coming to terms with the vicissitudes of immigrant life, Buddhists at Sa Chal utilize their own coethnic group as a framework through which they measure their self-worth and create new selves by recasting the Korean American Christian majority in the role of the other, which is then identified as the psychological minority.

NOTES

1. All personal names in this study have been changed to protect the identities of participants from the temple.

2. I use the generic term "Sa Chal" (Korean word for "temple") to refer to this religious organization throughout this essay.

3. The Chogye Buddhist Order refers to the Zen Buddhist sect that emerged from the unification of nine earlier sects of Zen Buddhism in Korea during the fourteenth century.

4. Although Korean Christian churches developed immediately after the initial wave of immigration to the Hawaiian Islands in 1903 and continued to play a central role in the adjustment of Korean immigrants to the United States, the first Buddhist temple was not established in the United States until 1972. For a history of the early Korean American church, see Yang, "Koreans in America, 1903–1945," and Kim Hyung-Chan, *The Korean Diaspora: Historical and Sociological Studies of Korean Immigration and Assimilation to North America* (Santa Barbara, CA: ABC-Clio, 1977).

5. From my own observations, I noted that from the period between June 1997 and June 1999, the Buddhist youth group attendance dropped more than 50 percent, from twenty-five students to just under fourteen students. According to the remaining

students, those who left either went to church, which offered better opportunities to meet up with friends, and because English was the primary language of communication. At this stage, it is difficult to ascertain how many of these students who attend church may in fact return to the Buddhist temple for worship in the future.

6. Following the Japanese occupation of Korea (1919–1945), Korean Buddhism was divided into eighteen sects, the largest of which is the Chogye order. Historically, Chogye-jong (order) has been associated with celibate monks, in contrast to the married clergy associated with the newer Taego order that had split from Chogye-jong. The Taego and Chogye orders comprise the largest of the eighteen sects. The other sixteen sects in Korea include the Maitreya sect, the Lotus sect, and the Tantric sects. For more information, see Mok Chong-bae, "Korean Buddhist Sects and Temple Operations," *Korea Journal* 23(9) (September 1983): 19–27.

7. I taught classes in Tibetan Buddhism for one semester at the request of the abbot.

8. Only 1.5 percent according to Won Moo Hurh, *Korean Americans* (New York: Greenwood, 1998), 114, although the abbot of Sa Chal places the number at around 10–15 percent.

9. According to one study, there were 2,050 Christian churches in Seoul in 1979. By 1981, the number doubled to 4,700. By 1990, of the 49 percent of Koreans who reported to be religious, 54 percent reported that they were either Catholics and Christians, while 42 percent claimed to be Buddhist. See Harvey Cox, *Fire from Heaven: the Rise of Pentecostal Spirituality and the Reshaping of Religion in the Twenty-First Century* (New York: Addision-Wesley, 1995), 213–41.

10. Ai Ra Kim, *Women Struggling for a New Life: The Role of Religion in the Cultural Passage from Korea to America* (Albany: State University of New York Press, 1996), 66. The everyday reality of Korean Buddhists living in the Korean American communities of Los Angeles can be characterized as increasingly Christianized. This situation becomes readily apparent through a cursory drive down the busy Wilshire Center district of Koreatown, where churches dot both the commercial and residential streets that make up this urban sector catering to Korean immigrants. South of Beverly Boulevard and north of Olympic Boulevard (the prime sections of Los Angeles's Koreatown), Korean Christian churches dominate the religious landscape of the neighborhood. Some churches are established within large-scale mainline American Protestant churches and have their services after English services of the churches that they rent. Others are located in small residential homes that, on Sunday mornings, are lined with cars crammed into the driveways and on the streets. Some Korean churches are even located in commercial buildings, with signs out front welcoming visitors and members with Korean language signage.

11. Taken from the *1999 Korean Community Directory* published by the *Korea Times* and *Korean Central Daily* newspapers in Los Angeles.

12. Hurh, *Korean Americans,* 106.

13. Ibid., 31.

14. Based on informal conversations with Abbot Lee and the Korean Buddhist magazine *Modern Buddhism* 107 (May 1999).

15. Hurh, *Korean Americans,* 107.

16. Briefly, these reasons can be attributed to the predominantly Christian immigrant population comprised of urban middle-class individuals who first came to the United States during 1903–1905, when newly converted Christians comprised 40 percent of the nearly 8,000 Korean immigrants to first land in Hawaii. Hurh, *Korean Americans,* 107.

17. Ibid., 109.

18. Hyung Park and Eui Hang Shin, "An Analysis of Causes of Schisms in Ethnic Churches: The Case of Korean American Churches," *Sociological Analysis* 49 (1988): 234–48. Anthropologist Kyeyoung Park further attributes the growth of Korean Christianity to the dual role of promoting economic success and attainment of the American dream and the preservation of ethnic identity. According to Park, "Korean devotion to small business success is ideologically intensified at the church," where rotating credit clubs (*kye*) are established among church members to finance businesses and where labor pools and business networks abound. See Kyeyoung Park, *The Korean American Dream: Immigrants and Small Business in New York City* (Ithaca, NY: Cornell University Press, 1997), 186–87.

Chapter Three

The Religiosity and Socioeconomic Adjustment of Buddhist and Protestant Korean Americans

Okyun Kwon

INTRODUCTION

Throughout the history of Korean immigration to the United States, more Christians than any other religious group have immigrated. After immigration, Koreans participate in religious activities more actively than they used to in their home country. The majority of Koreans in the United States (three-fourths) now identify themselves as Christian, although Christians barely maintain a numerical majority status in Korea.[1] Selective process of international migration and the religious climate and plausibility structure of the United States affect Koreans' religious affiliation after immigration, while their religiosity characteristics and practice style affect their way of thinking and socioeconomic adjustment. This might be a good example of the improvisation of cultural adjustment that many Korean immigrants have adopted after their immigration to the United States.

A large number of Koreans who did not practice religion before immigration have joined their ethnic religious organizations after immigration. Whether immigrants become more religious or not after their immigration or whether their immigration experience makes them more religious, joining their ethnic religious organizations has become an important part of the cultural adjustment of Korean immigrants in the United States.

According to a predeparture survey conducted in the mid-1980s when Korean immigration to the United States reached a peak, more than half of Korean immigrants were Christians (41.6 percent non-Catholic Christians and 12.3 percent Catholics), while only a minority were either Buddhists (12.8 percent) or were without religious affiliation (32.5 percent).[2] However, a nationwide survey conducted with the adult population (ages eighteen to sixty-eight) in Korea one year before the predeparture survey showed that the Christian population (21.1 percent, 4.9 percent of whom were Catholic) was smaller than the Buddhist population (24.4 percent). A recent census also shows that slightly more than half of the total population in Korea (51 percent) is religiously active, and among the religiously active, approximately half are Buddhist (45.6 percent) and the other half Christian (51.8 percent), including Catholics.[3] Many studies disclose that less than 5 percent of Koreans in the United States are Buddhist.[4]

Korean immigrants' high rates of religious participation and dramatic alteration of religious affiliation after immigration draw attention to the relationship between religion and immigration. This also reminds us of the debate about differences in the influences of Eastern and Western religions on religious practitioners' lives after immigration. But because most studies of Koreans' religions have focused on the functions and roles of religious organization at a collective level, less attention has been paid to the role of individual practitioners' belief characteristics and their effects on the nonreligious sphere of life.

RELIGIOSITY

Religiosity is a more practice-oriented concept than spirituality. While spirituality refers to an imaginary mental state or attentiveness toward the greatness of religious objects (e.g., supernatural powers), religiosity refers to the level of actual practice of belief in both religious and nonreligious settings. Spirituality thus seems to be a prerequisite condition for religiosity, but many religiously passionate practitioners manage to maintain a high level of religiosity regardless of their spirituality level. This also seems to be true for first-generation immigrants, many of whom struggle for a new life and a new source of spirituality. Most practitioners search for personal sacredness, values, meanings, and rewards in their religiously constructed cosmology, which is symbolically linked to their believed-to-be supernatural power(s). Religious practitioners who maintain a high degree of religiosity are thus apt to think of everyday life in a uniquely religious way, searching for the meanings and values from what happens in their lives. In search of meaning, they also make sure that what is happening in their lives and in the world makes sense to them in their religious cosmology.

Largely due to differences in practice style and the perceptions of supernatural power between Buddhists and Protestants, however, it is sometimes hard to apply this concept of religiosity to both religious groups in an invariable manner. It is true that the aforementioned definition of religiosity is readily applicable to practitioners of Western-style monotheistic religions but not to Buddhists, who are often perceived as atheistic, polytheistic, or pantheistic.

However, as Rodney Stark and William Sims Bainbridge point out, Buddhists maintain two versions of Buddhism: folk version and philosophical. "Folk versions of Buddhism tend to treat the Buddha as a god, while more philosophical versions focus on cosmic principles that seem devoid of personality and desire."[5] Most Buddhists I interviewed and met in their temples appear to keep both versions of Buddhism in mind. They view Gautama Siddrartha (Sakyamuni Buddha), the founder of Buddhism, as their god, while at the same time they also view him as one of many truly enlightened persons who envisioned and practiced the Buddhist version of truth (or dharma). For many Buddhists, therefore, Buddha is a source of supernatural power and at the same time is a perfect model for religious practice.

In part due to unfamiliarity with religious doctrines of non-Western religions, prolific interpretations of the doctrines of all religions, and differences in practice style and emphasis points of each religious tradition, scientific studies about comparison of religiosity characteristics of more than two religious groups and their impact on practitioners' daily lives are very rare. Peter C. Hill and Ralph W. Hood's anthology *Measures of Religiosity* (1999), which compiles 147 social science studies of the measurement of religiosity from 1935 to 1999, shows that only a few studies compare religiosity of two or more religious traditions. Many social scientists also agree that the concept of religiosity overlaps that of spirituality.[6] This is another difficulty that social scientists encounter when they study religiosity and its impact.

Because of the difficulties involved in soliciting the nature of religiosity of two different religious groups, two types of religiosity—collective and private—are particularly important. These two types of religiosity help illuminate the nature of the religiosity orientation and also highlight the similarities and differences in religiosity characteristics of the two religious groups. They also help to explain how the differences in religiosity characteristics of the two religious groups inspire differences in daily living.

RELIGIOSITY: BETWEEN-GROUP PERSPECTIVES

Although most Korean Buddhists consider Sakyamuni Buddha as their god, viewed from the perspective of Western religious traditions, Buddhists and Protestants avow different perceptions of religiosity in their respective religious communities. As with most practitioners of Western-style religions, Protestants possess a clear idea of a supernatural being and its exertion of higher spiritual power. Buddhists, however, do not view a supernatural being and its exertion of higher spiritual power as much as their Protestant counterparts do. Buddhists maintain a relatively weak notion about the necessity of an ideal relationship between themselves and the supernatural being in order to uphold religiosity. Influenced by the philosophical version of Buddhism, many Buddhists also retain a faith-free religious belief and practice, although it sounds very nonreligious to their Protestant counterparts and those within the Western intellectual tradition.

Unlike their Protestant counterparts, many Buddhists search for the sources of their religious power in nature and themselves. In their search for the sources of religious power, they try to emulate Sakyamuni Buddha's deeds and ways of thinking in a belief that practitioners also become a Buddha once they practice sincerely. They believe that Gautama Siddhartha—popularly known as Sakyamuni Buddha—is an outstanding religious leader who accomplished true enlightenment and thus was able to transcend the cruel karmic circle into which common practitioners inevitably fall. They also tend to believe that Sakyamuni is just one of many Buddhas who have come and gone in eternal space and time. For many Buddhists, Sakyamuni Buddha is a symbolic figure who is revered by them in this particular sense, not in the sense that he becomes a Buddhist god. Nevertheless, it is also true that many Buddhists worship Sakyamuni as their symbolic god.

Many Buddhists also have shrines in their homes. Buddhists' holding of religious space in their homes makes them emphasize less the importance of regular, collective service provided by temples. Keeping their own sacred space in their homes, many Buddhists try to keep up their religious mindfulness by performing rituals whenever they feel like it, minimizing the restriction of collective organizational regulations. Most Protestants, however, consider their regular presence at religious services at their designated religious space (church) as the most important way of keeping up their religiosity. These basic differences in the perception of religious mindfulness between the two groups also suggest that Buddhists emphasize an individually (or privately) grounded type of religiosity more than their Protestant counterparts. The two religious groups' perceptive differences in religiosity therefore make it difficult to apply a conventional scheme in order to fathom their religiosities. Religiosity of a particular religious group could be best measured only when their particularity in practice and cosmology is taken into account.

RELIGIOSITY: WITHIN-GROUP PERSPECTIVES

Another complicating factor in measuring religiosity is individual differences within the same religious group. Individual practitioners of the same religious tradition not only perceive the meaning of religiosity in an enormously different spectrum but also put a different level of emphasis on certain forms of religious practice. For example, some Buddhists believe that prostration is the most important form of ritual in order to keep up their religiosity, while others believe meditation to be so. Also, some Protestants believe that frequent and regular service attendance is the most important to keep up their religiosity, while others believe praying to be so. Individual differences in the perception of religious mindfulness within the same religion also imply that individual practitioners' source of religiosity or religious sentiment vary. Keith Roberts argues that the sources of religious sentiment that directly affect the degree of religiosity vary in intensity, frequency, context, content, value and expectation, and interpretation.[7] The diversity in practitioners' source of religiosity within the same religious group also makes it difficult to apply a standardized measurement scheme to all practitioners of the same tradition invariably.

THEORETICAL FRAMEWORK

Buddhists demonstrate different sets of religious values and emphasis points that in due course affect their religiosity characteristics in comparison to their Protestant counterparts. Their differences in religious practices and value orientation are presumed to reflect their nonreligious conduct in their daily lives. Max Weber once argued that believers of Western religion, who are more likely to uphold a world-accepting religious idea, are apt to more actively participate in worldly activities than believers of Eastern religions, who are more likely to practice world-rejecting religious ideas.[8] An extreme expression of Eastern religion practitioners can be a withdrawal from worldly activities or an escapism, which lets no one except the practitioner guide religious and worldly action.

In addition to Weber's classical explanations, Lawrence Iannaccone, an economist, recently categorized world religions in accordance with their ways of consumption of religious goods. According to Iannaccone, "alternative risk reduction strategies lead to different styles of religion: one centering on collective production, exclusivity, and high levels of commitment; another centering on private production, diversified consumption, and fee-for-service transactions."[9] He thus argues that at the global level, Western religions (Protestantism in our example) can be categorized as collectivity-oriented, while Asian religions are individuality-oriented. He also argues in the case of American religions that conventional religions show a more collective tendency while New Age religions are individualistic. Within Protestant groups, sectarian-style religious groups show more of a collective tendency, while mainline religious groups are more individualistic. In the Greco-Roman religious traditions, the Jewish-Christian tradition displays more of a collective tendency, while Pagan traditions are more individualistic.[10]

Most pertinent to our study is Iannaccone's argument about possible differences in levels of religious activity participation between practitioners of Western and Eastern religions. He claims that the private-style religion practitioners generally show a lower level of religious activity participation than those of the collective style.[11] According to his theoretical argument, Protestants maintain a higher level of religious activity participation in general than their Buddhist counterparts.

Presenting various historical examples, Barrington Moore Jr. recently argued that monotheistic religions tend to exercise a stronger and more straightforward way of upholding collectively driven religiosity than any other types of religion.[12] According to him, a monotheistic religion tends to practice religious rituals and beliefs in a much more unified and collective manner within the group, which helped it succeed in maintaining moral purity and exclusivity. Moore's historical argument also suggests that practitioners of monotheistic religions show a higher tendency toward collectively oriented religious participation. Monotheistic religions therefore tend to impose a higher degree of in-group–oriented social pressure upon individual practitioners, which makes them avow a higher degree of religiosity than do practitioners of other types of religion.

Viewed from the cross-sectional common denominator of these three theoretical arguments, Protestants are presupposed to maintain a higher religiosity than their Buddhist counterparts. Without a doubt, Buddhism has been viewed as one of the most representative Asian (or Eastern) religions. The Christianity that Korean Protestants believe in is the most representative Western religion and has no doubt been viewed as a monotheistic religion. The Buddhism that the Korean Buddhists believe in shares its cultural roots with Hinduism, which is animistic, polytheistic, and at times monotheistic. The Buddhism in Korea has also been syncretized with both the indigenous shamanistic religious elements and Confucianism.[13] Although Korean Christianity also experienced syncretism with long-standing indigenous religious ideas, especially with shamanism,[14] Korean Christianity is still claimed to be a monotheistic religion by the practitioners themselves.

METHOD

To understand the nature and characteristics of religiosity of the two religious groups in a comparative perspective, this study employed both qualitative and quantitative data analysis. The qualitative data concerning practitioners' thoughts and beliefs were collected through in-depth interviews and observations. The quantitative data were collected through surveys.[15] Participant observation of two congregations (one Buddhist temple and one Presbyterian church) was also conducted to augment insights into the surroundings of these two religious groups. The two congregations were selected because each is one of the most active and representative of its respective religious community.[16] Respondents were also selected from the religiously active members. They were selected with the help of lay leaders and clerics who were able to determine the members' degree of religious participation and sincerity.

SELECTED INDICATORS

Thirteen indicators are selected in order to compare practitioners' way of presenting religiosity in their respective religious communities. They include offerings, scripture studies, participation in religious activities during the week in addition to Sunday services, attitudes toward religious service attendance, personal identity preference (religious vs. national), proselytization experience, views of the scripture, perceived importance in religion practice, spiritual experience, belief in miracles, degree of dependence on religious belief or scientific knowledge, change of mental state in accordance with the amount of an offering, and reference to religious instruction for important decision making.

Although most indicators overlap the collective and individualistic components of religiosity to some extent, the first six indicators are considered to be more associated with collective tendencies, while the latter seven indicators are more private or individualistic.

SIMILAR ASPECTS OF RELIGIOSITY HELD
BY BUDDHISTS AND PROTESTANTS

Although the two religious groups are considered to maintain different religious tenets, worldviews, and methods of salvation, they share some similarities in their religiosity characteristics. The two groups showed a similar view on more than half (seven) of the thirteen indicators (e.g., scripture study, offerings, scripture, amount of offering, experience of spirituality, reference to religious instruction for important decision makings, and perceived importance in religion practice) in their respective religious traditions (table 3.1).

A similarly high proportion of both religious groups (88 percent of Buddhists and 93 percent of Protestants) believe that the contents of their religious scriptures are absolutely true, and a similar proportion of both groups (78 percent of Buddhists and 73 percent of Protestants) also stress a regular study

Table 3.1. Religiosity indicators similarly emphasized by Buddhists and Protestants (%)

Indicators of Religiosity	Attribution of Source	Buddhists	Protestants
Study scripture regularly	Collective = Private		
Yes		78	73
No		22	27
Offering regularly	Collective = Private		
Yes		90	92
No		10	8
Refer to religious instruction whenever an important decision is made	Collective < Private		
Yes		80	80
No		20	20
Content of scripture is absolutely true	Collective < Private		
Yes		88	93
No		6	5
Don't know		6	2
Ever have a spiritual experience	Collective < Private		
Yes		88	86
No		12	14
Change of mental state in accordance with the amount of offering	Collective < Private		
Yes		28	37
No		70	63
No answer		2	0
Having a religious faith is important for life	Collective < Private		
Very important		88	92
Moderately important		10	8
Not so important		2	0

of religious scripture. However, in general more Buddhists than Protestants express ambivalence about their scripture and study of it.

An identical proportion of both religious groups (80 percent) replied that they always refer to religious instructions whenever they have to make an important decision. The two religious groups' manifestation of a high degree of reference to their religious instruction indicates that their religious instructions provide them with their reference (or guide) points in their daily life. However, a good portion of respondents of both religious groups (20 percent) does not refer to their religious instructions to assist with their worldly concerns. This also indicates that secular lifestyles exist even among the devout practitioners of both religious groups.

For another aspect of religiosity, the two religious groups show similarity in their view on offerings. A similarly high proportion of both religious groups (90 percent of Buddhists and 92 percent of Protestants) replied that they pay offerings regularly to their churches and temples. Quite a few respondents of both religious groups (28 percent of Buddhists and 37 percent of Protestants) also responded that they experience changes in their mental states in accordance with the amount of the offering they make to their churches or temples.

Besides individual practitioners' sense of self-esteem in relation to their amount of offering, it is also true that in the church and temple those practitioners who make offerings receive more attention from their church or temple authorities. They also become important players in their respective religious communities because both church and temple readily confer lay leadership positions upon them in return. Since many religious leaders of both groups believe that only those who uphold a high degree of religiosity are able to offer a sizable amount, church and temple alike confer lay leadership positions upon them more readily than upon those who offer less. In this exchange relationship, religious organizations and the donors seek a reciprocal reward. In this regard, the two groups display a similar behavior pattern despite their dissimilarity in religious tenets and worldview.

In addition to regular offerings (e.g., Protestants' tithes and Buddhists' seasonal holiday offerings), many practitioners of both groups give extra offerings, which sometimes they cannot afford easily. This is a major reason that numerous Korean churches and temples in the New York metropolitan area are able to sustain themselves financially. Many Korean churches in this area have budgets of over $1 million. The Buddhist groups are similar. Although many Korean Buddhists do not go to their temples regularly, Korean Buddhist temples in this area usually send out invitations to their registered members whenever important Buddhist holidays approach. Many Buddhists make offerings to their temples on these holidays. As one of their important rituals, many Buddhists buy lotus flower lamps in May, near the Sakyamuni Buddha's birthday, and hang them on the ceiling of their temples' main service halls with their important prayer lists. The price of a lamp is determined by the temple authority, and no one argues about it. One Buddhist mentioned that the amount of money collected through the sale of lotus flower lamps is large enough to cover a significant portion of temple budgets.

Another facet of religiosity that is similarly viewed and emphasized by the two religious groups is spiritual experiences, which include Christians' speaking in tongues (glossolalia), unusual psychological states felt during deep meditation or prayer, prophesies appearing in dreams, and sudden cures of chronic illnesses. A similar proportion of both religious groups (88 percent of Buddhists and 86 percent of Protestants) have had spiritual experiences since they began to practice their religions. Only a few respondents replied that they have never had any spiritual experiences in their lives.

Most respondents who have spiritual experience also reported remarkably similar circumstances surrounding their experience regardless of their religious identity. Most of them, Protestants and Buddhists alike, stated that their spiritual experiences occurred when they had concentrated their minds on certain issues quite intensively. Most of them disclosed that they had sought solutions to their personal issues through their respective religious beliefs by concentrating their minds on the issues for quite a long time. They agreed that their mental concentration on important life issues brought forth the spirituality ever more intensively. According to them, the spiritual experience was preceded by their concern with certain issues. All respondents of both religious groups who had spiritual experiences brought unique stories that form a similar pattern. They agreed that they strongly upheld a belief that their supplications would eventually be answered if they prayed hard. The religion they practice does not seem to affect the degree and frequency of their spiritual experience, but individual practitioners' concentration of mind on their particular issues does.

A differential aspect that the two religious groups show in their spiritual experience is that Buddhists rely more on their own personal mental power to reach their spiritual experiences, while Protestants rely more on external agencies or sources of higher symbolic power, such as scripture, the cross, or images of God.

The last aspect of religiosity that the two religious groups similarly view and emphasize is the perceived importance of practicing religion. Most respondents of both religious groups (88 percent of Buddhists and 92 percent of Protestants) think that practicing religion in their respective religious tradition is very important for their lives, while only a few of them (10 percent of Buddhists and 8 percent of Protestants) do not do so.

Both religious groups also tend to believe that religious practice helps them obtain better lives after immigration to the United States. The majority of them admit that they have become more religious after immigration. Hardship, search for the meaning of life involved in immigration, and restoration of their mental energy for daily life are the major reasons they became more religious after immigration. They also agree that religious practice helps them maintain a good, healthy mental state for their daily lives after immigration.

Despite their featured differences in religious identities, tenets, and world-views, the two religious groups share some similar views and emphases on the source of religiosity. The similarities are driven by their religious symbols such as scriptures and offerings, which are presumed to exert an explicit religious function (confidence, conviction, comfort, truthfulness, keeping up a healthy mental state, psychological rewards, and social status). The two religious groups exhibit a high degree of similarity in that religiosity helps them uphold their material and psychological well-being in the real world. In this sense, the two religious groups at the very least share a similar aspect of religiosity that provides a basis for their religious power.

DISTINCTIVE ASPECTS OF RELIGIOSITY HELD
BY BUDDHISTS AND PROTESTANTS

Distinctive aspects of religiosity largely stem from differences in essential religious tenets and practice styles. For example, the two groups display distinctive views on miracles, presentations of religious identity, science, proselytization activities, and religious activity participation. The survey results show that Buddhists in general emphasize individualistically oriented sources for religious power, while their Protestant counterparts emphasize collectively oriented ones.

According to the survey results, almost all Protestants (98 percent) believe that miracles can occur, while a substantially lower proportion of Buddhists (84 percent) does. The two groups' difference in view of miracles is not strikingly large but is substantial enough to tell the difference in their viewpoint (table 3.2).

The different view of miracles between the two religious groups is largely due to their differential belief in the source for religious power. For instance, Buddhists' lower degree of belief in miracles is largely due to their self-reliant practice style, which renders them less likely to believe that religious power comes from external sources. For this very reason, a large proportion of Buddhists believe in the possibility of miraculous happenings once they practice their religion sincerely. However, they tend not to perceive this possibility as a miracle from a higher power but rather as their real life situation acquired by their own efforts.

When Buddhists pray in a private setting, many of them seek religious power from and in themselves, identifying themselves as the most important source for their religious power. As we have indicated earlier, however, it is also true that quite a few Buddhists in fact pray to Buddha near his image, regarding it as their source for a higher power. Buddhists' method of prayer in particular and

Table 3.2.   Religiosity indicators distinctively emphasized by Buddhists and Protestants (%)

Indicators of Religiosity	Attribution of Source	Buddhists	Protestants
Believe that miracles can happen	Collective < Private		
Yes		84*	98*
No		14*	0*
Don't know		2	2
Between religious belief and scientific knowledge, which is more relied on	Collective < Private		
Religious beliefs		58**	83**
Scientific knowledge		12	12
Equally		30**	5**
Between religious and national identity, which is more emphasized	Collective = Private		
Religious identity		42**	75**
National identity		40**	19**
Equally emphasized		18**	7**
Participate in religious activities during weekdays	Collective > Private		
Yes		62**	88**
No		38**	12**
Proselytization experience	Collective = Private		
More than 10 people		8**	31**
Few (1 or 2) people		46**	56**
Never		46**	14**
Have to attend Sunday service every week	Collective = Private		
Yes		12**	97**
No		88**	3**

*$p < .05$; **$p < .01$.

their religious practice in general look dualistic in this respect. They have Buddha in their minds as a symbolic religious power conferrer and as their most trustable exemplary of enlightened practitioners, but at the same time they perceive themselves as the most important source for their religious power. In general, Buddhists try to model after Buddha individually, while Protestants try to use themselves as an instrument for conveying the religious power conferred by the supernatural being. The two religious groups' differences in their view of miracles certainly reflect their differences in ways of identifying and conveying the source for religious power.

The two religious groups' difference in their views of miracles also suggests that the goals they pursue—religious salvation—might be same, but the paths might not. As an example, in order to achieve their religious goal, Buddhists are more likely to use a self-reliant course, which they consider as a religious power-producing process. Protestants are more likely to lean on a readily available external religious power source. Buddhists perceive that miracles can happen once individual practitioners seriously exemplify what Buddha did. Buddhists tend to believe that a miracle is something they can achieve. On the other hand, Protestants believe that miracles are not something they can achieve but are bestowed upon them in the form of grace from a higher power. Protestants often claim that miracles are virtually everywhere, but practitioners are not aware of their presence due to lack of faith.

How then do the two religious groups seemingly react to scientific knowledge, which is in general perceived to be more objective than religious claims or knowledge? In order to compare the two groups' views on religious beliefs and scientific knowledge, I asked the respondents if they relied more on religious beliefs or scientifically verified knowledge in their daily lives. A majority of Protestants (83 percent) replied that they rely on religious beliefs, while slightly more than half of Buddhists (58 percent) do so. Quite a large proportion of Buddhists (30 percent), however, replied that they rely on both religious beliefs and scientific knowledge equally. Many Buddhists interviewed also asserted that Buddhism is more scientifically oriented than any other religions, while Protestants assert that everything is under God's control, including scientific discoveries. Many Buddhists claimed that Buddhism had originated with critical views on both social and natural phenomena. Many Buddhists also claimed that Buddhism deals with matters of life in a more realistic view than any other religion. According to Buddhists' claim, Buddhists are more speculative in utilizing religious beliefs in their daily lives. This also suggests that, as the survey results disclose, Protestants are more likely to maintain a more religious way of thinking when they interpret the ways in which things around them exist and work.

The two religious groups exhibit quite distinctive presentations of their personal identity. In order to see their differences in identity presentation, I asked respondents which identity—religious or national—they emphasize more when they present themselves to others. A much higher proportion of Protestants (75 percent) than Buddhists (42 percent) replied that they rely on their religious identity rather than their national identity. Only a few Buddhists (18 percent) appeared to rely on both their religious and national identities equally, while fewer Protestants (7 percent) did so. It may be too early to conclude that

Protestants are more religious than Buddhists. The three indicators (views on miracles, science, and religious identity) we have examined, however, show that Protestants hold a higher degree of religious mindfulness in these areas. Percentage differences between the two groups concerning these three indicators are large enough to tell their distinctiveness in these areas of religiosity (see table 3.2).

The two religious groups display a very distinctive view on religious activity participation and proselytization. By and large, Protestants emphasize these areas of religiosity more strongly than do Buddhists. The survey results show that in addition to their regular religious service participation on Sunday, a large proportion of both religious groups (62 percent of Buddhists and 88 percent of Protestants) participate in extra religious activities during the week, such as dawn prayer meetings, Wednesday evening services, cell group meetings, scripture studies, and Friday evening prayer meetings. Protestants, however, show much higher participation rates than Buddhists in these extra religious activities. Buddhists' weekday religious activity participation rates, however, appear to be much higher than expected.

Consistent with the large difference in the rate of weekday religious activity participation, the two religious groups maintain a remarkably different attitude toward regular religious service attendance. Almost all Protestants (97 percent) believe that they need to attend religious services regularly, while only a few Buddhists (12 percent) believe in regular attendance. The majority of Buddhists instead view regular service attendance as the individual practitioners' choice in accordance with personal situations.

Compared with Protestants, Buddhists stress the importance of individual practitioners' mental freedom over other types of benefits they can possibly obtain through religious practice. Buddhists in general place more emphasis on individualized pace of religious practices. Many Buddhists also argue that their mundane life goals should be identical with their ultimate religious goals, because their ultimate meaning in life is also the main focus of their lives: a full, personal maturation, which is also known as Buddhahood in their own version of religious salvation. In this respect, for many Buddhists, Sunday service should not be considered their primary religious activity but rather just one of many methods of religious and spiritual discipline. A Buddhist shares his ideas about attending religious services:

> There are a lot of regulations that Buddhists have to observe. But they are not designed to restrict our behavior and ways of thinking, but to set us free from these means for an ultimate enlightenment, to the highest degree possible. Participation in the service on Sunday should not be perceived as practitioners' obligation that eventually restricts their ideas. Buddhism originally did not have churchlike services. Attending Sunday service is an adaptation from the Christian

tradition, which regulates believers' behavior and thoughts quite strictly. For me, service participation is to replenish my spiritual energy. It could be any day, not just Sunday, although it is greatly recommended for me to participate in all religious services held in the temple. Our Greater Vehicle Buddhism (Mahayana Buddhism) is also apt to praise the choice of individual practitioners in accordance with their personal situation. Practitioners can use their own judgment in solving problems if the solution is appropriate and the best alternative for their life situations. Some people might think this is arbitrary or lacking in standard. Buddhism, however, pursues the best choice in accordance with the given situation. We do not blindly follow often unrealistic religious rules. We don't believe that spiritual or religious dictates flow one way from Buddha, but we do believe that acquisition of spirituality should be a reciprocal process. I practice Buddhism for a practical reason. I personally put more values on earthly meaning of life than on heavenly ones.[17]

Unlike their Buddhist counterparts, Protestants put more stress on their standardized church order. Most Protestant churches encourage every church member to participate in services regularly. Protestant religious leaders also repeatedly urge church members to attend Sunday service every week by teaching that it is one of nonnegotiable religious regulations that Protestants are required to observe. Protestants become very conscious of their obligation to attend Sunday service from the very beginning of their church enrollment. Most Protestants also believe that earnest and consistent attendance at religious services is an important precondition for religious blessings, which are considered to be an important sign for their religious salvation. A Protestant, explaining the rationale of regular participation in Sunday service, stated that "I believe that regular service attendance is an important way of presenting my religious mindfulness. In my opinion true Christians must attend service regularly. No matter how solemnly I live in this world, I feel that some kinds of sinful or repugnant ideas penetrate my mind everyday. We Christians have to wash out these disgraceful ideas from our minds in order to keep our mind clean, just as we take a shower every day in order to keep our body clean. If time allows, I like to participate in religious services as many times as possible during the week. Once I felt God's grace, I could not wait until Sunday to express my gratefulness to God."[18]

Reflecting these differences in attitude toward regular service attendance, only a minority of Buddhists (33 percent) who are registered members of temples appear to attend Sunday service regularly, while a majority of their Protestant counterparts (75 percent) do so.[19]

In part reflecting their differences in presentation of religious identity, the two religious groups display quite a large difference in their proselytization experiences. They were asked about the frequency of proselytization experiences, measured by the number of people they eventually proselytized into their own religions. A relatively large proportion of both religious groups (54 percent of Buddhists and 87 percent of Protestants) have proselytized to a number of people of other religions or to nonpractitioners. Contrary to public beliefs, our survey results show that a relatively large proportion of Buddhists had proselytization experiences. However, the proportion of respondents who proselytized more than ten people is significantly different between the two groups. Many Protestants (31 percent) proselytized to more than ten people, while only a few Buddhists (8 percent) did so. Approximately half of Buddhists (46 percent) never proselytized, while only a few Protestants (14 percent) never did so. This is a direct reflection of differences in essential religious tenets that the two religious groups maintain. This also resonates with a Buddhist's comment on proselytization: "Proselytization is not [the] Buddhist way of practice. Developing my own Buddhahood is more important than proselytizing Buddhism to non-Buddhists. For me, becoming a good Buddhist [is] much more important than introducing my religion to others."[20]

DISCUSSIONS AND THEORETICAL IMPLICATIONS

Despite their two different religious traditions and essential tenets, the two religious groups display both similar and distinctive aspects of religiosity. Their similarities in religiosity largely stem from their emphasis on a common religious source from which practitioners obtain values, confidence, conviction, comfort, truthfulness, and psychological rewards. Their characteristic differences in religiosity, however, are more salient in the arena where practices are associated with collective activities and thoughts (e.g., religious identification, effort for expansion of their religions, and regular participation in religious services). Protestants show a much higher degree of religiosity in these areas than their Buddhist counterparts. But in some uniquely, personally grounded religiosity indicators (e.g., the sense of importance of practicing religion, spiritual experience, and trust in religious scripture), Buddhists maintain as high a degree as their Protestant counterparts.

Their differences in degree of religiosity mostly stem from differential emphasis and viewpoints on the sources for religious power, which are typified by their respective religious traditions. For instance, it is a well-known fact that Buddhism is a religion of self-reliance or of dharma (its own truth), while Christianity is a religion of supernatural reliance or of its external force of omnipotence. Buddhism also claims to be pantheistic and at the same time polytheistic, while Protestantism claims to be monotheistic.

Reflecting their emphasis on self-reliance in religious practice, Buddhists are more likely to believe that their religious commitment to personally oriented activities is more important, while Protestants are more likely to believe that a regular participation in collective religious gatherings is more important. Buddhists' emphasis on a self-reliant practice style also leads them to apply a more individual-based liberal idea to their daily concerns and practice of religion. On the other hand, Protestants' emphasis on an external, supernatural-reliant practice style leads them to apply a more standardized and collective idea to their daily concerns and practice of religion.

Largely due to the lack of comparative studies about the two religious groups' practice styles and religiosity characteristics, it is hard to generalize our findings. However, our survey and interview results suggest that the ways and the degree in which the two religious groups express their religious mindfulness differ substantially. As other researchers agree, Buddhists are by and large more subjective, inward looking, and self-responsible for things around them, while Protestants are more faith-conscious toward the divine power.[21] Buddhists also maintain a more accepting attitude toward cause-and-effect reasoning.[22]

How then do the differences in their ways and degree of presentation of religiosity possibly affect their nonreligious spheres of life, if any? Since religious practitioners tend to extend their religious beliefs to their nonreligious spheres of life,[23] the two religious groups' differences in religiosity to some extent affect their nonreligious aspects of life. One plausible observation point is the behavior that is considered to be closely associated with their socioeconomic status (e.g., educational level, income, saving rate, occupational type, social class background, etc.). The next question, then, is how are we able to secure the causal link between the two groups' religiosity characteristics and the behavior patterns associated with their socioeconomic status indicators?

According to our survey results, socioeconomic status indicators of Buddhists are a little bit higher than those of Protestants. Since the respondents are drawn from relatively devout members in their respective religious community, comparison of their socioeconomic status is less meaningful to portray than that for the respective populations of the two religious groups. Nonetheless, the survey results at least contribute to abate some stigmatized images associated with Buddhists, who once were depicted as otherworldly ascetics or world escapees.[24]

With regard to the relationship between religiosity characteristics and socioeconomic achievement of the two groups, two points of observation need to be made. First, Buddhist immigrants are different in many respects from their fellow Buddhists in Korea. Proportionally, more Buddhists than Protestants are concentrated in the rural areas of South Korea, and Buddhists are more densely concentrated in the southeastern region of the Korean peninsula, which is more industrialized than the rest of the peninsula except for the Seoul metropolitan area. Almost all of our Buddhist respondents (96 percent) lived in the four largest cities in Korea before they immigrated to the United States, whereas slightly more than three-fourths (78 percent) of Protestant respondents did so. This suggests that more Buddhist respondents than their Protestant counterparts were drawn from the most industrialized urban areas in South Korea. Buddhists' higher urban concentration rate before emigration is the most suggestive nonreligious, preemigration factor that in part explains their socioeconomic achievement after emigration. This also suggests that among the general Buddhist population in South Korea, urban Buddhists are as highly industrialized as their urban Protestant counterparts. Selectivity of international emigration can thus be as important as the two groups' religiosity characteristics in explaining their socioeconomic achievement after immigration.

Buddhists put a stronger emphasis on individualistically based sources of religiosity, and at the same time they maintain a weaker bond with their religious organizations. This is one of the major reasons many Buddhists switch their religion to Christianity upon their immigration to the United States.[25] Besides the negative images associated with their religious identity switch, Buddhists' emphasis on self-reliant practice style can have a stronghold in the arena where they utilize liberalized ideas in daily life.

Weber once sought theoretical clues to the development of modern capitalism from European Protestants' more individualized effort to affirm the grace of God, despite their belief in an insurmountable religious precept of predestination. In the sense that Buddhists apply their religious beliefs to their daily lives in a more individualized manner, they are closer to the early European Protestant immigrants than to Catholics in their application of religious beliefs to socioeconomic aspects of daily life. Buddhists' belief in the law of the karmic circle and reincarnation substitute for their Protestant counterparts' belief in predestination and resurrection, respectively. Both the early European Protestant immigrants and Korean Buddhists are ready to protest against the stricter religious and organizational regulations of Catholicism and homeland Buddhism, respectively, in order to protect what they believe is right. Like the early European Protestants, their immigration experience helps them effectively protect their beliefs, although their immigration was not motivated for religious reasons.

Encountering the different religio-cultural plausibility structure in America, some Buddhists, keeping a strong religio-cultural identity after immigration in reaction to the host society, are also more likely to maintain a more mission-oriented attitude as religious and cultural pioneers in the new world.[26] In addition to their liberal application of religious belief to their daily lives, which allows them more independence in their adjustment, their pioneer-like immigration experience also helps them more actively engage in and venture into the business world after immigration. Many active practitioners also tend to carry on an ascetic lifestyle in order to keep up a high fidelity in belief and a better application of religious beliefs to nonreligious spheres of life. The survey results display that Buddhists and Protestants alike become more religious and espouse an ascetic lifestyle more strongly after immigration. The two religious groups show no difference in daily life concerns and their value orientations, such as hard work, frugality, trust, and future orientation.[27] Buddhist respondents' income level and engagement in professionalism are higher than those of their Protestant counterparts. Buddhists' average annual personal income was $53,130 (N = 23), while Protestants' was $44,016 (N = 32). Reflecting their premigration socioeconomic backgrounds, a much higher proportion of Buddhists had managerial and professional types of occupations before and after immigration (30 percent and 18 percent, respectively) than their Protestant counterparts (7 percent and 14 percent, respectively).

Regardless of their religious devoutness, most first-generation immigrants strongly bear a success-oriented mind-set even before they immigrate to the United States. Once their immigration ethos is reinforced by their religious ethics, whether they are Buddhist or Protestant the effect seems to increase greatly. Active practitioners' high level of religious activity participation also provides them with a good opportunity for forming a close-knit social network through which they promote social capital.[28] This is an implicit effect of a religious immigrant community on its members' socioeconomic achievement in the host society. This area of study, however, has not been elaborated fully.

NOTES

1. The research and findings of this essay are based in part on Okyun Kwon, *Buddhist and Protestant Korean Immigrants: Religious Beliefs and Socioeconomic Aspects of Life* (New York: LFB Scholarly Publishing, 2003), 227–40.

2. Ibid., 50, 52–53, 83–84.

3. Insook H. Park, J. Fawcett, F. Arnold, and R. Gardner, *Korean Immigrants and U.S. Immigration Policy: A Pre-Departure Perspective,* East-West Population Institute Paper Series, No. 114 (Honolulu: East-West Center, 1990), 60–61. See also Korean Government, National Statistical Office, *Korean Statistical Yearbook,* 43rd ed. (Seoul: Korean Government National Statistical Association, 1996), 23; Yi Heum Yoon, ed., *The Yearbook of Korean Religions,* Vol. 1 (Seoul: Korea Research Institute for Religion and Society, 1993), 122–208.

4. Approximately 17 percent of first-generation Filipinos in the United States, 32 percent of Chinese in Chicago, 37 percent of Japanese in Chicago, and 65 percent of Asian Indians and Pakistanis in Canada attend religious services at their ethnic religious centers, according to Won Moo Hurh and Kwang Chung Kim, "Religious Par-

ticipation of Korean Immigrants in the United States," *Journal for the Scientific Study of Religion* 29(1) (1990): 19–34. See also Kwon, *Buddhist and Protestant Korean Immigrants,* 5.

5. Rodney Stark and William Sims Bainbridge, *A Theory of Religion* (New Brunswick, NJ: Rutgers University Press, 1996), 112.

6. Robert J. Taylor, J. Mattis, and L. M. Chatters, "Subjective Religiosity among African Americans: A Synthesis of Findings from Five National Samples," *Journal of Black Psychology* 25(4) (1999): 524–43.

7. Keith A. Roberts, *Religion in Sociological Perspective,* 3rd ed. (Belmont, CA: Wadsworth, 1995), 88–89.

8. Max Weber, *The Sociology of Religion,* translated by E. Fischoff (Boston: Beacon Press, 1993), 166, 173; Max Weber, *The Protestant Ethic and the Spirit of Capitalism* (London: Hyman, 1930), 118.

9. Lawrence R. Iannaccone, "Risk, Rationality, and Religious Portfolios," *Economic Inquiry* 33(2) (1995): 285.

10. Ibid., 290.

11. Ibid.

12. Barrington Moore Jr., *Moral Purity and Persecution in History* (Princeton, NJ: Princeton University Press, 2000), 65, 81, and 102.

13. James Huntley Grayson, *Early Buddhism and Christianity in Korea: A Study in the Explanation of Religion* (Leiden, Netherlands: E. J. Brill, 1985), 61–62.

14. Andrew E. Kim, "Korean Religious Culture and Its Affinity to Christianity: The Rise of Protestant Christianity in South Korea," *Sociology of Religion* 61(2) (2000): 117–33.

15. Data reported are from the combination of in-depth interviews of 40 members of the two congregations, closed-ended interviews of 109 respondents of the two religious communities, and participant observations of the two congregations. Interviewees are divided by their religious and gender identities. Among them, 50 are Buddhists and 59 Protestants, 57 are males (26 Buddhists and 31 Protestants), and 52 are females (24 Buddhists and 28 Protestants). The respondent range in age from twenty-four through sixty-five years.

16. The selected congregations are the Korean Buddhist Won Kak Temple (Wonkaksa in Korean) and the Grace Korean Presbyterian Church (Han-Min Kyo Hoe in Korean). The Buddhist temple is located in Salisbury Mills, Orange County, New York, and the Protestant church is located in Bayside, Queens, New York.

17. From an interview with Mr. J. S. Kwak on August 23, 1997.

18. From an interview with Mr. Y. B. Kim on March 21, 1998.

19. According to my survey of Korean Protestant churches and Buddhist temples in the New York metropolitan area, the average number of registered members of Protestant churches was 237, and that of Buddhist temples was 258. The number of regular service attendees of Protestant churches was 166 (75 percent of the registered members), and that of Buddhist temples was 43 (33 percent of the registered members).

20. From an interview with Ms. M. S. Cho, September 23, 1998.

21. Stephen S. Fugita and Marilyn Fernandez, "Religion and Japanese Americans' Views of Their World War II Internment," Paper presented at the 1999 Association for Asian American Studies Conference, 11, 26.

22. Kwon, *Buddhist and Protestant Korean Immigrants,* 198–99.

23. Gerhard Lenski, *The Religious Factor: A Sociological Study of Religion's Impact on Politics, Economics, and Family Life* (Garden City, NY: Doubleday, 1961), 8; Weber, *The Protestant Ethic and the Spirit of Capitalism,* 27.

24. Weber, *The Protestant Ethic and the Spirit of Capitalism,* 118, 228.

25. Kwon, *Buddhist and Protestant Korean Immigrants,* 181.

26. Ho-Youn Kwon, Kwang Chung Kim, and R. Stephen Warner, ed.s, *Korean Americans and Their Religions: Pilgrims and Missionaries from a Different Shore* (University Park: Pennsylvania State University Press, 2001), 5, 68; Helen Rose Ebaugh and Fenggang Yang, "Religion and Ethnicity among New Immigrants: The Impact of Majority/Minority Status in Home and Host Countries," *Journal for the Scientific Study of Religion* 40(3) (2001): 367–78.

27. Okyun Kwon, "Religious Beliefs and Socioeconomic Aspects of Life of Buddhist and Protestant Korean Immigrants," PhD diss., City University of New York, 2000, 449.

28. Eric Woodrum, "Religion and Economics among Japanese Americans: A Weberian Study," *Social Force* 64 (1985): 191–204.

PASSAGES

If religious traditions represent the more formal and organized nature of religion, then various passages suggest something of how religion and spirituality take shape in the lives of people. Jae Ran Kim has ably shown how religion factored into the experiences of Korean adoptees to the United States. Some adoption agencies have operated from an explicit goal of placing Korean children into American Christian homes, even as this population has rarely been part of the phenomenal growth of Korean American churches. For those within immigrant congregations, Sang Hyun Lee employs the concept of liminality to assess how Korean Americans have navigated worship within the Christian context. Although the position of being in-between can be a source of pain and loss, Lee suggests that it can also serve as a source of positive transformation and creative action for Korean Americans.

Jung Ha Kim writes about never-married women, underscoring how this particular subset of women operates as religious practitioners as well as theological innovators. The status of being never married also illustrates the diversity of women's experiences and how multiple social locations can be occupied at the same time. Ruth Chung and Sung Hyun Um also take up the theme of marriage but from the perspective of religiosity as a predictor of marital commitment and satisfaction among immigrant, 1.5-generation, and second-generation couples. Their findings suggest that more frequent church attendance contributes to greater marital commitment. Such was not necessarily the case for marital satisfaction. In varied ways, then, these essays in this section explore the role of religion and spirituality in the context of life passages.

Chapter Four

Waiting for God

Religion and Korean American Adoption

Jae Ran Kim

Some children see Him almond-eyed,
This Saviour whom we kneel beside
Some children see Him almond-eyed
With skin of yellow hue!

Alfred Burt, "Some Children
See Him," lyrics
by Wihla Hutson, 1951

Historically speaking, adopted Koreans are the unacknowledged, forgotten children of the Korean diaspora. In discussions of Korean America we are rarely invited to the table. We are the physical manifestations of shame and embarrassment in South Korea, where the stigma and control that exists around women's sexual activities have resulted in hundreds of thousands of abandoned or relinquished children, and in the countries that have received us, where we become replacement children for infertile couples or social experiments in color-blind theory. Americans know little about the Korean War, which was the major contributing factor in the phenomenon of Korean adoption. To many Americans, Koreans are the late-bloomer cousins to the neon-colored industrial, high-tech Japanese or the nameless, mute citizens scurrying about the background in the movie and television show *M*A*S*H*. Our civil conflict was not played out on television as the Vietnam conflict was. So, historically, American perceptions of wars fought against Asians tend to leapfrog from the Japanese who bombed Pearl Harbor to the Viet Cong guerrillas and the Tet offensive in Vietnam.

Flip through the texts of Frank Wu's *Yellow*,[1] Ronald Takaki's *Strangers from a Distant Shore*,[2] or *Asian American Dreams* by Helen Zia,[3] and we are relegated to a footnote or excluded entirely. Perhaps that is due to our shorter history as Americans, having just passed our fifty-year anniversary in the United States. Maybe it is a result of our scattered geographical displacements, where we become the lone representation of Asia America in the tiny hamlets of Small Town, USA. Or it could be the consequence of the assimilation necessary to survive for so many of us that have whitened away our racial, ethnic, and cultural identities as Koreans. As stated in the introduction to *Religion and Spirituality in Korean America,* adopted Koreans represented such as one-third of the immigrants entering the United States during the postwar period, sandwiched between Korean military brides and college students. Our total numbers today are about 10 percent of the total Korean American population.[4]

How do Korean adoptees in the United States experience religion and spirituality? What we know exists only from the limited published works written by a few Korean adoptees. The few research studies on Korean adoptees in the United States have focused mostly on the themes of adoptee racial identity construction or social and psychological adjustment.[5] When it comes to how we express and experience faith, we have been largely silent.

The information we have about Korean adoptee experiences of faith, religion, and spirituality come from personal essays and memoirs. Most of what is written, however, are descriptions of what it was like to grow up with Christian or Catholic parents. In her memoir *Ten Thousand Sorrows,* Elizabeth Kim vividly recounts her isolated, grim childhood with an abusive Christian fundamentalist minister and his wife, who forced her to marry a deacon in the church many years her senior.[6] In *The Language of Blood,* Jane Jeong Trenka writes about the small northern Minnesota town she was adopted to and provides a poignantly accurate description of the German Lutheran church where her mother made casseroles for church-basement potlucks and her father passed the offering plates.[7] What we don't hear from Trenka is how growing up in this religious community affected how she looked at the concept of God as a child and now as an adult. We don't know how she integrated her experiences into her overall identity. Adoptee narratives sometimes mention a belief in God or a line or two about being a Christian or Buddhist, but few expand beyond the self-identifying label.

From the written words of Korean adoptees on the subject of religion and spirituality, we have learned that the individual racial and religious identities of adopted Koreans are constructed within the framework of our adoptive families' racial and religious identities. Most adoptees, like myself, grow up in isolation in communities without Asian Americans, much less Korean Americans. Very few adoptive families have understood or had access to the connection of the Korean American community on racial, cultural, and spiritual levels. While many adoptive parents these days bring at least a token element of Korean culture into their homes, it is rare that a Christian adoptive family takes the step to attend a Korean church despite the opportunity for the growth of their adopted children's cultural as well as spiritual connections.

Despite the limited amount of information on adopted Korean American experiences with religion and spirituality, we do know that the Korean adoptee diaspora has been more isolated than other Korean American immigrants. Military brides who came to the United States often faced extreme isolation and ostracism in their communities but still came to the United States as partners in a relationship. Adoptees had to navigate from a space of being outsiders of their own family as well as society. Adoptees were allowed to enter the United States during a time when federal immigration laws barred other Asians. This position as a "special" and protected classification of immigrants may have been more accepted because as children we were easy to assimilate into the dominant society. Until recently, we did not have the language to position ourselves as members of a larger Korean American community.

There have been different phases, or eras, of Korean adoptions in the United States. The first is the Missionary Era, from 1953 to 1969, based on the identification, processing, and proselytizing of the so-called Korean orphan problem by evangelical Christians. The second era might be termed "Shifting Markets" and occurred during the 1970s and 1980s, when white American parents had a limited supply of domestic children available for adoption and thus turned to developing countries for children. South Korea in particular was a favorite choice because of the precedents set by the previous decades. For instance, South Korea was the only sending country that did not require the adoptive parents to travel to the country and pick up their child in person. The paperwork required for adoption, moreover, was fairly straightforward. The years since 1990 represent a third phase in which adoptive parents have had many more choices, especially influenced by China's adoption program. These newer adoptive parents have blended and tempered the humanitarian and entitlement frameworks of international adoption and have been much more likely to adopt the culture as well as the child, although at times the boundary between appreciation and appropriation is unclear.

Although the experiences of Korean adoptees have been largely absent from history texts and other works in the humanities and social sciences, there have been recent efforts by adoptees to bring an insider perspective to bear upon this topic. I include myself among these authors who have taken ownership of their own histories and social realities.

My Journey "Home"

The statue of Mary rises from the ground, her arms stretched out, palms upward in prayer. The deep folds of her long gray robes melt into the foliage of a half-dead winter garden. It is nearly the end of March and still jacket chilly. The whole landscape before me seems washed in sepia; the sky and Mary are cold and gray; the brittle fallen leaves from last autumn gather at Mary's feet and parched brown grass licks up to the garden's stone border. The church buildings surround me in a half circle. Directly behind Mary is the daycare that used to be Paek Paek Hap, White Lily. Once it was an orphanage, my orphanage. Thirty years ago under the blank gaze of Mary I arrived as a 14–month old infant, one of six kids found abandoned that day, passed from a city official at Daegu City Hall to the waiting arms of a nun. Once I was Catholic, and like all of the babies and children of Daegu who came through the doors of White Lily, we baptized ourselves with holy tears and became one of God's and an American family's sacrificial lambs.

I have come to this garden and this statue to exhale. Running away from the faith and churches of my childhood led me to this hibernating garden of the Sisters of St. Paul Chartres. Had I truly abandoned my faith, was not my presence here in this garden, in this city, in this country more than six thousand miles from my home and family in Minnesota faith that this place would provide the answers I was searching for?

One of the Sisters has just given me my file. It holds one single document, the same one I already possess, nearly blank. "Sorry, there is no more information," she tells me. "Nothing else I can do." Pausing before Mary one last time, I picture the garden in bloom and wonder if white lilies are among those flowers that ornament Mary's robes throughout the spring and summer.[8]

THE MISSIONARY ERA

The Sisters of the St. Paul Chartres, a group of French apostolates, established White Lily in Korea in 1888 to take in and care for thirty orphan children, and White Lily continued to operate as an orphanage until 1991, at which time the orphanage shut down and a daycare center was established in its place.[9] White Lily is typical of many Catholic and Protestant missionary programs in South Korea, serving the needs of children through a variety of services. Unlike the United States, South Korea does not have a government-run child welfare system. South Koreans have depended upon the charitable efforts of religious institutions and privately operated agencies to take care of orphaned and abandoned children who were not taken in by relatives. Like thousands of others, I was just one of many children abandoned or relinquished on the steps of a church, police station, or train platform; cared for in orphanages or foster homes; and eventually placed in the arms of a family in North America, Europe, or Australia. The official count varies anywhere from 150,000 to 200,000 Korean-born children who have been adopted to other countries. The United States alone accounts for at least 105,994 Korean children adopted between 1953 and 2005.[10]

In September of 1950, as General Douglas MacArthur commandeered American troops toward the city of Incheon, a Christian missionary by the name of Dr. Bob Pierce was unfolding his plan to help the Korean children orphaned as a result of the war. His plan was World Vision, an organization that would provide humanitarian aid to children in China and Korea.[11] Dr. Pierce traveled around the United States to church sanctuaries and school gymnasiums, campaigning on behalf of the "orphaned" Korean children through World Vision's child sponsorship program in which an individual or families could send a monthly sum to support a Korean child. Many of these children truly were orphaned, but the orphanages were also overflowing with Amerasian children, a different kind of war casualty. These Amerasian children were not literal orphans but rather were abandoned or relinquished because of the stigma and shame associated with being mixed race and of having white or African American fathers. Although the official war began in June of 1950, American troops had been in South Korea since 1945.[12] Thus, American GI's had at least five years to father and abandon children with local Korean women before the rest of the world realized that the problem existed. According to Eleana Kim, more than 90 percent of children adopted out between 1953 and 1960 were mixed race.[13]

It was at one of Pierce's lectures at the high school in Eugene, Oregon, in 1954 that *Other Sheep,* a grainy, black and white film of Korean children, inspired a local farmer named Harry Holt and his family. As Bertha Holt writes in her memoir, *The Seed from the East,* "Then came the scenes that shattered our hearts. We saw before us the tragic plight of hundreds of illegitimate children . . . GI-babies . . . children that had been hidden by remorseful mothers until it was no longer possible to keep their secret."[14]

For ten dollars a month, a sponsored child would receive food, clothing, and shelter, and, most importantly according to Bertha, "this small sum would provide Christian education and supervision."[15] The Holt family signed on to support ten children. The combination of Dr. Pierce's vision and Harry Holt's tenacious determination fueled by their evangelical beliefs transformed the concept of adoption not just for Koreans but for the rest of the world as well.

In many ways, Holt embodied the cultural narrative of the American ideal of the time period. Together with his wife Bertha, the Holts are presented as the archetype of the 1950s. Harry is usually portrayed as paternal, hardworking, and masculine, a man of the earth and the unquestioned spiritual and authoritative head of the household. Despite his many health problems, he often dictated orders from bed. Bertha is described as the ideal caretaker, mothering their six biological children and eight adopted children and often administering medical treatments to Harry.

Holt has long been mythologized as being "just a plain, humble farmer" by the media and the Holt organization in an attempt to disguise the ambitious and dogmatic nature of his agenda to promote Christianity. As Bertha Holt writes in their biography *Bring My Sons from Afar,* "It must surely be true that in the beginning God created a plan to rescue the Amerasian children of the Korean conflict. . . . They were the backwash of war, the outcasts of society . . . but God did not forsake them. . . . [H]e chose a fifty-year-old weakened by a long scar on his heart."[16] In fact, Harry Holt was a businessman, and a successful one at that. In addition to his sawmill business in Oregon, he had been proceeding with plans to expand his business in South America. After a heart attack in 1950, he sold his business and purchased farmland. It was also during this time that his foray into Christianity grew into a zealous fervor.

By the summer of 1955, Harry was on his way to Korea to look into adopting the Korean orphans that the Holt family had been sponsoring under the ministrations of World Vision. Experiencing insomnia during a layover in a Tokyo hotel room, Harry reached over to the hotel nightstand and pulled out the Gideon Bible. According to Bertha, "In the darkness he thumbed through it and put in his finger and turned on the light. His thumb was on Isaiah 43:5. *Fear not for I am with thee.* At that moment he was assured that it was not Harry Holt, it was the Lord Himself who was doing this. He wept for joy, then he read two more verses, 'I will bring thy seed from the east, and gather thee from the west; I will say to the north, give up; and to the south, keep not back: bring my sons from afar, and my daughters from the ends of the earth.'"[17] It was a calling, he believed, to facilitate adoptions between all the orphaned children and American parents. Holt rechanneled his former enthusiasm for business toward a new horizon: to bring Korean "war orphans" from the "cold and misery and darkness of Korea into the warmth and love of your homes."[18]

The federal law that governed the adoption of foreign-born children to the United States in 1955 was the Refugee Relief Act. Children adopted to the United States from Germany and Japan had been the primary beneficiaries of the Refugee Relief Act, but children from other countries, including South Korea, had also been adopted through this law. The Holts, in seeking to adopt their eight sponsored "orphans," were asking for six more children than the Refugee Relief Act allowed. Since the Refugee Relief Act limited American families to adopting two children, the Holts appealed to Senator Richard Neuberger, the U.S. senator from Oregon. The Holts asked Senator Neuberger to help them navigate the adoption of all eight children.

While Harry Holt was in Korea meeting the family's sponsored children, Senator Neuberger successfully passed HR 7043 as part of the Refugee Relief Act through Congress on July 31, 1955. The provisions in HR 7043 allowed the Holts to proceed with the adoptions.[19] It is important to note that the Immigration Act of 1924 had barred immigration to the United States for Chinese, Japanese, Koreans, and South Asian Indians,[20] and the Immigration and Nationality Act of 1965, which lifted these restrictions, would not be passed for another ten years. HR 7043 did not change immigration restrictions for other Asian immigrants; it only provided an exception for Korean-born children whose immigration to the United States was for the purpose of adoption. Holt's ability to adopt Korean children during a time when Asian immigration was severely restrictive is in itself a remarkable feat.[21]

On October 14, 1955, Holt returned from Korea with his eight adopted children and the Holt's immediately began helping other Americans adopt. In 1956, the Holt Adoption Agency opened for business.[22] The media surrounding the Holts' adoptions and vocal evangelism created such a frenzy that the number of children adopted from Korea rose from 59 in 1955 to 671 by the end of 1956.[23] Holt had tapped into the zeitgeist of middle-class America's desire toward humanitarian aid framed within a Protestant ethic.

SHIFTING MARKETS

The civil rights era blossomed in the 1960s, during which there was tremendous societal upheaval that influenced the world of American adoptions. In 1972 *Roe v. Wade* legalized abortions, and in that same year William T. Merritt, president of the National Association of Black Social Workers, spoke out against the adoption of black children into nonblack homes, calling it "racial and cultural genocide."[24] A few years later, Congress enacted the Indian Child Welfare Act of 1978, prohibiting what had been the routine practice of putting Indian children in non-Indian adoptive homes and Christian boarding schools, which was, according to the National Indian Child Welfare Association, an action to "terminate the very existence of all Indian tribes."[25] The Indian Child Welfare Act of 1978 stated that "there is no resource that is more vital to the continued existence and integrity of Indian tribes than their children."[26] The African American and American Indian communities had recognized that these transracial adoptions meant the loss of future members of their cultural and racial communities. White adoptive parents were not instilling racial and cultural pride; in fact, most of the experiences of American Indian children prior to 1978 were of being prohibited to speak or practice their native languages or cultural traditions.

The societal shifts around female reproductive rights, including the feminist movement, *Roe v. Wade,* the widespread availability of birth control pills, and an increase in women postponing marriage and childbirth, contributed to the decrease in both fertility and births rates among white child-bearing women. In addition, the stigma of being a single mother had decreased in the United States. As a result, it became more difficult for prospective white adoptive parents to find healthy white infants. At the same time, agency and government

Table 4.1.   Number of children sent overseas
for adoption by decade

Decade	Adoptions
1953–1959	2,899
1960–1969	6,166
1970–1979	46,035
1980–1989	66,511
1990–1999	22,925
2000–2005	10,579

policies restricting the availability for African American and American Indian children meant that there were also fewer children of color available for adoption. Americans who wanted to adopt looked to foreign countries.

The demand for children was high, and South Korea had a large supply. Poverty remained a factor for why some Korean families relinquished children, but as often happens when a country becomes industrialized, young women moved to urban areas for employment and were vulnerable to sexual exploitation.[27] South Korea's economy was on the rise, as were the number of babies born to unwed women.

While a thread of humanitarian or rescue perspective may have continued to influence adoptions during this period, the larger driving force was that American couples wanted to adopt and felt entitled to experience parenthood. It is during this era that the number of Korean adoptions grew to more than 66,500 children in 1980s (table 4.1).

THIRD PHASE

The 1988 Olympic Games in Seoul was South Korea's chance to show the world how far the country had come since the end of the Korean War in 1953. Instead, the American media portrayed South Korea as a country that "exported their children"[28] for economic gain, as reported by television media and Matthew Rothschild's *Progressive* article "Babies for Sale: South Koreans Make Them, Americans Buy Them."[29] The government reacted quickly, setting goals to reduce the number of adoptions each year until they ended all together, although that goal was never realized. After 1990, the number of adoptions decreased dramatically, and adoptions to the United States remained at around fifteen hundred. The only time since 1990 that adoptions to the United States rose to more than two thousand was 1999 and may be explained by the economic crisis that occurred in South Korea in late 1997.[30] South Korea may have decided to reduce the number of children allowed to be adopted to the United States and other countries, but the demand for children did not decrease. South Korean children dropped to the third spot behind China and Russia on the U.S. list of immigrant visas for "orphans" by 1995, and by 2000 Guatemala pushed South Korea to the fourth-largest sending country.

Adoptive parents today are much more likely to consider their families in a multicultural and multiracial context. Adopted Korean children had now reached their thirties and forties, and many were parents themselves and were beginning to inform the world about their experiences.

Racial Re/construction—In God's Image

Some children see him Lily white,
    The baby Jesus born this night,
Some children see him lily white,
    With tresses soft and fair.

Some children see Him almond-eyed
This Saviour whom we kneel beside
Some children see Him almond-eyed
    With skin of yellow hue![31]

It is fitting that my early experience as a child of God was at White Lily, as the family, church, and community that I was adopted into was "lily white." The hymn above, which was sung each Christmas Eve in my childhood church, goes on to describe Jesus as "bronzed and brown" or "dark as they,"[32] presenting a theme of the universality of Jesus. As one of only two adopted Asians in my church, I represented a weekly reminder of the success of God's presence in faraway heathen countries. I had, after all, in the words of Harry Holt, been delivered from the "cold and misery and darkness of Korea."[33] I have at times believed that my parents adopted me for the purpose of adding bonus points to their heavenly tally. It is no secret that many of the first agencies to actively recruit families for the adoption of South Korean children were faith-based organizations such as Holt's. "It is our personal desire that these children go into Christian homes," stated Holt's *Adoption Handbook*. "We want to let these children we serve come to know Jesus."[34]

According to the Adoption History Project, the Holts "were happy to accept couples who had been rejected, for a variety of reasons, by conventional adoption agencies."[35] In short, the Holts bypassed the traditional home study standards set at the time by the U.S. Children's Bureau and the Child Welfare League of America. The Holt's believed that the only qualification prospective adoptive parents had to have was a personal belief in Jesus Christ. The form letter Holt sent to prospective parents states, "In the enclosed application you are asked to state in your own words what your faith is and what Jesus Christ means to you personally."[36] Close friend Senator Neuberger, the politician responsible for changing federal laws enabling adoptions from Korea, referred to them as modern-day "Good Samaritans" in a speech before the U.S. Congress.[37]

Many in the adoption field are uneasy with the relationship of agencies such as Holt's and their Korean affiliates because of their emphasis on Christianity. Robert Ackerman, the Immigration and Naturalization Service officer in charge of adoptions at the U.S. embassy in Seoul during the 1980s, worried that the more extreme religious adoption agencies viewed adoptions as "a quick means of spreading the Gospel, a head start on proselytizing."[38] Ackerman had reason to be concerned. Following Holt's example, adoption agencies with unabashed religious agendas flourished and continue to operate today. An Internet search for "adoption" and "Christian" brings up web pages by organizations with names such as Christian World Adoption Agency[39] and All God's Children Adoption Agency.[40] The Holt Adoption Agency, now going by the name Holt International, still operates within an evangelical framework. Its mission statement is that "Holt International Children's Services is dedicated to carrying out God's plan for every child to have a permanent, loving family."[41]

Korean children were not the only children whose spiritual lives were an important factor in assimilating a group of people. Native American children had been forcibly removed from their homes and placed into Catholic and Protestant boarding schools[42] or adoptive homes since the mid-1800s in order to "Kill the Indian, save the Man."[43] The underlying theme among Protestant Christian philosophy in the welfare of children of color is one of "saving the heathen" from the "dark or savage" ways of their native cultures.[44] Harry Holt, in his 1955 "Dear Friends" newsletter, wrote, "We would ask all of you who are Christians to pray to God that he will give us the wisdom and strength and the power to deliver his little children from the cold and misery and darkness of Korea."[45]

Holt's letter reveals much about the sentiments that Americans had toward people of color: Korea is a country of "misery and darkness," and people of color are not willing or able to take care of their own. Holt's letter also echoes Andrew Sung Park's assessment that the history of the Christian church has often "offered positive endorsement[s] of racism." Park writes that "the church has often promoted the perception among its (usually white) members that they are superior to adherents of other religions, and this has in turn often been extended to perceptions of racial superiority as well."[46]

Korean children adopted by white parents in the 1950s and 1960s were often subject to intense racial prejudice inside their own places of worship. Church was not a sanctuary from the eye-pulling, ching-chong chants and racially charged epithets that I received from the children in my school. Some churches were active participants in the racial reconstruction of adopted Korean children, either through denigrating Koreans and Korean culture or by placing an importance on a universal identity (i.e., white) as a Christian. Either way, both overt and covert biases led to adopted Korean children distancing themselves from their ethnic heritage in order to fit in with the dominant culture. In my own Sunday school classes, I was subject to name calling and eye pulling. I endured racist descriptions of naked African tribes practicing voodoo, sinister Russian officials ready to kill Christians in the Soviet Union, and backwards Chinese and Koreans who practiced idol and ancestor worship. Missionaries, I was told, were the gatekeepers through which unsaved racial others could enter heaven. Since the majority of Korean children adopted to the United States are placed in European American homes, we are given a quasi status as not truly white but not Asian either. We are neither refugees nor immigrants in the traditional definitions. Due to our special immigration status, we are exempt from being a racial other.

Christianity also has a tendency to breed a kind of color blindness by promoting a "we are all God's children" mentality that is often as dangerous as overt racism to a child of color. This is especially true for an adopted child who is the sole representation of other in a white congregation. It is easy for a church community to forget our racial, cultural, and ethnic heritage. In Christianity, all human beings are God's children. My own parents, for example, did not recognize or acknowledge the racism I encountered because they did not see me as a Korean person. Racism could not exist in a place where everyone was the same.

The irony of the hymn "Some Children See Him" was that I did not see Jesus as "almond-eyed" with a "skin of yellow hue." For as long as I could remember, every picture of Jesus—from my little white leather-bound children's Bible to the paintings hung in the church—was the same: a white Jesus with long wavy brown hair and wearing a white robe and sandals. This universal view of Jesus being white reinforced a framework that white people are our saviors.

SPIRITUALITY AS A CULTURAL CONNECTION

Why is it that most adoptive parents discount the Korean churches as places for cultural, social, and spiritual growth? The idea that church provides more than just an individual's spiritual foundation might be a clue. White adoptive parents who attend a Korean church become the racial minority in that setting.

Some families choose places of worship that reflect their own social identities, without thinking about how their adopted Korean children experience being racial minorities on a daily level. Even if the doctrine and liturgy of the Korean church is the same as a non-Korean church, it is telling that most adoptive parents would prefer the comfort of their own social community with whom to share their religious and spiritual beliefs and practice. Lack of access to a Korean American church is another reality that many adoptive families face, but for those adoptive families who do have a Korean American spiritual community close by, there is the language barrier to overcome. For many Korean American churches, the development of English-language services or ministries is a relatively new practice.

What happens when the adoptive parents' religious and spiritual faith is also deeply tied to ethnic and cultural identities? In "A Daughter of the Commandment," Eileen Deitcher, an adoptive mother, reflects upon the day when she tells her five-year-old daughter about "their [Jewish] ancestors," and her daughter responds, "Not *my* ancestors." Deitcher writes, "Back then you were a sensitive, perceptive little girl who was beginning to explore your complex heritage—Korean, American, Jewish, and blend of Danish, Irish and Swedish as well. So when you heard about these Biblical ancestors who are so important in Jewish tradition, you were asking, 'What does this have to do with me?'"[47]

Deitcher negates her daughter's concerns about participating in a religious faith based on the importance of genealogical ancestry. The mother uses her own ethnic cultural aspects of being "American, Jewish, . . . Danish, Irish and Swedish" to illustrate that her daughter's Korean ancestry is but a small part of her overall heritage. Embracing these European American and Jewish ethnic and cultural identities assumes that the Korean adopted daughter must subvert her Korean ancestry, which does not trace back to Jewish ancestry, in order to be a member of the adoptive family's spiritual community.

Sometimes it is not as simple as chastising adoptive parents because they do not choose to attend a Korean church. The diaspora of adoptees is reflected in the large numbers who grow up in small towns where no Korean community exists. Some might question why adoptive parents would consciously choose to raise Korean American children in areas devoid of Korean communities, but the reasons behind those choices are complex and often justified or simplified as meeting the needs of the parents over the needs of the adopted Korean child. As a result, Korean adoptees attend the churches, synagogues, and other religious institutions that reflect their adoptive parents identities. It is also easier for adoptees living in isolated or rural areas to assimilate to the dominant culture, whereas Korean American immigrant families represent a group of Asians versus an individual person.

As a whole, Korean Christian churches have not taken a stand in the issue of adoption, and if adoptees are mentioned at all, it's often in the context similar to how Pastor Jin S. Kim, a Korean American minister and the director of the Korean Adoptee Ministry (KAM), writes in his sermon "Jesus the Adoptee." "I am convinced that adoptees have a unique and natural insight into the heart of Jesus Christ who is the adoptee par excellence, the archetype of all adoptees in the world ever born."[48]

Kim advises adoptees to "understand from the earliest age that their only true father is their Father in Heaven" and suggests that Jesus as a son of God adopted by humans was the first "cross-cultural" adoption.[49] Kim uses the framework of a spiritual identity as primary over cultural, ethnic, and even biological/family identities, a parallel to those who claim that the only race is the human race.

Kim is one of the few leaders in the Korean American Christian community who have recognized the identity struggles of adopted Koreans, including their unique spiritual needs. Kim created KAM at a Korean Presbyterian church in Minnesota, which advertises its services to adoptees and adoptive families with the catch phrase, "Blood is thicker than water! Jesus' love is thicker than Blood!"

The paradox for some is that KAM believes the way to "heal" the pain of adoption is to figuratively become adopted yet again, that is, "to become a child of God."[50] However, some adoptees find comfort in groups such as KAM and the community of the church. Jamie Kemp found the commonalities among the first- and second-generation Korean Americans and adoptees at her church a salve for her bitter feelings toward the country that abandoned her. "Although our backgrounds divide us to a certain degree," writes Kemp, "they all seem to accept me because we share the same heritage and faith. Our common Christian way of thinking binds us closer together."[51]

Kemp's experience is a reminder that not all adopted Koreans feel that Christianity is racist or has reinforced or exacerbated racism. Some, such as Stephen C. Morrison, openly express the importance of their religious faith in their lives and want to use their faith to help adoptees. Morrison was adopted to the United States in 1970 at the age of fourteen and is the founder of Mission to Promote Adoption in Korea (MPAK), an organization whose aim is to reframe the concept through the adoption of Korean children by Koreans and Korean Americans. Acknowledging during a 1999 speech in Seoul that Koreans and Korean Americans were not adopting Korean children, Morrison stated that "I have given many testimonies at various Korean churches regarding my adoption experience, and shared the love I have received from my parents and from God. . . . I have tried to be an instrument to give God the glory. . . . As a Christian, I have especially tried to reach out to the

Korean Christians to look at such children with the compassion that Christ felt for them."[52]

One of the most engaging accounts of an adoptee's personal spiritual journey comes from James Straker, who after years of struggling with "the dilemma presented by two opposing natures, one . . . that wants an Asian identity and the other that wants to avoid all of the complications and intense emotions associated with Asian identity," and "the world of abandonment and of adoption." Straker recounts how a Benedictine monk saved his life through "the gift of faith." For three years Straker lived as Brother Titus in the Benedictine tradition, and during this time he found a measure of solace and peace in his life. Straker writes that he devoted "a lot of time and prayer to finding a peaceful resolution to the unanswered questions that my adoption had brought into my life. And God's gift to me was to find the answers to these questions in the . . . Biblical themes of abandonment, adoption and redemption. . . . I believe it is this kinship of human experience and being which somehow transforms the vagaries of life into important discoveries; enduring discoveries of just how far the human spirit can soar."[53] Jamie Kemp's faith also enabled her to work toward bringing a sense of peace about her abandonment. "Through fellowship with church members and through prayer," Kemp writes, "I have found great comfort and strength that in due time, in my walk with God, I will forgive a country that can't seem to forgive itself."[54]

The Korean adoptee community is very diverse, but our shared experience of being adopted has driven many of us to look at one another. In 1999, the first Gathering of Adult Korean Adoptees was held in Washington, D.C., and four hundred adopted Koreans from around the world attended the conference. For many, it was the first time they had been in a room with other adopted Koreans. Since then, Korean adoptees have begun to take a critical look at our representations in art, literature, and scholarship. Today, adopted Koreans in the United States are participating as authors, and not just subjects, of the current body of research.

An adopted Korean American friend of mine, quoting poet Marilyn Chin, once told me that in an artist's journey, he or she first writes about the self, then about politics, and then about God. If so, then adopted Korean Americans are well on their way with the first two through adopted Korean American memoirs,[55] anthologies,[56] and documentary films such as Deann Borshay's film *First Person Plural*.[57] We have demanded that adoption narratives include our own voices. Adopted Korean Americans are politically active and aligning in greater numbers to larger Korean and Asian American communities and issues. We have written about the self. We are working through the politics of our unique identities. At this point in our adopted Korean American journey, then, we are waiting for God.

NOTES

1. Frank H. Wu, *Yellow: Race in America beyond Black and White* (New York: Basic Books, 2002).

2. Ronald Takaki, *Strangers from a Different Shore: A History of Asian Americans* (New York: Back Bay Books, 1998).

3. Helen Zia, *Asian American Dreams* (New York: Farrar, Straus and Giroux, 2000).

4. Jessica S. Barnes and Claudette E. Bennett, *The Asian Population: 2000,* Census 2000 Brief, U.S. Census Bureau, February 2002, www.census.gov/prod/2002pubs/c2kbr01-16.pdf.

5. See Amanda L. Baden and Robbie J. Stewart, *The Cultural-Racial Identity Model: Understanding the Racial Identity and Cultural Identity Development of Transracial Adoptees,* 1996, Unpublished manuscript available at http://www.transracialadoption.net/; S. P. Kim, S. Hong, and B. S. Kim, "Adoption of Korean Children by New York Couples: A Preliminary Study," *Child Welfare* 58 (1979): 419–27; Rita Simon and Howard Alstein, *Transracial Adoptees and Their Families: A Study of Identity and Commitment* (New York: Praeger, 1987).

6. Elizabeth Kim, *Ten Thousand Sorrows: The Extraordinary Journey of a Korean War Orphan* (New York: Doubleday, 2000).

7. Jane Jeong Trenka, *The Language of Blood: A Memoir* (St. Paul, MN: Borealis, 2003), 19.

8. Jae Ran Kim. This piece was first published in Jane J. Trenka, Sun Yung Shin, and Chinyere Oparah, eds., *Outsiders Within: Writing on Transracial Adoption* (Cambridge, MA: South End Press, 2006), 151–52. Reprinted with permission from South End Press.

9. Sisters of St. Paul of Chartres, 2004, http://www.spctaegu.or.kr/eng/index.php.

10. Eleana Kim, ed., *Guide to Korea for Overseas Adopted Koreans* (Seoul: Overseas Koreans Foundation, 2004). The Korean Ministry of Health and Welfare reports that 100,858 children were sent to the United States during 1953–2002. The U.S. Department of State reports that during 2002–2005, another 5,136 children from Korea were adopted to the United States. Information about immigrant visas issued to the United States can be found at http://travel.state.gov/family/adoption/stats/stats_451.html.

11. Information about Dr. Bob Pierce and World Vision can be found on the World Vision website at http://www.worldvision.org.

12. Bruce Cummings, *Korea's Place in the Sun: A Modern History* (New York: Norton, 2005), 185.

13. Kim, *Guide to Korea,* 15.

14. Bertha Holt, *The Seed from the East* (Los Angeles: Oxford Press, 1956), 25.

15. Ibid., 26.

16. Bertha Holt, *Bring My Sons from Afar* (Eugene, OR: Holt International Children's Services, 1986), 1.

17. Ibid., 4.

18. Ellen Herman, "Harry Holt's Dear Friends Letter, 1955," The Adoption History Project, June 22, 2005, http://darkwing.uoregon.edu/~adoption/archive/Holt DearFriendsltr.htm.

19. Holt, *Seed from the East,* 115.

20. Zia, *Asian American Dreams,* 34.

21. Restrictions on Asian immigration began back in 1882 with the Chinese Exclusion Act, which began a precedent of tight limitations on the number of immigrants from Asian countries who were allowed to enter the United States. See Takaki, *Strangers from a Different Shore,* 14.

22. The Holt Adoption Agency (now Holt International) incorporated in 1956, according to Holt International. Holt did not comply with all of the U.S. licensing requirements until 1962. See Holt, *Bring My Sons from Afar,* 200.

23. Kim, *Guide to Korea,* 9, table 1. Statistics from Korean Ministry of Health and Welfare, Seoul.

24. Rita J. Simon and Howard Altstein, *Transracial Adoptees and Their families: A Study of Identity and Commitment* (New York: Praeger, 1987), 143.

25. National Indian Child Welfare Association, Testimony of the National Indian Child Welfare Association regarding proposed amendments to the Indian Child Welfare Act, S 569 and HR 1082 (1997), http://www.nicwa.org/policy/legislation/HR2750/index.asp.

26. Indian Child Welfare Act of 1978, PL 95-608, 92 Stat. 3069.

27. Kim, *Guide to Korea,* 15.

28. Ibid. Bryant Gumbel, then host of NBC's *Today* show, reported that Korea's largest export was children. From "Adoption History: Adoptions from South Korea," *First Person Plural,* 2000, http://www.pbs.org/pov/pov2000/firstpersonplural/historical/skadoptions2.html.

29. Mathew Rothschild, "Babies for Sale: South Koreans Make Them, Americans Buy Them," *The Progressive* 52(1) (1988), available at http://modelminority.com/modules.php?name=News&file=article&sid=478.

30. Cummings, *Korea's Place in the Sun,* 331–36.

31. "Some Children See Him," by Wihla Hutson and Alfred S. Burt, 1951, http://www.alfredburtcarols.com/burt/Web%20Pages/This%20Is%20Christmas/Childrensee.htm.

32. Ibid.

33. Herman, "Harry Holt's Dear Friends Letter, 1955."

34. Rothschild, "Babies for Sale."

35. Ellen Herman, "Bertha and Harry Holt," The Adoption History Project, June 22, 2005, http://darkwing.uoregon.edu/~adoption/people/holt.htm.

36. Ibid.

37. Ibid.

38. Rothschild, "Babies for Sale."

39. Christian World Adoption, Inc., "A Christian International Adoption Agency," http://www.cwa.org/.

40. All God's Children International, "Adoption and Relief Services," http://www.allgodschildren.org/.

41. Holt International Children's Services, "Introduction to Holt," http://www.holtintl.org/intro.shtml.

42. Vine Deloria Jr. and Clifford M. Lytle, *American Indians, American Justice* (Austin: University of Texas Press, 1983), 240–41.

43. "Official Report of the Nineteenth Annual Conference of Charities and Correction (1892), 46–59," in Richard H. Pratt, "The Advantages of Mingling Indians with Whites," *Americanizing the American Indians: Writings by the "Friends of the Indian," 1880–1900* (Cambridge: Harvard University Press, 1973), 260–71, http://socrates.bmcc.cuny.edu/bfriedheim/pratt.htm.

44. David Wallace Adams, *Education for Extinction: American Indians and the Boarding School Experience, 1875–1928* (Lawrence: University of Kansas Press, 1995); Andrea Smith, "Soul Wound: The Legacy of Native American Schools," *Amnesty Magazine,* http://www.amnestyusa.org/amnestynow/soulwound.html.

45. Herman, "Harry Holt's Dear Friends Letter, 1955."

46. Andrew Sung Park, *The Wounded Heart of God: The Asian Concept of Han and the Christian Doctrine of Sin* (Nashville: Abingdon, 1993), 65.

47. Eileen Deitcher, "A Daughter of the Commandment: One Mother's Bat Mitzvah Reflections," *Korean Quarterly* 4(3) (2001): 19.

48. Jin S. Kim, "Jesus the Adoptee: A Contextual Theology of Liberation for the Adoptive Community," *Church of All Nations Discipling for Outreach,* January 16, 2003, http://www.cando.org/resources/sermon.asp?contentid=61.

49. Ibid.

50. The Korean Adoptees Ministry, "Welcome to Korean Adoptees Ministry," http://www.kam3000.org.

51. Jamie Kemp, "Abandoning Disgrace," *Korean Quarterly* 4(2) (2000/2001): 21.

52. Stephen C. Morrison, "Adoption . . . Isn't It Our Responsibility?" http://www.mpak.com/HomeEnglish.htm.

53. James Straker, "Abandonment and Adoption: How Understanding the Journey Is a Gift to the World," *Korean Quarterly* 4(2) (2000/2001): 16.

54. Kemp, *Abandoning Disgrace,* 21.

55. See Kim, *Ten Thousand Sorrows;* Trenka, *The Language of Blood;* Katy Robinson, *A Single Square Picture: A Korean Adoptee's Search for Her Roots* (New York: Berkley Books, 2002).

56. See Susan Soon-Keum Cox, ed., *Voices from Another Place* (St. Paul, MN: Yeong & Yeong, 1999); Tonya Bishoff and Jo Rankin, eds., *Seeds from A Silent Tree: An Anthology by Korean Adoptees* (Glendale, WI: Pandal, 1997); Jane Jeong Trenka, Sun Yung Shin, and Chinyere Oparah, eds., *Outsiders Within: Writing on Transracial Adoption* (Cambridge, MA: South End Press, 2006).

57. Deann Borshay, *First Person Plural,* http://www.pbs.org/pov/pov2000/firstpersonplural/, is an account of Borshay's search for her Korean family and identity.

Chapter Five

Liminality and Worship in the Korean American Context

Sang Hyun Lee

When I worship at Korean American churches, I often find myself having two strong feelings that appear to be at odds with each other. On the one hand, I feel at home. Every one is Korean, and I don't stick out. We sing familiar hymns in Korean that I used to sing as a young boy back home. I don't have to wonder what anybody may think about the presence of an Asian person in their midst. I am not a stranger any more but "one of us" for a change. At the same time, I sense an uneasiness in me. I notice that everything about the worship experience is so traditionally Korean. In the prayers, sermons, or anywhere else, I do not find any aspect of their actual life in America significantly reflected or addressed. Invariably, pastoral prayers will mention the president and other leaders of the Republic of Korea, but one waits in vain for any intercession for the president of the United States, where most of them are now citizens and where their children are growing up. I feel uneasy about this hyper-Korean atmosphere at Korean American worship services because I worry that such worship might be functioning, at least in part, as one hour of escape from reality rather than as a time of being empowered to face up to that reality.

Korean Americans, whether the first or the later generations, live very much in an in-between world, in a predicament where they are located in the socio-cultural worlds of both Korea and America. They are not in Korea anymore, nor do they feel that they really belong to the mainstream America. They are in-between their two worlds and, therefore, on the edges of both. They live in ambivalence and often find that their self-identity has become ambiguous. This positioning of Korean Americans resonates with the themes of race and improvisation raised by the editors in the introduction. The racialization of immigrants and their children in the United States means a marking as the other in which racial difference sets them apart from the normative European American standard against which all others are judged. That difference in the case of Asian Americans is not temporary but rather has endured over time and worked against structural assimilation.

In the face of such realities, Korean Americans have had to fashion their own place in the United States, and improvisation has very much been part of that process. Churches have been an important place in the carving out of space and meaning in an often inhospitable land. How men and women and different generations (first, 1.5, and second) have done this speaks to the pressures as well as the creativity that such ambivalences can generate. Where in Korean worship services is this ambivalence of their in-between existence expressed and in some way addressed?

But, then, we should probably ask the prior question of why Korean Americans worship services should pay any attention to their sociocultural in-between predicament at all. I address this question by exploring the intriguing fact that the Asian American experience of in-betweenness has something in common with the in-betweenness or liminality, which some scholars believe is an essential element of the experience of worship. We think about worship as a liminal experience. What does such a conception of worship mean in the context of the Korean Americans' sociocultural experience of in-betweenness or liminality? The implications of such a conception of worship are relevant for some of the often-discussed issues in Korean American churches. Namely, to what extent is it desirable that Korean American worship services try to celebrate the Korean cultural heritage, as some believe they should? What are the first-generation Korean American churches to think of the emergence of independent second-generation churches? How can Korean and Caucasian American joint services be more meaningful for the participants than they usually appear to be? What is the essential requirement, in other words, of a successful cross-cultural and multicultural worship?

THE KOREAN AMERICAN CONTEXT: MARGINALITY AS COERCED LIMINALITY

The Korean Americans' experience of in-betweenness in actuality does not exist in its purity but rather in the context of the racist realities in American society. Korean Americans, like other nonwhite peoples, are not just in-between but rather are coerced to remain there by the barriers (nowadays quite subtle but as real as ever) erected by certain social structures and attitudes of the dominant center. So the in-betweenness of Korean Americans is a coerced in-betweenness. To refer to this twin situation of nonwhite persons' being in-between and being coerced to remain there, the literature in social sciences has used the concept of marginality, or marginalization.[1] The marginality of Korean Americans, in other words, is an experience with two dimensions—namely, in-betweenness and being forced to stay there by the dominant group—and the effect of the coercive element in this experience makes the whole experience of marginality an oppressive one. The terms "marginality" and "marginalization" have often been used broadly to refer to oppression, dehumanization, etc. In this essay, I use "marginality" to refer to the Korean American experience of being in-between and also of being coerced to remain in-between by the dominant group. Marginality is thus coerced liminality.

Now I want to lift up briefly the creative potentials inherent in the in-between situation considered apart from the oppressive dimension. The experience of being in-between or on the edge is called liminality (from the Latin word "limen," meaning threshold) by the anthropologist Victor Turner, who has used liminality as a key concept in his well-known studies of change processes.[2] The first creative function of liminality is an openness to what is new. All social and individual changes, according to Turner, involve three stages: separation, liminality, and aggregation. A change involves leaving something or some place behind, being in transition or in-between, and then finally arriving at or achieving a new state of affairs. The middle, or the liminal and in-between, stage is usually an ambivalent time, but this stage, according to Turner, is what makes all creative changes possible. Turner emphasizes the antistructural nature of liminality. That is, in liminality, one has left behind the "culturally defined encumbrances of . . . role, status, reputation, class, caste, sex or other structural niche."[3] Liminality is "structural ambiguity" in which the usual hierarchy and status in society are momentarily suspended. In liminality, persons are freed up temporarily from all that binds them in society. Thus, liminality is "a realm of pure possibility whence novel configuration of ideas and relations may arise."[4] Freed from the usual ways of life and thought, the liminal person has an inherent openness to new possibilities and new ways of thinking about life.

Second, according to Turner, liminality is conducive to genuine community or, to use Turner's own terminology, communitas. Communitas is the egalitarian relationship among persons in which people "confront one another not as role players but as 'human totals,' integral beings who recognizantly share the same humanity."[5] Released for a moment from social structure, persons in liminality can relate to each other simply and fully as human beings and experience an intense quality of human communion that is usually impossible in structured society.

Communitas is a "generic bond underlying or transcending all particular cultural definitions and normative ordering of social ties." Such a human community with a complete acceptance of each other as whole human beings cannot be programmed or manufactured but instead spontaneously "breaks in through the interstices of structure, in liminality; and at the edges of structure in marginality; and from beneath structure, in inferiority."[6]

The third dimension of the creativity of liminality is its capacity to rise to a constructive critique of the existing structure and thus to a visioning of an alternative ordering of life. This is liminality's prophetic function. Liminality is the creative space where one has the freedom to break down the status quo and also the freedom to rebuild it in a different way. "Liminality," Turner points out, "raises basic problems for social structural man" since it "invites him to speculation and criticism."[7] And the very nature of communitas that liminality brings about is a challenge to the existing social structure.

In actual life, however, Korean Americans' liminality does not always lead to creative consequences. There are two reasons that Korean Americans' liminal creativity usually remains suppressed or distorted. For one thing, there is the general human tendency to avoid open-endedness and ambiguity. It is much easier for anyone to elude from or try to ignore an ambiguous situation than to face up to it directly. The traditionalist Korean Americans (usually the first generation) try to avoid an explicit awareness of liminality by clinging unrealistically to their Korean past. They are often more Korean in their outlook and actions than Koreans in Korea because the Korea they left years ago has not stood still but instead has been rapidly changing. Thus, we witness the hyper-Koreanness in many of the first-generation Korean immigrant churches. The assimilationists (often some of the second- or later-generation persons), on the other hand, may try to forget their Korean side and believe that they are white.[8] This second response to the in-betweenness may sometimes lead to self-hatred.[9]

This escapism is exacerbated by the racist hegemony of the dominant group who do not accept the in-between people as whole human beings but instead consider them as not just different but also inferior. The so-called blatant discrimination against nonwhite people happens less often now than in previous years. But what sociologists call the subtle and isolated discrimination has not disappeared and continues to have an impact upon the victims that is just as dehumanizing, if not more so, as the blatant and organized acts of racism.[10]

So the sociocultural context in which Korean American Christian worship occurs is marginally understood as a coerced liminality. And in coerced liminality, the inherent creative possibilities in Korean Americans' in-betweenness is frustrated, suppressed, and distorted. Indeed, Korean American worship often tends to be used as an opportunity toward hyper-Korean escapism.

WORSHIP, LIMINALITY, AND COMMUNITAS

Theologically speaking, worship is the Christian community's ritual in which people participate in the Triune God's activity of redeeming the fallen creation and thereby communicating in time and space God's own internal glory. What we are directly concerned with here is not a doctrinal discussion of worship but rather a conceptualization of the psychosocial factors involved in worship. God is directly involved in worship, but God works in and through the believer's active participation. Thus, an understanding of the human dimension is a necessary component in any theological reflection on worship.

In the scholarly conception of worship as liminality and communitas, all of the three dimensions of the creative powers of liminality are involved. First of all, worship, according to the Turnerian theory, is a time of liminality, that is, an experience of being freed up from the social structures (such as hierarchy, status, and role playing). Liminality is antistructural in the sense that the usual social conventions are momentarily suspended. Worship as a liminal experience is a "time out of time" when what does not happen in society can happen.[11] Worship is a time when men and women are freed at least temporarily from the existing social structure and become available for the new ways of thinking about the meaning of life and about the manner of their social relating.

Worship, secondly, is also a time of communitas, which is facilitated by worshipers' liminal condition. The worshipers' experience of liminal communitas functions as the "containment," to borrow Robert L. Moore's term, in which they feel safe to bring to the surface their hidden anxieties and fears, examine the status quo of their individual and social existence, and envision new ways of thinking and living.[12] Liminal communitas, according to Turner, is society's "subjunctive mood, where suppositions, desires, hypotheses, possibilities, and so forth all become legitimate."[13]

Thirdly, the creative powers of both liminality and communitas in worship naturally implies a prophetic function of worship. In liminal communitas, the worshipers are free and open to consider alternative ways of social order. The worshipers can experience a profound transformation and, as J. Randall Nichols puts it, are "able to carry the fruits of that transformation back into the world of structure, perchance to work toward its reformation."[14] In short, when worship is an experience of liminal communitas, the ritual acts and words can change individual lives as well as the world in which worshipers lead their daily lives. What this means is that worship by its very nature can be an experience that leads the worshipers to become change agents in the actual society. Worship and social action are internally related. Bobby C. Alexander, who has studied Pentecostal worship as a liminal experience, has also observed that it is when a theology or ideology of a prophetic participation in the reform of the existing society is effectively preached and taught in a congregation that the liminal experience more easily leads the worshipers to an active participation in social reform. In this way, Alexander emphasizes the role of the theological content in the effective elicitation of prophetic action from the liminal experience of worship.[15]

WHAT KOREAN AMERICAN WORSHIP CAN BE

Korean Americans in general, we observed above, do not have an easy time in facing up to their existential predicament of being in the ambiguous in-between liminality, which is made to remain seemingly permanent by the dominant group's racist barriers. But we could still ask, what could it mean to think of Korean American worship as a liminality/communitas experience that happens in the particular context of coerced, suppressed, and often avoided context of sociocultural in-between liminality?

The first thing to note is that in Korean American worship, liminality and communitas would have a dialectically reinforcing relationship. On the one hand, Korean Americans' existential liminality, at least in principle, could function as a factor that would facilitate their experience of worship as liminality. This possibility of course assumes that the manner and content of worship are designed in such a way that they deliberately lift up the worshipers' lives in the ambiguous but exhilarating predicament of in-betweenness. The self-conscious awareness of their existential liminality could heighten the intensity of their experience of worship as a liminal time. Such an experience of worship as liminality, in turn, would bring about an intense experience of communitas, which is a true community experience and not an experience of togetherness that results from escaping from their liminal reality.

On the other hand, Korean American worship would also have an inherent communitas element that would provide the marginalized Korean Americans a safe space in which to face up to their existential predicament. The Korean American church as a Christian church inherits in its liturgy and its message certain elements of communitas that were originally formed in the early church as a community of believers. Then, there is also the psychosocial fact that in Korean American worship, people gather together with a keen sense of comfort in knowing that they fit in and do not stick out. In spite of all the internal strife and conflict in many Korean American churches, no one can deny that Korean Americans' experience, in most cases, a deep feeling of being accepted on the most fundamentally human level by everyone present there, an experience that is virtually impossible in the churches of the majority population. An ethnic togetherness, however fragile and narrow, could still provide a degree of safety in which the worshiper might be willing to become conscious of the ambiguity of her or his in-between predicament in American society. In this way, the liminal predicament of Asian Americans and the Christian worship's inherent elements of communitas could work together to bring about a more explicit experience of liminality in Korean American worship, which would in turn intensify the communitas experience.

How do the three creative potentials of liminality mentioned above function in Korean American worship? First, Korean American worship can be a time when Korean Americans' own liminal existence can be honestly faced and thereby be open to new ideas about the meaning of their lives and destiny. Most Korean immigrants come to the United States with very mundane purposes: to give their children a better education, to attain a better financial future for themselves, etc. In the liminal openness to the new experience, Korean American worshipers could entertain the possibility that their existence in this country as strangers may have a theological meaning: namely, their life as pilgrims and pioneers, their vocation as God's creative minority in the United States and the world, etc. In the liminal openness of Korean American worship, a new identity that is neither just Korean nor just Caucasian American could be entertained: a new identity as Korean American with its own meaning and dignity.[16]

In these and other ways, Korean Americans' experience of liminality and the liminality in their worship connect with each other. In other words, Korean American worship conceived as a liminal time directly addresses the essence of their existential question. Korean American worship can indeed be a transforming time.

But then we must not forget that Korean Americans' liminality is a coerced and oppressive liminality with its dehumanizing consequences. A great deal of comforting and healing must happen in worship and in the life of the church if Korean American worshipers are to have the courage to face up to their liminal reality with all of its painful ambiguity and in spite of the maginalization they have experienced precisely because of their liminal (neither fully Korean nor fully American) existence.

Second, the creative power of communitas is its conduciveness to communitas. The experience of liminality in Korean American worship, therefore, can lead to an experience of a genuine community in which persons are accepted unconditionally without regard to their social status or racial or ethnic origin. Such a communitas experience in Korean American worship would certainly be a rehumanizing and empowering force for a people who have experienced so much nonacceptance and alienation in American society at large.

The communitas that emerges from liminality would also have an important difference from the togetherness that results simply from racial or ethnic commonality. Communitas emerges from a situation where all social roles, hierarchy, and distinctions are left behind. In other words, communitas by its very nature transcends all boundaries. Korean American Christian communitas born out of the liminality in worship is deeper than racial or ethnic togetherness and thus has the capacity to embrace persons of other racial and ethnic backgrounds. Communitas that is born out of liminality is not a voluntary racial or ethnic confinement or ghettoization but instead is an inherently inclusive and open community. I am not in any way denying the necessity of racial or ethnic churches; they are of an absolute necessity under the present social conditions. What I am saying is that racial and ethnic churches with a communitas experience derived from liminal awareness would have an ecumenical edge and outreach.

Third, liminality and communitas have a prophetic function vis-à-vis the existing order of human life. Freed temporarily from the existing social hierarchy and statuses and experiencing communitas, the participants in Korean American worship become capable of critiquing the status quo and of envisioning a new way of ordering life in the American society in general and in Korean American communities in particular. As we noted above, however, the preaching and teaching of a social critique would have to accompany the experience of liminality and communitas in worship if the inherently prophetic thrust in liminality and communitas is going to be expressed in human thought and action. Korean American churches are exceptionally diligent in holding worship services, usually at least a few times early in the morning every week, on Sunday mornings, on Sunday and Wednesday evenings, and in small group meetings. If these worship services provided the experiences of liminality and communitas and if a Christian prophetic concern about the society is effectively communicated, Korean American churches could have an enormous capacity to empower their members to be agents of social change.

In short, what Korean American Christians often try to avoid in worship (namely, an awareness of liminality) is precisely what is needed. Christian worship can both enable Korean American worshipers to become aware of their own existential situation of liminality and also liberate the suppressed and frustrated creative powers of their liminality so that the exercises of those powers can be aligned with the purposes of God. The conception of worship as involving the experiences of liminality and communitas, therefore, enables us to see how worship is directly related to Korean Americans' existential predicament and also to their Christian vocation.

What is being suggested here is far from any romanticization of the experience of marginality itself. What is being proposed is that if the creative potentials of the liminal side of marginalization could be freed from suppression and also be empowered to function through worship, then those creative powers of liminality could be exercised precisely in struggling against all coercive and oppressive forces of dehumanizing racism. Marginality as we have defined it is not desirable. But the liminal dimension in that marginalization is a nascent power that should be freed up and put into service for social change.

IMPLICATIONS FOR SPECIFIC ISSUES IN KOREAN AMERICAN CHURCHES

The understanding of Korean American worship as essentially involving the experiences of liminality and communitas sheds light on concrete issues in regard to worship in Korean American churches. The first issue has to do with the demand in Korean American churches for a greater presence in worship of Korean cultural values and practices. This demand is made for a variety of reasons. Some are deeply concerned that the younger generations are so thoroughly Americanized that they may completely lose any sense of self-identity as Koreans. Others point out that Koreans in the United States are marginalized by the dominant group for their Koreanness and that the churches must affirm precisely the dignity of their Koreanness. Still others maintain that the Christian faith in a God who became incarnate into a particular culture and society calls for the enculturation or indigenization of the Gospel and of the Christian worship. We must overcome, it is argued, the over-Westernization of the Christian worship and introduce to it Korean cultural forms and expressions.[17]

For all these reasons, many Korean American churches have Korean-language schools to teach their youths Korean. A small number of those churches try to use rice cakes in communion services. Korean holidays such as chu-suk (the harvest festival in the fall) and the lunar New Year are celebrated as part of the life of the church. There is a growing use of hymns and anthems written and composed by Koreans.

From the perspective of the interpretive frameworks we are working with in this essay, there is both merit to this cultural mandate and also some danger signals. Korean Americans are indeed marginalized for their Koreanness, and thus the Christian affirmation of them as human beings would have to involve a positive lifting up of their Korean heritage in the life of the church, including worship. However, Korean culture also involves a strong emphasis on social and economic hierarchy, occupational and other kinds of status, and patriarchy. In the name of preserving Koreanness, these cultural structures are brought into the worship of many (certainly not all) Korean American churches. Hierarchy, status, and role playing are precisely what have to be left behind if worship is to be an experience of liminal communitas.

For example, during the Eucharist, potentially the most liminal communitas-generating ritual, many Korean American churches allow only the elders (usually only the male elders) with white gloves to have the privilege of serving the elements to the seated members of the congregation. Only the elders handle the white sheet covering the Eucharistic elements. Elders and the minister serve each other as other members passively watch. In this way, even the Eucharist may end up reinforcing the dehumanizing aspects of the Korean culture instead of evoking life-changing liminality and egalitarian communitas.

Certainly, I am not arguing against the existence of elders and other officers in the church. Rather, I am saying that elders and other officers are often deployed in worship services in such a way that hierarchical superiority and status achievement of an ecclesiastical sort are paraded and reinforced. In this regard, the practice of having some members of the congregation hold the elements at the front of the sanctuary with all others coming up in single or double files to take the elements might have considerable merit. Forming a circle around the communion table (or circles around tables for larger congregations) also may be conducive to liminality and communitas.

The Christian worship with liminality and communitas can be a transforming ritual that motivates the participants to try to reform the existing social order. But as Timothy L. Carson points out, worship, when it is not freed from social status and hierarchy, can degenerate into a mere ceremony that only reinforces the existing culture and social structure.[18] In short, Korean American churches do need to affirm their Korean heritage for all the reasons mentioned earlier. However, Korean culture (and any culture, for that matter) should not be affirmed in such a way that all the existing elements in that culture are unthinkingly reinforced.

The second issue about worship much talked about in Korean American churches has to do with the differences between the worship styles of the first and second generations. The first-generation Korean American churches have become acutely aware of the ministry needs of their highly Americanized English-speaking second generation. Many Korean American churches have instituted English-speaking worship services to occur alongside the first-generation worship in Korean. Some second-generation Korean Americans have organized their own English-speaking congregations completely independent from first-generation churches.

This latter development (which some have called the silent exodus) worries many first-generation Korean Americans for two reasons. The worship style of those independent Korean American churches (with their use of Gospel songs rather than hymns from the hymnal, for example) appear too informal and not proper in the eyes of the first generation. And some first-generation churches feel that their youths' independence is a betrayal of their ethnic loyalties and cultural heritage.[19]

This is indeed a complex issue with many angles to it. Here we simply ask what light our conceptions of worship and of the Korean American context might shed on the matter. Second-generation Korean Americans often do not find the English services at their parents' churches satisfying, and one of the reasons for this could be that those services are not effective in evoking liminality and communitas for the second generation. When English services are held as a part of the first-generation church's program, English is spoken, but the order, music, and all other aspects of worship are usually exact copies of the first-generation worship. It is possible that the very traditionally Korean worship style of the first generation is not conducive to liminality and communitas for the second generation.

Second-generation Korean American Christians typically spend a lot of time before and during worship singing Gospel songs. If these songs engender liminality and communitas for the second generation, then those songs should be used, assuming that they have no theological problems in content. The order of worship, the way things are said, and the body language especially of the worship leaders can all be factors that may or may not evoke a sacred and transforming experience for second-generation Korean Americans just as for first-generation Korean Americans.

Thus, second-generation Korean Americans' desire to have their own kind of worship and even establish their own independent congregations does not have to be viewed as a betrayal either of their ethnic and family loyalties or of the proper way that Christians should do things, again assuming that the acts and words in their worship ritual are fundamentally Christian in content. The indispensable need for liminality and communitas in worship constitutes at least one legitimate reason for the independent second-generation churches and ministry.

The third issue has to do with multicultural or cross-cultural worship. Korean American congregations, especially those that share facilities with white American congregations, are occasionally invited by their white American host churches to a joint worship. Such invitations are usually taken as a friendly gesture by Korean American church people. But, according to my limited experience, Korean Americans' attendance at such joint worship services is usually very poor, and I have rarely heard Korean American church members speak of their cross-cultural worship experiences as moving or in any way memorable. Why are such so-well-intended cross-cultural worship services so often found wanting? The language barrier and other cultural gaps are part of the problem, as every one says. I suspect, however, that the problem goes deeper. Our conception of worship as liminality would imply that if a truly cross-cultural or multicultural worship occurred, the people of both cultural backgrounds should be led by their joint worship to an experience of being freed up from their own cultural structures as well as from their status in the society as a whole. White American church members and Korean Americans must be thrown into a wilderness together if a sense of communitas is to occur. Multicultural or cross-cultural worship, in other words, requires leaving home, a pilgrimage. They must all become liminal.

But the dynamics of Asian Americans' marginalization by the white dominant center would require something more. White Americans and Korean Americans occupy quite different social and cultural status in American society, with the white Americans occupying a higher rung than Korean Americans in the hierarchy. Sociologically and culturally, white Americans are the center, while Korean Americans are marginal and peripheral. If this is the case, then white Americans would have to give up more, be freed up more, than Korean Americans if they are to experience genuine liminality and communitas. Turner, as far as I know, does not speak about this kind of issue. His theory would seem to imply, however, that the culturally and socially privileged would have more status to leave behind than the culturally and socially marginalized.

But what would it mean in concrete terms for the white American church people to let go or leave behind especially their status that is higher than that of Asian Americans? One idea would be for white Americans to leave their comfortable and beautiful sanctuaries and come down, so to speak, to the Korean American church building for a joint service. Whether the worship is in English or Korean, the leadership in the service could consist of more Korean Americans than white Americans. Instead of having the Korean American church be represented only by its choir (as is often the case), the sermon could be preached by the Korean American pastor even if the sermon has to be simultaneously translated into English.

However, the act of white American Christians relinquishing their superior status so as to experience liminality together with nonwhite Christians is actually a much more subtle task than just walking over to the Korean church building. The root of the problem in the interaction between white and nonwhite peoples is not the fact that the white people are white people. The problem is rather that white people as a people consider themselves a super or at least a superior race. Social, economic, and cultural factors are of a secondary consideration in this matter. Nonwhite persons as nonwhite persons—whether they are rich or poor, highly educated or illiterate, successful in society or not—are thought of as inferior by most of the white population.

Thus, white people's first step toward an experience of liminality together with nonwhite people would be to acknowledge that they are not a superior

race or ethnic group but simply a particular ethnic groups, one of many ethnic groups. White people's road to authenticity is to become a particular ethnic group for the first time. Benjamin Reist, a fine theologian who used to
teach at San Francisco Theological Seminary, once wrote, "And so the road
to inexhaustible freedom for whites involves becoming neither black nor red,
but white, for the first time. It involves becoming white as liberated into particularity, the particularity of being one component in the full mosaic that is
humanity; becoming white in such a way that white cannot be white unless red
and black are equally present in the historical space that is human liberation."[20]
Without this basic shift in white people's self-conception, they could not genuinely leave behind their social roles and their place in the social hierarchy and
become liminal as they gather together with nonwhite persons for worship.

I once witnessed a lone white American person participating in communion
service at a national meeting of Korean American pastors and their spouses.
Here was a top white American leader of the Presbyterian church at an all-
Korean Presbyterian gathering. Let us call him Dr. Smith. I noticed that at
the beginning of the conference, Dr. Smith appeared understandably quite
isolated as he awkwardly walked among the groups of Koreans talking to
each other in Korean. Few seemed to know who this white person was, and he
seemed somewhat at a loss as to how to act in this kind of situation.

At the opening worship of the conference there was a communion service,
and I noticed Dr. Smith receiving the elements of the Eucharist surrounded
by about five hundred Korean American clergy and their spouses. There he
was, a white American of a high status all by himself partaking in the Lord's
Supper with Korean Americans. I know that he did not understand a single
Korean word throughout the service. But he was probably a man of sufficient
grace not to take offense at this situation. He probably was also sensitive
enough to know that all those Koreans who now at this worship make up
the majority have suffered much alienation in American society. At the same
time, of course, he must have known the tunes of the hymns sung in Korean
and also the meaning of much of what was going on. Although the service
was in Korean, the worship was still for him a Christian ritual. Nevertheless, this was a highly unusual situation for a white Anglo person; for about
an hour, much of Dr. Smith's social, cultural, and ecclesiastical status was in
suspension. Most importantly, Dr. Smith, I know, is a man who was deeply
aware of the problematics of the white people's superior race consciousness,
and he was probably quite aware that he was just one particular human being
and not a superior being, just like the Korean American individuals around
him. He had become self-consciously and genuinely liminal together with
all other Korean American worshipers. And because of his liminality, he was
in the sacred space of communitas. He was in communion with five hundred

Korean American persons who were now equal with him in Christ. And in and through this liminal communitas, the symbols of the Eucharist could exercise their efficacious power.

After the communion service, I accidentally passed by Dr. Smith talking enthusiastically with several Korean American pastors. I could not hear exactly what he was talking to them about. But I did not have to hear what he was saying to know that his demeanor had been completely changed. He did not appear awkward interacting with Korean Americans. He was at ease with himself and with his Korean American clergy. They were no longer strangers to each other. Perhaps this experience also made Dr. Smith want to make a change, more than ever before, in the existing social order.

But such an act of letting oneself be freed even for a few minutes from status and role playing is difficult for any group of human beings. The people at the center are reluctant to give up any power and thus are prone to be protective of the existing social structure. The people on the edge have a hard time facing up to their experience of liminal ambiguity and will often cling to the comfort zones of their ethnic enclaves. Turner himself noted that when those in a socially marginalized group experience communitas with the people of their social or ethnic category, they can easily turn inward with an exclusive attachment to their own kind of people and thus paradoxically go against the "drive to inclusivity" inherent in communitas.[21]

Thus, worship and especially multicultural worship with authentic experiences of liminality and communitas are not easy to bring about. But then, worship in the final analysis is not something that is achieved. Only God can bring about the human participation in God's own communion with himself. In short, it is all grace. Nevertheless, liminality and communitas are among the important ordinary means of that grace.

NOTES

1. For sociological discussions of marginality and my earlier attempts to appropriate this concept in my own theological reflection, see, for example, Everett V. Stonequist, *The Marginal Man: A Study in Personality and Culture Conflict* (New York: Russell & Russell, 1937); Alan Kerchkoff and Thomas McCormick, "Marginal Status and Marginal Personality," *Social Forces* 34 (October 1977): 48–55; H. F. Dickie-Clark, *The Marginal Situation: A Sociological Study of a Coloured Group* (London: Routledge, 1966); Won Moo Hurh, "Comparative Study of Korean Immigrants in the U.S.: A Typological Study," in B. S. Kim et al., eds., *Koreans in America* (Montclair, NJ: Association of Korean Christian Scholars in North America, 1977); Won Moo Hurh and Kwang Chung Kim, *Korean Immigrants in America: A Structural Analysis of Ethnic Confinement and Adhesive Adaptation* (Rutherford, NJ: Fairleigh

Dickinson University Press, 1984); Sang Hyun Lee, "Called to Be Pilgrims," in S. H. Lee, ed., *Korean American Ministry: A Resourcebook* (Louisville, KY: Presbyterian Church, USA, 1987), 90–120; S. H. Lee, "Pilgrimage and Home in the Wilderness of Marginality: Symbols and Context in Asian American Theology," *Princeton Seminary Bulletin*, n.s., 16(1) (1995): 49–64.

　　2. Victor Turner, *Ritual Process: Structure and Anti-Structure* (New York: Aldine, 1969), 94.

　　3. Victor Turner, *From Ritual to Theater: The Seriousness of Human Play* (New York: Performance Art Journal Publications, 1982), 48.

　　4. Victor Turner, *The Forest of Symbols: Aspects of Ndembu Ritual* (Ithaca, NY: Cornell University Press, 1967), 97.

　　5. Victor Turner, *Dramas, Fields, and Metaphors: Symbolic Action in Human Society* (Ithaca, NY: Cornell University Press, 1974), 269.

　　6. Ibid., 68; Turner, *Ritual Process,* 128.

　　7. Turner, *From Ritual to Theater,* 47.

　　8. See Stonequist, *The Marginal Man,* 159–209.

　　9. See Peter I. Rose, *They and We: Racial and Ethnic Relations in the United States* (New York: McGraw-Hill, 1997), 175–76.

　　10. See Joe R. Feagin, *Racial and Ethnic Relations* (Englewood Cliffs, NJ: Prentice-Hall, 1989), 14–17.

　　11. Robert L. Moore, "Ministry, Sacred Space, and Theological Education: The Legacy of Victor Turner," *Chicago Theological Seminary Register* 75(3) (1985): 1–10.

　　12. Turner, *Ritual Process,* vii. See also Victor Turner, "Passages, Margins, and Poverty: Religious Symbols of Communitas," *Worship* 46 (1972): 390–412, 482–94.

　　13. J. Randal Nichols, "Worship As Anti-Structure: The Contributions of Victor Turner," *Theology Today* 41(4) (1987): 405.

　　14. Bobby C. Alexander, *Victor Turner Revisited: Ritual As Social Change* (Atlanta: Scholars Press, 1991), 43, 95–99.

　　15. On the idea of Korean American as a new identity, see Won Moo Hurh, "Toward a New Community and Identity: The Korean American Ethnicity," in B. S. Kim and S. H. Lee, eds., *The Korean Immigrant in America* (Montclair, NJ: Association of Korean Christian Scholars in North America, 1980), 1–36.

　　16. See Greer Anne Wenh-in Ng, "The Asian North American Community at Worship: Issues of Indigenization and Contextualization," in David Ng, ed., *People on the Way: Asian North American Discovering Christ, Culture, and Community* (Valley Forge, PA: Judson, 1996), 147–75. For a description of worship in the Korean tradition, see Paul Junggap Huh, "The Making of a Book of Cross-Cultural Worship: Resources for Korean American Churches" (PhD diss., Drew University, 1999).

　　17. For a similar critique, see Tom Driver, *The Magic of Ritual: Our Need for Liberating Rites That Transform Pour Lives and Our Communities* (San Francisco: Harper San Francisco, 1991), 152–60.

　　18. Timothy L. Carson, *Liminal Reality and Transformational Power* (Lanham, MD: University Press of America, 1977), 87.

19. For a good discussion of the issues facing ministry with the Korean American second generation, see Sukhwan Oh, *The Ministry of 2nd Generation in 21st Century: Korean Americans, Arise and Take the Land!* (Bellflower, CA: Christian Han-Mi Association, 1999).

20. Benjamin Reist, *Theology in Red, White and Black* (Philadelphia: Westminster, 1975), 183.

21. Turner, *From Ritual to Theater,* 51.

Chapter Six

The Restoried Lives

The Everyday Theology of Korean American Never-Married Women

Jung Ha Kim

Telling our stories to one another is what women have always done—over the garden fence, at the food co-op, down at the pump. . . . By telling our stories, we must force our churches to hear what we have suffered and the way we have gotten through. We must pull them away from their domesticity and other worldly preoccupations and force them to deal with the nitty gritty of bread and justice. . . . Our stories are of individuals, but only as they are told collectively do they move us forward. In the process of telling our stories as a conscious, political act, we begin to define ourselves and our reality. We cease, thenceforth, to be defined by the men who run our churches, by the corporations who project our images, or by the men in Washington who seek to control our destinies.

Sheila Collins, "Theology in the Politics of Appalachian Woman"

I understand what feminists are saying about the inclusive language, because God cannot possibly be a man or a woman. But I personally have no problem believing God and Jesus as male. In fact, it makes better sense for me to believe that God is male. Otherwise . . . otherwise, I can't explain why the world is how it is in now. Wars, suffering, pain, destruction. . . . I am not saying that God [is the one who] caused all these disasters or [that] only men are capable of causing so much pain. But I'd prefer relying on this image of [a] male God who is mysterious and [is] in charge of everything. It may sound like an antifeminist thing to say, but I'm a feminist in my own ways. But more than a feminist, I am a romanticist, I think. I want my God to be male, even if it'll kill me to depend on a man to solve all my problems [laughs]. Besides, all my life He's been a man and I've gotten used to thinking of God as the provider of big things in my life, while I work on small things every day. Isn't that what partnership is all about?

C. J. Lee (pseudonym), interview conducted on May 2, 2000

When I wrote *Bridge-makers and Cross-bearers: Korean-American Women and the Church,*[1] a deceptively simple question was the center of the study: How do Korean American women experience their own church? By employing various qualitative methodologies, such as in-depth interviews and site visitations as an observing participant,[2] I attempted to delineate Korean American women's experiences of their own church as both oppressive and liberatory at the same time. On the one hand, the Korean American church, as a racial-ethnic minority community, provides the much-needed socioreligious refuge for its adherents who are displaced and marginalized in the mainstream America. On the other hand, the Korean American church is a deeply gendered institution, and both its maintenance and growth are often predicated on sacrifices of its women adherents to preserve the Korean culture in the material-istically abundant land flowing with milk and honey, the United States. While endowing its members with the religious purpose to sojourn in God's promised land as faithful flocks, the Korean American church renders its women's contributions and sacrifices invisible and their leadership as secondary to that of its male adherents. Consequently, the agency of Korean American women portrayed in *Bridge-makers and Cross-bearers* (and other previous works) is based on centering their everyday negotiation to counteract the multiple layers of patriarchy in their lives: Confucian cosmology, Christian orthodoxy, and (religious) institutional sexism against women. And I argued that Korean American women's survival and the quality of life in the context of the church heavily relies on negotiating and mastering what James Scott has called the everyday "hidden transcripts" and "subversive obedience" of the oppressed.[3] Since "no people is ever willingly, or without resistance, colonized,"[4] those who seek to uncover experiences of oppression must learn to spot remnants of resistance that are often hidden and disguised. To borrow a Korean American woman's own words, "we don't have much choice, but to make do with whatever is out there for our own advantage."

The current study[5] is an exploratory attempt to document what Korean American women say and think about their own experiences of the sacred, be it Christian, organized religion, New Age spirituality, or unnamed, based on selected autobiographical interviews (both formal and informal) with Korean American never-married women. When relevant, insights from the selected (auto-)biographical writings of or by Korean American women will be also utilized. As such, this study makes the following assumptions: (1) Korean American women are both active participants in the organized religious insti-tutions and spiritual agents who recognize the sacred presence in their own everyday life, (2) Korean American women are both practitioners and experts of religious rituals (both within and outside of their own religious organiza-tions) and also are theological innovators who struggle to name and celebrate the sacred in their own terms, (3) Korean American women are both inter-generational transmitters of the ethnic and religious traditions and also moral agents who are ceaselessly engaged in telling and retelling their own storied lives to reflect the past and to envision the future,[6] and (4) Korean American never-married women are heterogeneous and also conscious contemplators of various social locations that they simultaneously occupy as spiritual, Korean American, Asian American, never-married, and women.

Some of these assumptions seem obvious and understandable, but brief explanations may be in order. The seemingly clear distinction between what Korean American women experience in organized religion and what they think of religion and the sacred experiences in their own everyday lives is based on both heuristic and political reasons. In other words, when sharing their own life stories, Korean American women themselves tend to make a differentiation between the institutionalized and the everyday experiences of the sacred. And while Christian theologians also point to praxis and theory as two sides of the same coin and that doing theology entails both reflec-tion and action, Korean American women's stories of the experienced sacred remind us that practice and theory are, after all, the two main mediums for human beings to make (better) sense of the lived reality. Thus, practices and reflections of religion, each and both, deserve systemic probing. Further-more, the political nature of a peculiar historical amnesia in human societies often necessitates repeating the obvious—that women are human beings and that all human activities entail both praxis and theory—from time to time. To name just one such political forgetfulness in the context of the (Korean American) Christian church is to look at the historical tendency to render women primarily as practitioners (i.e., mundane and everyday), and men as theologians (i.e., sacred and abstract). In spite of the recent proliferation of the literature on Korean Americans' and Asian Americans' experiences of religion and their faith communities in the past decade, challenging the perception that men are naturally fit to make theological reflections and decisions from the position of authority while women are innately good at preparing and carrying out religious and cultural practices in detail has been sporadic. It is with this awareness of historically constructed separation and dichotomy between the experiential and the reflective dimensions of religion based on gender identities that this study seeks to remember and learn from Korean American women's reflections of religion. In a broad sense, I am also interested in addressing Mary Farrell Bednarowski's question: "When women write and speak publically—and self-consciously as women—about religious ideas, what do they have to say?"[7]

A rather obvious claim—that Korean American women are active moral agents—is made specifically by analyzing their own life stories in this study.

As storytellers and story-reflectors, Korean American women position themselves as both observers of and participants in their own lives. Since life stories reveal the intersection between individual experiences and historical circumstances, telling a life story not only entails recalling an experience as a product but also discerning the process of evaluating what is worth remembering by telling. Memory is, after all, "not a passive depository of facts, but an active process of creation of meanings."[8] Remembering the person she once was in light of the present self thus highlights moral agency. While "stories are lived before they are told," Alasdair MacIntyre also asserts that human beings are essentially "story-telling animals."[9] Judy Yung, who compiled the oral histories of Chinese women in San Francisco in *Unbound Feet* (1996) and *Unbound Voice* (1999), also emphasized the importance of taking women's life stories seriously. Yung states that "oral history allows ordinary folk like my subjects to speak for themselves, fill in historiographical gaps, and challenges stereotypes, as well as validate their lives. For too long Chinese [and other Asian American] women have silently borne the maligned images imposed upon them by dominant culture—the exotic China Doll, erotic Suzy Wong, and diabolical Dragon Lady."[10]

The main methodological and conceptual challenges for writing this essay, however, are rooted in the very awareness that Korean American women are essentially storytellers and that as they restory their lives, Korean American never-married women traverse neatly drawn analytical and categorical boundaries between the sacred and the everyday, the East and the West, and the center and the margin. And this crisscrossing in Korean American never-married women's life narratives presents the challenge of placing and integrating their religious thoughts within the larger framework of (Korean) American religious thoughts. Moreover, the paucity of recorded life stories of Korean American women in general, and Korean American never-married women in particular, pushed me to rethink the problem of silence as not so much a problem of the oppressed but rather of the dominant for not being able to listen to the stories told by the marginalized. For they have been telling, and never cease to tell, their life stories in their own terms. Confronted by the reality of not having a substantial amount of data to compare and contrast this particular study with other similar studies, I was faced with the following questions. How would I (and others) account for the historical silence and the erasure of women's stories in Korean America? Is it mainly the problem of "voice" and a methodological issue of how to strategically make oneself heard? If "coming to one's own voice" is the product of inner agency and "cultivating the power to speaking for oneself" is the "prerequisite for maturity,"[11] as some European American feminists insist, what roles do varied compositions of the listening communities play in the process of acquiring one's own voice? To what extent do we listen to the stories that Korean American women tell and risk being changed ourselves by what we hear?

Well knowing that a single study to uncover storied and restoried lives of Korean American never-married women and their religious thoughts will not be sufficient to address the foregoing questions, I turn to Gary Y. Okihiro's notion of family album history for both conceptual and methodological insights. "As a new way of documenting a history," Okihiro argues that "a family album history is inspired by the strands in Asian American history that reach to those regularly absent from the gallery of 'great men,' to activities excluded from the inventory of 'significant events,' and to region usually ignored by the worlds of science."[12] As such, it overcomes limitations imposed by deeply patriarchal accounts of historical recordings, communal histories written by outsiders, and forgotten and omitted stories of the dispossessed. Just as individual family albums may "help to define a personal identity and locate its place within the social order and to connect that person to others, from one generation to the next, like the exchanging snapshots around family friends,"[13] the racialized, gendered, and stigmatized Korean American never-married women's family album may help to uncover the intricate relationship between the individual's social locations and experiences of the sacred. For the storied lives of Korean American never-married women demonstrate their consciousness of the significant roles that race, ethnicity, gender, and marital status play in constructing religious thoughts. With the hope that what we hear from their life narratives can point to newly emerging themes and paradigms for further understanding people's religious thoughts in general, I now turn to discussing largely two narrative sources of the Korean American never-married family album: the selected discussion of findings from the survey study and autobiographical interviews with four Korean American never-married women.[14]

FINDINGS FROM THE SURVEY

In writing this essay, I decided not to recapitulate much of the standard discussions of research methodology that would be applicable in social scientific projects. Instead, I offer a brief discussion of how I determined appropriate research methods that can assist inquiries about Korean Americans, spiritual, never-married, and women. Approaching this essay from several perspectives as a researcher, a Korean American, a woman, an interviewer, churched, and never-married, I also feel the need to disclose both the intention and the type of energy I invested in the larger project that this paper is based on. The original intent of the larger study was to document the lives of never-married Asian

American women in the United States and write a book that I would enjoy reading and learning from. As a never-married woman myself, the breadth of my own curiosity about other never-married women's lives and the depth of the urgency I felt about spreading the good news about how most never-married women are happy,[15] normal, and contributing members of society were so great that I put no special emphasis on surveying the religious or spiritual dimension of the never-married women's lives in designing the questionnaires. As part of the demographic sketch of survey respondents, I included one question on respondents' religious affiliation. The survey was meant to be a pretest to the larger nationwide study to measure and examine the extent of conscious self-understanding among Asian American never-married women as racialized, gendered, and single (especially never-married) people. Started with only seven participants, the snowball sampling technique enabled me to identify eighty-one potential participants and send out the questionnaires to them during the period of September 1999 to May 2000. With an exceptionally high return rate of 74 percent, Asian American never-married women provided richer information about themselves than the questionnaire originally intended. For example, virtually all respondents answered the question on religious affiliation by checking one or more religious categories, and some wrote on the margin to describe or explain their own answers. One woman wrote on the margin "but not practicing" next to her check mark on "Christian" as her religious identity. Another woman checked both Christian and Buddhist as her religious identity without any explanation, and another checked the "other" category and wrote that "I am spiritual, not religiously based." Yet another wrote that she "used to be Christian but don't know now."

Korean American never-married women in general are more likely than any other ethnic Asian American women to report that they are Christians (either Protestant or Catholic) and also specified later in the survey that they receive community support from their own religiously affiliated groups or meetings than from any other sources. Inundated with rich data from the survey, I formulated some open-ended interview questions to uncover the seemingly shared sense of ambivalence among Korean American never-married women's understanding of their own religious and spiritual identities. What follows is a brief discussion of the selected findings from the survey.

Among fifty-nine usable responses of the survey, eleven were self-identified as Korean American women of thirty-two years and older. Out of the eleven Korean Americans who returned survey questionnaires, five came from the West Coast (including California, Washington, and Oregon), three from the East Coast (such as Massachusetts and New York), two from the Midwest (Illinois), and one from the South (Georgia). The occupations of these women also vary: computer programmer (2), flight attendant (1), university affiliated

Table 6.1.   A Demographic chart of Korean American never-married women

Age		Generation		Length of Stay		Education*		Income	
32–34	4	First	7**	0–10 yrs.	0	High school	0	$20k or less	1***
35–40	1	Second	3	10–15 yrs.	0	2 yrs. college	0	$20–38K	3
41–50	6	Third	1	16–20 yrs.	2	4 yrs. college	4	$38–65K	6
51–60	0	Fourth	0	21–25 yrs.	3	Master's	2	$65–80K	0
61+	0	Fifth	0	26–30 yrs.	2	Prof. Doc.	2	$80K or more	1
				31–35 yrs.	0	PhD	2		

*Not all respondents answered the question about their highest educational attainment.
**Among the first generation, three women specified and wrote on the margin that they are "1.5 generation."
***One woman who reported that her annual income is less that $20,000 also provided a written explanation for her "temporary poverty" as "working only half-time" as a student.

(3), architect (1), consultant (2), and ordained minister (1). Other demographic information of the respondents are presented in table 6.1.

Between the extremes of wealth and poverty, there seems to be a significant Korean American middle class across generational lines. While these Korean American women's annual income attests to their middle-class status, their high educational attainment is also noteworthy: all eleven respondents reported that they have at least a bachelor's degree in arts or sciences. And out of ten respondents, six reported to have higher academic degrees. In order to earn their annual income, they also work long hours. Only three reported that they work forty or less hours per week, while the rest work more than forty hours. Two women reported working more than sixty hours a week, and another wrote in "too many" as the number of hours worked outside the home. Of particular interest to this study from the overall findings based on the survey are (1) the respondents' religious identities and what they say about their own religious experiences, (2) the frequency of physical mobility (measured by the frequency of changing residency) in their lives, and (3) the perceived responsibilities and burdens they experienced as single women from their family and other groups (including the church).

In regard to the self-reported religious identities of Korean American never-married women, as mentioned earlier a majority of Korean American women—nine out of eleven—identified themselves as Christians. Along with them, five specified "Protestant"; one specified "Catholic"; one wrote "spiritual, but not religious"; one wrote "Christian, but not practicing"; and another wrote "both Buddhist and Christian." Rather than checking a religious category that was already provided in the survey, one woman wrote that she "used to be Christian but don't know now." Put simply, Korean American never-married women as a whole did not experience the question about their religious affiliations based on the common and conventional Likert scale as making either/or choices among the prescribed categories. They freely checked one or more categories that they felt fit better for describing their religious identities. By choosing more than one category and/or naming their own religious identities as hybrid, Korean American never-married women clearly point to the fact that there is more than one way to be affiliated with the organized religion and many ways to experience a meaningful spiritual life. This sense of fluidity and the openness to experience the sacred in the context of both organized religion and everyday life will be further delineated in the discussion of selected life stories later on.

Although frequent moving of one's residence is rather common among most of the Asian American never-married women respondents of the survey across ethnic lines, four out of eleven Korean Americans reported that they moved more than three times in the previous two years, and another three reported that they moved at least once in the previous two years. While the most frequently moved women tend to be rent-paying tenants of an apartment or a single family house, the fact that four out of five women who moved more than three times in the previous two years among fifty-nine respondents happened to be Korean Americans caught my attention. Although causal factors for the frequent change of residency may vary from person to person, there is a strong correlation between Korean American women's physical mobility and their own perceived and real responsibilities for taking care of others. Since adult status in Confucian cultures often is conferred through marriage and the birth of children, Korean American never-married women are perceived as self-centered and perpetually young.[16] Given this cultural perception, Korean American never-married women ironically report that they are often left alone to care for aging parents or to tend to other family emergencies. In a follow-up interview, one woman who moved three times in the previous two years to take care of her mother, who went through cancer treatments, said, "It's always me, you know, because [my sisters] have their own husband[s] and children. What really gets me is when they say 'you don't have family to take care of but we do' and 'it's hundredth times easier for you to take vacation days off or move because you are single.' I mean, when did their marriage license become a license not to care for their own mother? Since when did their mother-in-law become their only mother?"

To the question "To what extent are you responsible for caring for your elderly parents?" only four Korean American women reported that "such responsibility is well rotated among family members," one reported that "to some extent I am responsible for them," and the rest (six) reported that "to a great extent I am responsible for them." No one answered "I am not responsible for them." Since none of the eleven Korean American women respondents is the only child of their parents, the women's perceived and real responsibilities for taking care of their elderly parents are quite remarkable. Contrary to the common perception that never-married (and other single) women are free from family-related responsibilities and obligations, the everyday life of Korean American women is deeply rooted in their love and responsibility for family members.

This finding concurs with that of a nationwide study on the relationship of the person providing informal (i.e., unpaid) care to elderly persons in the United States. The U.S. Special Committee on Aging documented that 47 percent of such caregivers are women, most often daughters and wives.[17] Other studies that examine intergenerational social support also point to the fact that a "person who had at least one daughter is more likely to receive help than those who had just a son or two sons."[18] What seems to be intriguing from findings of my survey is that women are not only the kin keepers, but seemingly unattached never-married women in Korean America are playing an indispensable role in providing informal support to their aging parents as surrogate sons. As a never-married Korean American woman in her late forties puts it, "You are never really alone. All single women living alone by themselves, completely free from family responsibilities, is a myth. I may be the only one who lives in the house, but [the house] is ready for others to move in as a temporary shelter any time. Besides, my house is filled with my worrying about my mother, my sister who is going through a bitter divorce, my other sister who decided to go back to work, my brother's family, the pastor's wife in my church who needs surgery to remove her ovarian tumor."

Detecting the shared ambivalence in Korean American never-married women's religious thoughts and a meaningful correlation between their residential mobility and the real and perceived burdens they experience from their family of origin, I conducted follow-up autobiographic interviews with selected respondents of the survey. What follows is a selected discussion of the insights I gained from their life narratives.

INSIGHTS FROM FOLLOW-UP
AND AUTOBIOGRAPHICAL INTERVIEWS

The Center and the Margin

Making an argument that South Korea remains as a strong marrying country, Laurel Kendall in *Getting Married in Korea* cites an interview conducted by Kim Eun-Shil while she was doing her field research. "When I asked women why they got married, they laughed at my absurd question and said that they wanted to live a 'normal' life."[19] At the time of Kim's field research, "eighty-four out of every eighty-five women in their thirties would have been married" in Korea.[20] Also citing a scan of travelers' and missionaries' accounts that "marriage under the old Korean system was almost as certain as death," Kendall makes a convincing argument that "marriage has been an abiding Korean preoccupation."[21] While Korean American never-married women who participated in this study are not living in South Korea, they are keenly aware of the cultural ramifications of being single in the couple's world on both sides of the Pacific Ocean. A woman in her late forties confesses that "I used to think that I must be abnormal. When you are surrounded by all married people with kids, you wonder what is wrong with you. The thing that really got me is not what others may be saying about me but what I used to think of myself. I guess I was brainwashed to think that all normal people naturally get married." Another woman in her late thirties criticized what she called the Korean American conservatism: "I can't believe how conservative Korean Americans are. You'd think [that] they are more open to [accepting] different life-styles since they have been living in America. I heard that there are now many independent and single women in [South] Korea too. But here in America, [Korean Americans] have this archaic attitude about all-good-women-get-married. They think that all *no-cheo-nyeo* ('old maid' in Korean) must be either too picky or too loose to be a good marriage material." Another woman in her forties points to the "myth of sisterhood" among Korean American women: "I get a cold shoulder from some married women in the church and social gatherings. You become a threat to them, especially if you look attractive. Single women are seen as a being on the prowl." She adds, "I know that some of my married friends never invite me to their family gatherings because they feel this unspoken threat and anxiety about my being an unattached and free woman. I don't know if their fear is based on the lack of trust in their husband[s] or me, but we don't ever talk about it. And I just don't expect [my friends] to invite me over to spend any substantive time with their husband[s], ever."

Never-married women's experiences of prejudice, discrimination, and marginality against their marital status are not only from married people but also from other singles. As one woman in her fifties puts it, "I have several friends who went through some bitter and difficult divorce[s]. So I naturally think of them as all singles like myself. But even they try to tell me sometimes that I lack something important in my life just because I have not gone through a marriage. I mean, when I look at them, they don't seem to live an ideal life either. So to tell me that I'm missing out on this mysterious joy of being married to a man is a joke. Even my divorced friends differentiate me [from themselves]."

Whether Korean American women experience their never-married marital status as normal or not, they tend to be more conscious and contemplative about being single. For example, only one out of eleven respondents answered "rarely" to the survey question "How often do you think about your own marital status?" Another two responded "only on special occasions," and the rest of them reported that they either "almost always" or "to a great extent, at least once a day," think about their being single in the couple's world. One woman wrote on the margin "This question is annoying. I am more than just a single woman." Yet even she reported that she thought about her marital status "to a great extent, at least once a day." Just as Korean women in Korea automatically equate the life of a normal person to a married life, Korean American never-married women report that they also spend a lot of time and energy contemplating the meaning and ramifications of their own marital status. Indeed, as Elaine H. Kim asserts, the "Korean cultural construction of masculinity and femininity have shaped Korean American men's and women's experiences, which include the subordination of women in political, economic, social, and cultural domains."[22] And this extensive reflection of the marital status also influences and impacts Korean American never-married women's thoughts on religion.

A woman in her forties who specified that she is "more spiritual than religious" shares the following insight about Jesus Christ as a never-married man (*chong-gak*):

> Have you ever heard a pastor preaching about Jesus's marital status? [Pastors] sometimes mention the fact that Jesus was single. He was often misunderstood and rejected by his own people. The Bible clearly states that Jesus was often alone and felt utterly lonely. But pastors never spell out Jesus as a *no-chong-gak* [old never-married man]. He wasn't just a single man. At the time of Jesus, people used to get married early. Since Jesus was never married and he was well over thirty [years of age] at the time of his death, people probably talked about his marital status a lot. Was he too poor to get married? Did he have any physical deformity? Was he not interested in woman at all? I mean I have zillions of questions that I want to ask about him as a *no-chong-gak*. But no. We don't even talk about why he was single. If Jesus was fully a man and fully God, why don't we talk about his human side in the church? Rather than picking on *no-cheo-nyeo* [old maid] like myself as an exception, people should ask some serious questions about themselves, [such as] why they got married if they are really serious about following Jesus's footstep.

Another woman who "used to be a Christian" but doesn't practice it anymore shared the following:

> I think Jesus was able to care for so many people because he was single. If he was married and had a wife and children, he probably could not do all those things he did for the people. And all those women [who are] mentioned in the Bible were probably unable to assist him so closely. It was God's will that Jesus lived a single life. And when I compare Jesus's life with mine, I take comfort in knowing [that] God understands what it means to live a life as a single person. Just as Jesus relied on those women [who are mentioned in the Bible] to help

him, I rely on many people for their kindness and friendship. Because of them I rarely feel lonely. But when I do [feel lonely], I take comfort in knowing that Jesus was also alone. I think people who discriminate against single people don't really understand why God made Jesus to live alone in the first place. There are certain sacrifices and blessings that comes with living a single life. And only God-ordained people can live a single life. Single life is not better or worse [than married life], but it's just different.

In listening to the life narratives of Korean American never-married women, it is clear that they do not experience their marital status as a type of problem to be solved. Instead, it is a dimension of life that they are consistently and consciously aware of. While the surrounding culture tends to render Korean American never-married women as secondary citizens, they are able to recognize the marginal place and position that Jesus once occupied in his own historical time as another never-married person. Just as liberation theologians point to the theological privilege that the oppressed occupy, never-married Korean American women are aware of their marital status, which enables them to identify and understand the mystery of the Christian God who was/is never married. Moreover, regardless of one's own religious identities, there is yet another "dangerous memory" in the Korean immigration history that can further empower Korean American never-married women. Elaine H. Kim argues that Korean American women share a long legacy of female insubordination. "The first Bible women and the 'picture brides' who sailed for Hawaii at the turn of the century" and "women who did not want to marry, women who wanted careers, divorces, single mothers, childless women, survivors of scandals, artists, intellectuals, eccentrics" all came to the United States as immigrants, "because women could recreate themselves in new social environments, distanced from the discipline of the militarized masculine states and social mechanisms that maintain it."[23]

When we place Jesus's marital status at the center and the legacy of independent Korean female immigrants to the United States at the center to analyze the lived experiences of these Korean American never-married women, we can see them as innovative theologians and active agents of history making in Korean America. Indeed, the matter of occupying the center or marginal location in society, in religious organizations, and in one's own life is then largely a matter of the beholder.

THE SACRED IN THE INSTITUTIONALIZED RELIGION AND IN THE EVERYDAY LIFE

Whether they experience religious/spiritual lives as members of an organized religion or not and whether they make clear distinctions between and among religious categories such as Buddhism, Confucianism, and Christianity or not, Korean American never-married women's life narratives reveal a complex interplay between drawing community boundaries and community memberships in their lives. Some of the boundary drawings that women experience are explicit and imposed from their surroundings, such as the institutionalized religious confession of a doctrine or a creed, but some are drawn implicitly by women themselves. Referring to some of the commonly assumed binary oppositions that are already built into the everyday language, such as "Korean and American," "women and men," and "inside and outside" of the church (or other religious organizations), Korean American never-married women disclose their deeply ambivalent relationships with religious communities. And their life narratives testify that there is more than one way to stay in the faith community as well as more than one way to leave the community. What Mary F. Bednarowski calls "ambivalence as a new religious virtue" among American women can also describe Korean American never-married women's experience of their own faith communities: "Some of the women have remained active and visible in their communities. Other have said good-by without leaving. And still others no longer have any kind of formal association with former religious communities but continue to acknowledge their influences."[24]

Offering the perceptive critique against the (Korean American) organized religion and the keenly felt yearning for a fulfilling spiritual life, Korean American never-married women straddle various boundaries. A woman in her late forties articulated her reason for "attending the church but no longer as a committed member" in this way:

One of the reasons for the Korean church growth is because people still have a strong attachment to Korea that they have left behind. And I personally don't think this cultural attachment to Korea in and of itself is necessarily bad; just that they live here [in the States] as if they are still living in Korea. And I understand that the only place Korean men can attain some respectable social status probably is in their own ethnic church. Once I went to this small Baptist church to check out its new English [worship] service that they have just started. There were less than twenty people altogether [attending the service]. Out of this small number of people, do you know how many of them are elders and deacons of that church? At least twelve. I was introduced to twelve deacons, elders, or other leaders of the church during the fellowship hour. How can the church sustain itself with only a handful of laypeople and that many leaders? How is it that almost everyone in the church has to have some leadership titles? Something is wrong with this picture of the church. And if people can't become an elder in one church, they can always go to another [church] and become one. I think it's really sick how Korean men are single-mindedly driven to acquiring social status with all means possible. It seems like most Korean churches are catering to men's need to attain leadership roles. At some point Korean churches have to decide who they want to serve, Korean men or Christians.

Another woman in her forties offered the following thought on "Korean American churchgoers": "When I don't attend the [Korean American] church for a while, some church members call and tell me how important it is to keep the *Chu-il* ["Lord's day" in Korean] and live a life of piety. But when I go to the church, all they care and talk about is which family moved into their newly built house and whose family just opened another successful business. Then when they see me they talk about my marital status as if it's their own business. If they really want me to attend the church more faithfully, they need to make the church [a] comfortable place for me to go. I mean, if all you get from going to the Korean church is stress, you need to ask why you would want to go there again and again in your right mind. Don't you?" She also compares her own experiences of "being religious" with that of her mother. "My mother, till this day, never skipped the church on Sunday. Even when she had [a] 102–degree fever several winters ago, she went to the church. As if God really lives in the church, she went to the church every Sunday to pray and to worship. Being a religious person is the same as going to the church for my mother." Although she respects her mother's way of committing herself to the church, she tells her own understanding of the omnipresent God. "I get upset when my mother insists that I go to the church every Sunday no matter what. I don't believe that God really cares whether I attend the church every Sunday or not. I mean, I believe that God is everywhere and that God communicates differently to different people. Some people, like my mother, find God only in the church, [whereas] some other people, like myself, can find God everywhere and everyday. Sometimes I wonder how God of my mother and mine is still the same and yet so different at the same time."

Referring to what she calls "an excessive social concern" among Korean American Christians in general, a woman in her late thirties observed that some of her Korean American single women friends attend the church mainly to "check out and flirt with men." In her words,

The Korean American church has become too much of a social scene where people exchange business cards and other information about the immigrant life. The church is [also] a place where single men and women can check out and flirt with each other. My two friends [who are also never-married] changed their church membership several times in the last few years. Of course, they say that the minister's sermon isn't good or some other lame reason for hopping around from one [Korean American] church to the next. But I know that they are actively searching for their future husband. At one time [one of the two] went to two different churches every Sunday for several months. One in the morning and another in the afternoon. I don't blame them for trying so hard to find decent men to get married. What I don't understand is how Korean they have become as they get older. My friends grew up in the States and all had non-Korean boyfriends. When it's time to get married, though, they all of a sudden decide to listen to what their parents are saying and look for a Korean man to get married. And some ministers of the [Korean American] church actively take on the role of matchmakers in order to recruit and keep young members in their own church. Whenever I think about how the church has become too much of a social scene, I feel real bad. I don't go to the church any more. Not only because I refuse to participate in this meat market mentality of singles in the church, [but] I don't have any desire to dress all up and publically demonstrate how good and strong my faith is. Having a quiet Sunday morning all to myself and feeling grateful about my life is a religious experience I can have at my own home without going to the church.

Along with these articulations of Korean American never-married women's traversing across lines of the organized religion and the everyday, of women and men, and of Korea and the United States, a woman in her forties shares another seemingly contradictory realm of living a religious life and of getting married.

My mother went to this famous *chom-jang-i* ["fortune-teller" in Korean] in Korea [when she visited South Korea in 1989]. Not that I believe whatever that *chom-jang-i* said, but after that trip back to Korea, my mother decided not to bug me to get married any more. This famous *chom-jang-i* told my mother that I was supposed to get married in [my] late twenties, but since I missed the opportunity to be married, I shouldn't get married until I reach the age of forty-seven or forty-eight [laughs]. That's not all [still laughing]. If I can't get married by forty-eight, I should dedicate myself to the Buddha or something. You see, my mother didn't tell [*chom-jang-i*] that I live in the States. So, I guess if I lived in [South] Korea, I was supposed to become a Buddhist nun by now. I don't know anything about Buddhism. . . . I go to this Korean American church now. I actually turn[ed] to religion when I became forty-eight years old. I grew up in the Korean [American] church just like all other Korean Americans who grew up in America. But I left the church after I left [my parents'] home because I didn't see the point of going to the Korean church. The only . . . times when I went to the [Korean ethnic] church was the weekends when my mother was visiting me and some special occasions once in a while, like for the Easter morning service or something. . . . I didn't feel like going to the American [i.e., non-Korean American] church either. I tried a couple of times, but [it] didn't feel like my church. Maybe because I became a Christian in the Korean church, I really didn't feel at home in any other churches. . . . Now I go the [Korean American] church mostly for spiritual reasons. I don't care much about small group meetings or other fellowship activities at the church. I just want to have a place called my home church. I don't go to the church necessarily to meet God or something. The God I ever experience is when I am alone, thanking so many blessings in my life. . . .

I am sure my mother would refuse to hear this, but I really don't think much about men when I'm alone. I don't really feel lonely when I am alone. You know, sometimes, when I sit out in my balcony and think, what more can I ask for in this life?! I'm so content and grateful for what I have in my life. When I drink a glass of cold iced tea, when I watch flowers and plants growing outside my balcony, and when I feel the day has been a productive one, I feel God. I don't know how others experience God. But for me, if I can attend to many little things in my daily life, I know God is there with me. When I told my mother the other day that all I need is God and not a husband, my mother didn't know what to do with me [laughs]. You see, she can't tell me not to go the church any more, because she's a deacon. But she can't encourage me to get more religious because she's afraid that what *chom-jang-i* told her may come true. I thought about telling my mother a joke that I'm going to a seminary to get ordained but decided against it. It'll be too much for her to take it even as a joke. She doesn't bug me to get married any more, but I think she still secretly wishes for me to get married. So for her my turning to religion is a mixed blessing.

Some of what Korean American never-married women say about being religious in the context of their own ethnic faith community resonates closely with what others have said about the Korean American church in general: that the church tends to be schismatic and patriarchal. As a racial-ethnic institution, the church functions not only as a religious institution but also as a social institution for its adherents. These experiences of organized religion are shared across various marital statuses. Dora Yum Kim, the second-generation Korean American woman in her autobiographical book, for example, also points out what she calls "a ridiculous growth" of the Korean American church and states: "You know, there used to be only one Korean church when I was growing up—the Korean Methodist Church. I can understand the need to have different denominations represented, like the Korean Buddhist Church and the Korean Catholic Church, but the growth of Korean churches is ridiculous. A new church forms anytime anyone has a disagreement. This has been happening more and more in the past ten years with the influx of more Koreans. There are now over a hundred Korean churches in the Bay Area. Can you believe that? It's the men, of course. They fight and then start a new church. They just can't stay supportive of each other. Everyone needs to be the boss. It's like they're all on ego trips."[25]

Different from other general critiques of the organized religion, what is particular about Korean American never-married women's stories of the sacred experiences is their own conscious awareness of how significantly their marital status impacts their own religious thoughts. For example, Korean

American never-married women identified Jesus Christ not only as a man and God but also as a *no-chong-gak* (old never-married man) and God. As with other never-married people, they also are able to name the myth of living a single life as completely free of family and community responsibilities. Jesus, in fact, was "able to do so much for others" precisely because he was single, Korean American never-married women argue. Furthermore, the deeply heterosexual and couple-oriented socioreligious environment in Korean America also reinforces them to consciously and constantly reflect on their life experiences as singles. While demands of their presence and commitment in their family, church, and circles of friends are made on the grounds of love and spirituality, Korean American never-married women are often treated as secondary citizens in these communities. Given the fact that the women experience marginalization and inhospitality in their own communities, it is no surprise to learn that Korean American never-married women experience the sacred in the interiority of their own everyday lives rather than in the institutionalized religious setting.

The life narratives of Korean American never-married women thus offer testimony to more than one way to belong to a community and more than one way to leave that particular community. While maintaining a fluid sense of affiliation with organized religion, Korean American never-married women also reveal that they are more likely to experience the sacred in their everyday life context, such as "in the quiet moment of being by [themselves]," "when alone," and "when reflecting on my many blessings in life." This emphasis on dailiness in Korean American never-married women's religious thoughts is similar to what Mary F. Bednarowski calls "the ordinary." She argues that "the ordinary" is "not only . . . a descriptive category but . . . [also] a more complicated theological category, one that is acquiring depth of meaning as women . . . elicit details of their lives."[26] Indeed, Korean American never-married women's stories of daily life with their own details and particularities are the very sources of their own religious thoughts.

CONCLUSION

Throughout this study, I sought to remember what Judy Long lamented about understanding women's lives: "We still know very little about the shape of women's lives, and still less about how they are experienced. It is vital to listen intensely, and comment minimally."[27] One of the objectives in this study is to gain insight by intentionally engaging in in-depth listening to make selective knowledge claims of what Korean American never-married women say about their own religious thoughts. David D. Hall in his introductory remarks in *Lived Religion in America* also confessed that "we know next-to-nothing about religion as practiced and precious little about the everyday thinking and doing of lay men and women."[28] Thus, what I attempted to accomplish in this essay is to share the selected findings from the larger study about the religious thinking of Korean American never-married women as they reflect on their everyday lives. As racialized, gendered, and marginalized people based on their marital status, Korean American never-married women's life stories point to the importance of dailiness in constructing the sacred. Recognizing and celebrating the sacred in the stories told by them, I also identified two crisscrossing boundaries: (1) the center and the margin and (2) the sacred in organized religion and in everyday life. These and various other traversing boundaries in the lives and stories of Korean American never-married women point to the limitations and restrictions of relying on conventional categories to express not only religious thoughts but also excitement about and the need to rethink the notion of ambivalence altogether. To borrow Bednarowski's expressions, "ambivalence emerges much more as a virtue to be cultivated in creative and dynamic ways than a vice to be avoided"[29] when listening to stories that Korean American never-married women tell.

Because I am well aware of the fact that sampling pragmatics often determine generalizability of study findings, the main goal of this essay has been to provide a descriptive analysis of the everyday theology of Korean American never-married women. Thus, while I cannot claim that the ambivalence in the religious thoughts of Korean American never-married women is unique or generalizable, I concur with what Peter A. Dorsey offered as a justification for writing autobiographical and (religiously) confessional narratives. Dorsey states that the authors of these writings "assumed that all the faiths could benefit from the knowledge of one person's life: a single life was significant because it manifested universal pattern of experience of the holy."[30] Furthermore, Carolyn G. Heilbrun articulates the peculiar nature of women's search "for fellow beings who have faced similar struggles, conveyed them in ways a reader can transform into her life, [and] confirmed desires the reader had hardly acknowledged—desires that now seem possible. Women catch courage from the women whose lives and writings they read, and women call the bearer of that courage friend."[31] With a hope that Korean American never-married women's selected life narratives can also be beneficial to everyone who is struggling to come to terms with one's own ever-changing notion of the self and her encounters with the sacred in twenty-first-century America, I conclude by noting the wise advise of a never-married woman in her fifties: "In my twenties, I searched for the meaning of life by wishing to form a family of my own. In my thirties, I looked for the meaning in life in things that I can acquire and possess. In my forties, I thought my job and career [could] provide some answers and meanings. Now that I'm in my fifties, I turn to my inner-self for answers. I realize that the meaning of life is in my own everyday life, not from a man, material possessions, or the work I do, but in my own self. And knowing what I know now, I look forward to discover[ing] new changes in my sixties. Who knows, I may be able to say, I no longer think about the meaning of life any more because God is in me and I in God, by then."

NOTES

1. Jung Ha Kim, *Bridge-Makers and Cross-Bearers: Korean American Women and the Church* (New York and London: Oxford University Press, 1997). The first epigraph is from Sheila Collins, "Theology in the Politics of Appalanchian Woman," in Carol Christ and Judith Plaskow, eds., *Womenspirit Rising* (New York: Harper and Row, 1979) 152–53.

2. What social scientists called participant observation as a methodology to gain knowledge of the community that one studies is, in fact, predicated on the quality of the relationship(s) between the observer/researcher and the observed/researched. In order to make explicit this collaborative and cooperative endeavor of conducting participant observation, some social scientists refer to doing research from an observing participant perspective or as conducting participatory research. Raymond Brady Williams, *Christian Pluralism in the United States* (Cambridge: Cambridge University Press, 1996), for example, developed an observing participant relationship with the Asian Indian Christians when he studied their community.

3. The concept of the hidden transcript is coined and discussed in James C. Scott, *Domination and the Arts of Resistance: Hidden Transcripts* (New Haven, CT: Yale University Press, 1990). As a way for the oppressed to talk back at the force or people who oppress them, they use what they have available to subversively serve their own interests.

4. Sheila Collins, "Theology in the Politics of Appalanchian women," in Carol Christ and Judith Plaskow, eds., *Womanspirit Rising* (New York: Harper & Row, 1979), 157.

5. The term "restory" is borrowed from Jon Laid, "Women and Stories: Restorying Women's Self-Consciousness," in Monica McGoldrick, Carol Anderson, and Froma Walsh, eds., *Women in Families: A Framework for Family Therapy* (New York: Norton, 1989), 425–50.

6. The process of telling and retelling one's own life stories is what Laid, "Women and Stories," calls restorying.

7. Mary Farrell Benarowski, *The Religious Imagination of American Women* (Bloomington: Indiana University Press, 1999), e.g., 186 and 188, repeatedly asks the same probing question.

8. Alessandro Portelli, *The Death of Luigi Trastulla and Other Stories: The Form and Meaning in Oral History* (Albany: State University of New York Press, 1991), 52.

9. Alasdair MacIntyre, "The Virtues, the Unity of a Human Life, and the Concept of a Tradition," in Lewis P. Hinchman and Sandra K. Hinchman, eds., *Memory, Identity, Community: The Idea of Narrative in the Human Science* (Albany: State University of New York Press, 1997) 254.

10. Judy Yung, *Unbound Voices: A Documentary History of Chinese Women in San Francisco* (Berkeley: University of California Press, 1999), 511.

11. See, for example, Jill Ker Conway, *When Memory Speaks: Reflections on Autobiography* (New York: Knopf, 1998), especially chapters 5 and 6; Katharine Grham, *Personal History* (New York: Alfred A. Knopf, 1997); and Rebecca S. Chopp, *The Power to Speak: Feminism, Language, God* (New York: Wipt & Stock, 2002).

12. Gary Y. Okihiro, *Privileging Positions: The Sites of Asian American Studies* (Pullman: Washington States University Press, 1995), 93.

13. Ibid., 94.

14. The life narratives of all four Korean American never-married women who participated in in-depth interviews and who shared their life stories with me came from the larger nationwide study on never-married Asian American women. At the outset, an individual's marital status may not seem to be an important factor for identifying who she is or for determining how she experiences and thinks of religion. The stories told by never-married women, however, point to the intricacy of intersecting various variables in forming a self-identity, such as the marital status and religious experiences. If we agree that religion indeed is an important lens through which individuals construct meanings and negotiate their own identities, then the vast variety of life experiences as a whole must need to be taken together in its entirety to understand religion. For the larger study to document never-married Asian American women's lives in the United States, I sent out eighty-one questionnaire forms based on the snowball sampling technique during the period of September 1998 to May 2000. This survey was meant to be a pretest to a much larger nationwide survey to be conducted later. Among eighty-one mailed-out forms, sixty-two were returned (with three undeliverable addresses) by May 2000. Among fifty-nine usable responses, eleven are from Korean American women, and four out of eleven expressed an interest in participating in further interviews by providing their contact information. All names appearing in this essay are pseudonyms to protect the identities of the women.

15. Numerous studies of self-reported life-satisfaction studies demonstrate an interesting interplay of gender and marital status. Studies show that marriage as an institution provides more benefits to men than to women. For example, in terms of the status of mental and physical health, married men enjoy better health than married women. In fact, married women are twice as likely than married men to suffer from chronic depression and other mental disorders. The overall life satisfaction scale also ranked married men as happiest, followed by single (especially never-married) women. Married women's life satisfaction ranked third, followed by divorced and widowed women and men. For further discussions, see Frances Goldscheider, "Recent Changes in U.S. Young Adults Living Arrangements in Comparative Perspective," *Journal of Family Issues* 18(11) (1997): 708–24; and Andrew J. Cherlin, *The Changing American Family and Public Policy* (Washington, DC: Urban Institute Press, 1988).

16. For further discussions on gender roles and gender inequality in the context of Confucian culture, see Aira Kim, *Women Struggling for New Life: The Role of Religion in the Cultural Passage from Korea to America* (Albany: State University of New York Press, 1996); John Lie and Nancy Abelmann, *Blue Dreams: Korean Americans and the Los Angeles Riots* (Cambridge: Harvard University Press, 1997); and Keyoung Park, *The Korean American Dream: Immigrants and Small Business in New York City* (Ithaca, NY: Cornell University Press, 1997).

17. U.S. Senate, Special Committee on Aging, *Aging in America: Trends and Projections* (Washington, DC: U.S. Government Printing Office, 1988).

18. G. Spitze and J. Logan, "Sons and Daughters, and Intergenerational Social Support," *Journal of Marriage and the Family* 52(2) (May 1990): 420–30.

19. Laurel Kendall, *Getting Married in Korea: Of Gender, Morality, and Modernity* (Berkeley: University of California Press, 1998), 5.

20. An article written by Yeon-sun Khang, "Traditional Wedding Ceremony Convened by Rigid Rules," *Korea Herald,* June 22, 1992; cited in Kendall, *Getting Married in Korea,* 5.

21. Kendall, *Getting Married in Korea,* 5.

22. Elaine H. Kim, "Men's Talk," in Elaine H. Kim and Chungmoo Choi, eds., *Dragon Women: Gender and Korean Nationalism* (New York: Routledge, 1998), 68.

23. Ibid., 106–7.

24. Mary Farrell Bednarowski, *The Religious Imagination of American Women* (Bloomington: Indiana University Press, 1999), 5–6.

25. Soo-Young Chin, *Doing What Had to Be Done: The Life Narrative of Dora Yum Kim* (Philadelphia: Temple University Press, 1999), 127–28.

26. Bednarowski, *The Religious Imagination of American Women,* 116.

27. Judy Long, *Telling Women's Lives: Subject/Narrator/Reader/Text* (New York: New York University Press, 1999), 142.

28. David D. Hall, ed., *Lived Religion in America: Toward A History of Practice* (Princeton, NJ: Princeton University Press, 1997) vii.

29. Bednarowski, *The Religious Imagination of American Women,* 20.

30. Peter A. Dorsey, *Sacred Estrangement: The Rhetoric of Conversion in Modern American Autobiography* (University Park: Pennsylvania State University, 1993), 37.

31. Carolyn G. Heilbrun, *The Last Gift of Time: Life beyond Sixty* (New York: Ballantine, 1997), 138.

Chapter Seven

Korean American Religiosity As a Predictor of Marital Commitment and Satisfaction

Ruth H. Chung and Sung Hyun Um

Korean immigrant families face many challenges in the process of migration and adaptation to life in the United States. The economic pressures that bear upon families in the initial period of adjustment often exert undue strain on the familial and marital bond. As wives are compelled to work outside of the home to supplement the family income and promote economic stability, established gender roles and power relations may be disrupted. These and other stressors as well as more tolerant attitudes toward divorce contribute to a rate of divorce among Korean immigrants that is as much as eight times higher than in the Korean population.[1]

The acculturative stress that strains immigrant families and marriages is further complicated by disruption of kinship networks and other sources of social support. Within the diasporic experience with the multiple dislocations of geography, culture, and relationship, many immigrant families improvise and turn to religious communities as a pseudo-extended family.[2] Religion has played a singularly important role in the Korean immigrant community in the United States from its very inception to the present. In contrast to the early immigrants who came from China and Japan, Koreans came largely as in-tact families seeking not only a better life for themselves but also freedom to practice their newly adopted Christian faith. For these early pioneers, the ethnic church functioned as the primary means of social support, cultural maintenance, and political activism surrounding the Korean independence movement.[3]

Ethnic churches continue to serve as the focal point of immigrant life for post-1965 Korean immigrants. While approximately 20 percent of the population in Korea is affiliated with Christian churches, about 75 percent of Koreans in the United States are similarly affiliated, and of these 77 percent attend church at least once a week, a rate higher than any other Asian group except the Filipinos.[4] This increase in religiosity is motivated in part by social, psychological, and economic benefits derived from religious membership. The most common social functions of immigrant churches are (1) to provide fellowship, (2) maintain Korean cultural traditions (3) provide social services for church members and Korean community, and (4) provide a place of social status and position.[5] In addition, the psychological benefits of church affiliation include a higher degree of life satisfaction for immigrant men who hold staff positions in the church.[6]

Questions regarding the impact of religion on various aspects of marriage and family life have been explored by social scientists. On the whole, the existing body of research suggests that religion has a positive impact on family life,[7] which is not surprising given the mutually reinforcing nature of religion and family as core institutions of American society. This mutual reinforcement occurs in two different domains of social support and social control.[8] Religion as a means of social support for families include fostering familial love, stability, and satisfaction, whereas social-control functions relate to constraining divorce, sex outside of marriage, and exogamy. But what is notably absent from this body of research is exploration of the interrelationship of religion and family in immigrant populations.

Given the significance of the family itself as the impetus for migration and of religious communities as one of the primary agents of social support, we felt the need to examine the intersection of these two institutions. Based on the empirically supported view that the best predictor of overall satisfaction with family life is satisfaction with the marital relationship,[9] we examined two aspects of marriage that would have the greatest impact on the family: commitment to maintaining the marital unit and satisfaction with marriage. We also felt the need to expand the existing body of knowledge in this area by determining to what extent established findings linking religiosity to marital commitment and satisfaction would hold true for Korean Americans in particular. We now turn to a brief review of the broader literature in religiosity and marriage.

RELIGIOSITY AND MARITAL COMMITMENT

In examining the corpus of research on the relationship between religiosity and marital commitment, we discovered several related concepts such as marital stability, marital adjustment, and divorce. Regardless of the variations in constructs, on the whole there is consistent evidence to indicate that religiosity promotes marital commitment and stability. When religiosity along with number of children and family income were examined as predictors of marital adjustment, religiosity emerged as the strongest predictor. This relationship remained even when controlling for social desirability, leading to the conclusion that "religiosity was the most consistent and strongest predictor of marital adjustment."[10]

In a large-scale social and demographic analysis based on fifteen hundred respondents, religiosity, as measured by frequency of religious service attendance, was one of ten factors examined as predictors of divorce. Race was the strongest factor, with blacks having a higher rate than whites, followed by age at first marriage (the lower the age, the higher the risk), and religiosity, with higher frequency of church attendance predicting lower likelihood of divorce. Relatedly, those with no religious affiliation had the highest rate of divorce, whereas Jews and Catholics reported the lowest rates.[11]

Another larger-scale study of 4,587 married couples confirmed and extended these earlier findings by showing that frequency of church attendance was positively associated with marital stability, that those with no religious affiliation had higher rates of divorce than other groups, and that the lowest rate of divorce was found among Jews. In addition, they discovered that interfaith marriages increased the likelihood of divorce, and differences in frequency of church attendance within the marital unit also predicted higher rates of divorce. In fact, if the wife attended church on a weekly basis but the husband did not, their likelihood of divorce was actually higher than couples in which both did not attend church at all and almost three times as high in comparison to couples who both attended church on a weekly basis. The authors argued that "shared participation in religious activities is a critical aspect of religious experience that can sustain marriages."[12]

RELIGIOSITY AND MARITAL SATISFACTION

As with the literature on religiosity as a positive predictor of marital commitment, religiosity is also a positive predictor of marital satisfaction. However, the evidence of this relationship is somewhat more equivocal. Studies in a 1957 issue of the *American Sociological Review* provide some of the earliest empirical evidence of religiosity as a predictor of marital satisfaction.[13] Since then, a large-scale national study examining ten well-established predictors of marital happiness revealed that frequency of church attendance was the most powerful positive predictor. Other notable predictors were the presence of very young children and being middle-aged for females, both having a significant negative relationship. Surprisingly, contrary to conventional wisdom, socioeconomic factors failed to have an impact on marital satisfaction. However, the authors caution that on the whole, even the significant predictors account for very little of the total variability in marital satisfaction and thus do not offer a compelling explanation.[14]

A study by Ruth Hatch, Dorothy James, and Walter Schumm found that for wives, the only significant predictor of emotional intimacy and marital satisfaction was church attendance. Another indicator of religiosity used in the study, that of spiritual intimacy, had only an indirect impact through emotional intimacy. They also found some evidence in keeping with prior research that fundamentalism is negatively related to marital intimacy and satisfaction.[15] But in contrast to these studies, Alan Booth, David Johnson, Ann Branaman, and Alan Sica found no relationship between religiosity and overall marital quality. Although there was some evidence to indicate that frequency of religious activity slightly decreased the probability of considering divorce, it did not significantly increase marital happiness or marital interaction or decrease marital conflict.[16]

An extension of the religiosity and marital satisfaction literature is found in comparing couples that are heterogamous versus endogamous. Similar to the studies noted above reporting higher rates of divorce for exogamous couples, couples with different religious affiliations reported lower marital satisfaction than those with the same affiliation.[17] Complicating this trend, Constance Shehan, Wilbur Bock, and Gary Lee found that Catholics involved in interfaith marriages versus intrafaith marriages did not differ in their report of marital happiness. However, the authors did find that those who were homogamous reported greater frequency of attending mass than those who were exogamous.[18]

On the whole, there is enough evidence to suggest that religiosity has a positive impact on marital commitment and satisfaction, but further research is indicated to clarify some of the contradictions, particularly with regard to marital satisfaction, and also to determine if these patterns extend to Korean Americans. This combined with the significance of religious participation in the Korean immigrant community led to our empirical inquiry. Therefore, the purpose of this study was to determine to what extent religiosity predicts marital commitment and marital satisfaction for Korean Americans who are married. We also explored gender and generational differences in marital commitment and satisfaction. Given the preponderance of the literature indicating religiosity as a predictor of marital commitment, we hypothesized that this pattern would hold true for Korean Americans as well. But given the equivocal nature of the relationship between religiosity and marital satisfaction, we did not hypothesize a specific outcome for this relationship.

METHOD

Participants

A total of 181 Korean American married individuals responded to a survey distributed through twenty-four different Korean churches in the Southern

California area. In terms of demographic profile of the respondents, the overall mean age was forty-three with a range of twenty-two to sixty-three; gender composition was 37.6 percent male and 62.4 percent female; mean years of marriage to the present spouse was seventeen years, with only 4 percent being divorced; and mean number of children was two. Ninety-one percent of the sample was first generation, 6 percent was 1.5 generation, and 3 percent was second generation (native born). For those who immigrated, the mean number of years in the United States was sixteen years, with a mean age of twenty-seven years at immigration. Due to the comparatively smaller number of 1.5- and second-generation respondents, in subsequent analyses involving generation, they were combined and relabeled as 1.5/2nd generation.

Examination of socioeconomic data revealed that 15 percent had incomes of $20,000 or less, 29 percent had incomes of $20,001 to $40,000, 28 percent had incomes of $40,001–$60,000, and 29 percent had incomes over $60,001. Only 3 percent did not complete high school, while 22 percent completed high school, 61 percent completed either associate or bachelor's degrees, 10 percent completed master's degrees, and 5 percent completed doctorates.

Instruments

Data was collected through a self-report questionnaire that included basic demographic questions (age, gender, years in the United States, years of marriage, number of children, income, and educational levels), a measure of marital satisfaction, and a measure of marital commitment.

Religiosity. Religiosity, as assessed by frequency of church attendance, is one of the most prevalent measures of this construct. Most of the studies of religiosity reviewed previously in this study were based on this approach. Even when multidimensional indicators of religiosity were employed, frequency of church attendance was distinguishable as the strongest and sometimes the only significant predictor of marital and family variables.[19] The participants in our study had high levels of church participation, with 39 percent attending church more than once a week, 37 percent once a week, 13 percent nearly every week, 3 percent less than once a month, and only 7 percent once or twice a year. The average years of practicing religion was twenty-two for the overall group. In terms of religious affiliation, Methodists were the largest denomination, followed by Seventh-day Adventists, Presbyterians, Baptists, and Catholics.

Marital satisfaction. Marital satisfaction was measured by the Kansas Marital Satisfaction Scale (KMSS), a three-item questionnaire known for its brevity and high reliability.[20] The items—such as "How satisfied are you with your marriage?"—were presented using a seven-point Likert format, ranging from very satisfied to very dissatisfied. The measure has moderately high reliability estimates ranging from .81 to .98. The alpha reliability for the present sample was .94. This measure was selected because it has an established precedence of use with the Korean and other Asian populations.

Marital commitment. The Commitment Inventory (CI) consists of two sub-scales: dedication commitment and constraint commitment. Personal dedication "refers to the desire of the individual to maintain or improve the quality of his or her relationship," whereas constraint commitment "refers to forces that constrain individuals to maintain relationships regardless of their personal dedication."[21] To make the CI more culturally relevant for the Korean American population, three items were added addressing the notions of fate (under dedication commitment), will of God (under constraint commitment), and filial piety (under dedication commitment). Adding each of these three items yielded alpha coefficients that were higher than without (.79 vs. .77 for fate; .79 vs. .78 for will of God). The filial piety item left the alpha coefficient unchanged at .87.

Procedure

The data was collected through twenty Korean-speaking and four English-speaking Korean churches in Southern California. These twenty-four churches were selected based on personal networks of the second author. A data collection coordinator was designated for each congregation and was provided with standardized instructions on dissemination of the survey. Each questionnaire packet had a cover sheet explaining the purpose of this study, assurance of confidentiality, and other information in compliance with informed consent. Each packet contained both English and Korean versions of the questionnaires to enable participants to respond in their preferred language. To ensure comparability of the two versions, the English version was translated into Korean, back-translated into English, and then compared to the original version. Any discrepant items were reconciled to the agreement of the two translators. To ensure anonymity and promote a higher response rate, respondents were provided with postage-paid return envelopes along with the surveys.

RESULTS

To address the primary research question regarding the predictive relationship of religiosity to marital commitment and marital satisfaction, three sets of multiple regression analyses were conducted. Religiosity, as defined by frequency of church attendance, was the predictor variable, and constraint commitment, dedication commitment, and marital satisfaction served as the three criterion variables.

For constraint commitment, religiosity was a significant predictor for the overall group, with greater frequency of church attendance predicting higher constraint commitment (table 7.1). When the prediction model was examined separately by gender and generation, the same pattern of significance held for both men and women and for the first generation but not for the 1.5/2nd generation. An identical pattern was observed for dedication commitment, with increase in religiosity predicting higher dedication commitment for the group as a whole as well as for men, women, and the first-generation respondents.

In terms of marital satisfaction, religiosity was not a significant predictor, even when examined separately by gender and generational status. Given that religiosity was unrelated to marital satisfaction, follow-up analyses were conducted to explore the possibility that constraint and dedication commitment might be better predictors of marital satisfaction. Additional regressions performed with these two variables added resulted in a significant overall prediction model for men, women, and first-generation respondents. Interestingly, of the three variables, only dedication commitment was a significant predictor of marital satisfaction (table 7.2).

Secondary analyses were also conducted to examine gender and generational differences in marital commitment and marital satisfaction. Multivariate analysis of variance (MANOVA) failed to reveal any significant differences between men and women in constraint and dedication commitment. However, there was a significant difference by generation,[22] with the first generation reporting significantly higher scores on constraint commitment (M = 232.63)

Table 7.1. Results of multiple regressions for frequency of church attendance predicting constraint commitment and dedication commitment

Variables	R2	b	Beta	P
Constraint Commitment				
All groups combined	.08	3.68	.28	.001
Men	.08	3.71	.28	.022
Women	.08	3.59	.28	.003
1st Generation	.08	3.69	.28	.001
1.5/2nd Generation	.06	4.34	.24	.342
Dedication Commitment				
All groups combined	.07	5.55	.26	.001
Men	.10	6.56	.31	.010
Women	.06	5.36	.25	.007
1st Generation	.08	5.43	.28	.001
1.5/2nd Generation	.01	−2.06	−.05	.844

Table 7.2.   Results of multiple regressions for frequency of church attendance, constraint commitment, and dedication commitment predicting marital satisfaction

Variables	R2	b	Beta	P
Marital Satisfaction				
All groups combined	.20			.001
Frequency		.01	.01	.958
Constraint		.03	.01	.900
Dedication		.08	.44	.001
Men	.13			.025
Frequency		.22	.06	.622
Constraint		.04	.17	.227
Dedication		.04	.22	.111
Women	.30			.001
Frequency		−.18	−.05	.581
Constraint		−.04	−.13	.201
Dedication		.12	.63	.001
1st Generation	.18			.001
Frequency		−.03	−.01	.919
Constraint		.09	.03	.714
Dedication		.08	.41	.001
1.5/2nd Generation	.21			.369
Frequency		.252	.09	.752
Constraint		−.08	−.05	.904
Dedication		.03	.49	.213

than 1.5/2nd-generation respondents (M = 215.06). In contrast, the reverse was true for dedication commitment, with the 1.5/2nd generation (M = 225.59) having higher scores than the first generation (M = 200.57). In terms of marital satisfaction, there were significant differences by gender and generation, with men (M = 17.60) reporting higher marital satisfaction than women (M = 15.82), and 1.5/2nd-generation respondents (M = 19.35) reporting higher marital satisfaction than first-generation respondents (M = 16.19).[23]

DISCUSSION

The results of this study revealed a consistent pattern of religiosity predicting martial commitment but not marital satisfaction. As hypothesized, frequency of church attendance was predictive of greater marital commitment (both constraint and dedication) for all but the 1.5/2nd generation. This overall pattern is in keeping with the existing corpus of research conducted on European Americans and supports the assertion that religion and family serve to mutually reinforce each other as agents of social support as well as social control.[24] Scott

Stanley and Howard Markman's measure of constraint commitment reflecting the social control functions allowed us to test this mutually reinforcing relationship.[25] However, as our significant findings on dedication commitment suggest, the positive impact of religiosity on marital commitment is not limited to the control functions; frequency of church attendance also increases the desire to maintain or improve the quality of the marital relationship. This is encouraging news indeed for both the church institutions and those who attend church frequently. However, what is not clear in the context of this study is the precise mechanism by which an increase in religiosity contributes to an increase in marital commitment. Certainly, the most obvious interpretation is that the precepts of Christianity not only constrain couples to maintain their relationships out of duty and obligation but also strive to improve the quality of that relationship. But it is also plausible that social pressures and modeling effects within the religious community could be compelling factors.

Although our findings support the existing body of research on religiosity and its influence on marriage, a relatively small portion of variability in marital commitment was explained by religiosity, confirming the observation that "religion has generally been found to have a positive, if often modest, impact on the family."[26] This leaves us to speculate on what factors other than religiosity might account for marital commitment. In our study, follow-up analysis adding other sociodemographic indicators such as number of years in the United States, number of children, and years of practicing religion, as supplemental indicators of religiosity all failed to notably increase the predictive power of the overall model. Of the variables examined, frequency of church attendance remained the single most effective predictor. This finding adds to the established notion that even as a single item, this indicator is a robust indicator of religiosity. It appears that there is something about frequency of church attendance that captures the essence of religiosity.

The fact that the 1.5/2nd generation was the only group for whom religiosity did not predict marital commitment, combined with the finding that this group had higher dedication commitment and higher marital satisfaction than the first generation, is indicative of an acculturation effect. The 1.5/2nd-generation has internalized more of the host culture's greater emphasis on love, compatibility, and self-fulfillment rather than duty and obligation as prescribed by religious beliefs or Korean culture. If R. Bellah, R. Madsen, M. Sullivan, A. Swidler, and S. Tipton's assertion that excessive individualism weakens the sense of obligation in marriage is true,[27] then the increasing rate of divorce among Asian Americans may be attributable in part to acculturation to an individualistic value orientation. However, for Korean Americans who attend church on a regular basis, an increase in both constraint and dedication commitment may help to moderate the effects of values acculturation and thereby lower the rate of divorce.

The finding that religiosity did not predict marital satisfaction is not surprising given the inconsistencies in the existing literature. On one hand, Norval Glenn and Charles Weaver found religiosity to be one of the strongest predictors of marital happiness,[28] but others have found more modest indirect effects through intervening variables such as emotional intimacy[29] or homogamy and shared sphere of religiosity.[30] The findings of our study are suggestive of an indirect effect as well. Although religiosity did not predict marital satisfaction directly, religiosity did predict dedication commitment, which in turn was the only significant indicator of marital satisfaction. It is interesting to note that of the two types of commitment, only dedication commitment, and not constraint commitment or religiosity, predicted marital satisfaction.

CONCLUSION

The dual processes of control and support functions of religion appear to have parallel application for the Korean immigrant family as well as the community as a whole. Within a diasporic context characterized by discontinuity and disruption, religion serves as one of the primary means of maintaining continuity of the family and the ethnic community. Religion serves as a primary vehicle for providing meaning, a sense of belonging, and comfort as well as control functions to promote ethnic identity and endogamy.[31] The amplified and expanded role of religion for Korean Americans reflects the improvisations that can occur as a result of diaspora. In order to decipher the complexity of how this occurs and the underlying factors that contribute to these processes, future studies should include a nonreligious comparison group as well as a larger sample of 1.5– and second-generation subjects and expand the predictors to gain a better understanding of how to increase marital commitment and marital satisfaction in Korean Americans. For the purposes of our study, we found that greater frequency of church attendance predicted greater commitment to marriage but that marital satisfaction was unrelated to frequency of church attendance. The empirical evidence in favor of the protective function of religiosity in relation to marital commitment should serve to further encourage both religious institutions and Korean immigrant families.

NOTES

1. Siyon Rhee, "Separation and Divorce among Korean Immigrant Families," in Young I. Song and Ailee Moon, eds., *Korean American Women: From Tradition to Modern Feminism* (Westport, CT: Praeger, 1998), 151.

2. Illsoo Kim, *New Urban Immigrants: The Korean Community in New York* (Princeton, NJ: Princeton University Press, 1981).

3. Byong-youn Choy, *Koreans in America* (Chicago: Nelson Hall, 1979); and Wayne Patterson, *The Korean Frontier in America* (Honolulu: University of Hawaii Press, 1988).

4. Won Moo Hurh and Kwang Chung Kim, "Religious Participation of Korean Immigrants in the United States," *Journal for the Scientific Study of Religion* 19 (1990): 19–34.

5. Pyong Gap Min, "The Structure and Social Functions of Korean Immigrant Churches in the United States," *International Migration Review* 26 (1992): 1370–94.

6. Huhr and Kim, "Religious Participation of Korean Immigrants in the United States," 31.

7. Darwin L. Thomas and Marie Cornwall, "Religion and Family in the 1980s: Discovery and Development," *Journal of Marriage Family* 52 (1990): 983–92; Darwin L. Thomas and Gwendolyn C. Henry, "The Religion and Family Connection: Increasing Dialogue in the Social Sciences," *Journal of Marriage Family* 47 (1985): 369–79.

8. William V. D'Antonio, William M. Newman, and Stuart A. Wright, "Religion and Family Life: How Social Scientists View the Relationship," *Journal for the Scientific Study of Religion* 21 (1982): 218–25.

9. Jung Ja Rho and Walter R. Schumm, "Components of Family Life Satisfaction in a Sample of 58 Korean/American Couples," *Psychological Reports* 65 (1989): 781–82.

10. Erik E. Filsinger and Margaret R. Wilson, "Religiosity, Socioeconomic Rewards, and Family Development: Predictors of Family Adjustment," *Journal of Marriage and the Family* 46 (1984): 668.

11. Norval D. Glenn and Michael Supancic, "The Social and Demographic Correlates of Divorce and Separation in the United States: An Update and Reconsideration," *Journal of Marriage and the Family* 46 (1984): 563–75.

12. Virginia R. Call and Tim B. Heaton, "Religious Influence on Marital Stability," *Journal for the Scientific Study of Religion* 36 (1997): 390.

13. Lee G. Burchinal, "Marital Satisfaction and Religious Behavior," *American Sociological Review* 22 (1957): 306–10; and Paul Wallin, "Religiosity, Sexual Gratification, and Marital Satisfaction," *American Sociological Review* 22 (1957): 300–305.

14. Norval Glenn and Charles N. Weaver, "A Multivariate, Multisurvey of Marital Happiness," *Journal of Marriage and the Family* 40 (1978): 269–82.

15. Ruth H. Hatch, Dorothy E. James, and Walter R. Schumm, "Spiritual Intimacy and Marital Satisfaction," *Family Relations* 35 (1986): 539–45.

16. Alan Booth, David R. Johnson, Ann Branaman, and Alan Sica, "Belief and Behavior: Does Religion Matter in Today's Marriage?" *Journal of Marriage and the Family* 57 (1995): 661–71.

17. Timothy B. Heaton, "Religious Homogamy and Marital Satisfaction Reconsidered," *Journal of Marriage and the Family* 46 (1984): 729–33.

18. Constance L. Shehan, E. Wilbur Bock, and Gary R. Lee, "Religious Heterogamy, Religiosity, and Marital Happiness: The Case of Catholics," *Journal of Marriage and the Family* 52 (1990): 73–79.

19. Booth, Johnson, Branaman, and Sica, "Belief and Behavior"; Richard A. Hunt and Morton B. King, "Religiosity and Marriage," *Journal for the Scientific Study of Religion* 17 (1978): 399–406; and Margaret R. Wilson and Erik E. Filsinger, "Religiosity and Marital Adjustment: Multidimensional Interrelationships," *Journal of Marriage and the Family* 48 (1986): 147–51.

20. S. Mitchell, K. Newell, and W. Schumm, "Test-Retest Reliability of the Kansas Marital Satisfaction Scale," *Psychological Reports* 53 (1983): 545–46.

21. Scott M. Stanley and Howard Markman, "Assessing Commitment in Personal Relationships," *Journal of Marriage and the Family* 54 (1992): 595–608.

22. Generation: F(1, 154) = 8.01, p = .005.

23. Gender: F(1, 134) = 6.97, p = .009; Generation: F(1, 154) = 8.01, p = .005.

24. D'Antonio, Newman, and Wight, "Religion and Family Life," 218.

25. Stanley and Markman, "Assessing Commitment in Personal Relationships."

26. Hatch, James, and Schumm, "Spiritual Intimacy and Marital Satisfaction," 539.

27. R. Bellah, R. Madsen, M. Sullivan, A. Swidler, and S. Tipton, *Habits of the Heart: Individualism and Commitment in American Life* (New York: Harper & Row, 1985).

28. Glenn and Weaver, "A Multivariate, Multisurvey of Marital Happiness," 273.

29. Hatch, James, and Schumm, "Spiritual Intimacy and Marital Satisfaction," 539.

30. Shehan, Bock, and Lee, "Religious Heterogamy, Religiosity, and Marital Happiness," 73.

31. Pyong Gap Min, "The Structure and Social Functions of Korean Immigrant Churches in the United States," *International Migration Review* 26 (1992): 1370–94.

Section III

FROM GENERATION TO GENERATION

These essays are concerned with how 1.5-generation and second-generation Korean Americans, who are largely English-speaking, are expressing their religion and spirituality. Sharon Kim tracks the creative and varied ways that second-generation ministries are unfolding in Southern California and how they complicate standard categories of assimilation and religious pluralism that stress ethnic maintenance. Her findings point to a complex and fascinating interplay of race, ethnicity, generation, and religion.

Rebecca Kim moves her questions about the next generation to the college campus and asks why Korean American Christians have chosen to participate in ethnic-specific (Korean American) ministries. High levels of education and acculturation would suggest decreasing levels of racial-ethnic orientation, but Kim's research suggests otherwise. In the final essay, David K. Yoo takes a historical view of generational transition through a case study of a particular Korean American Christian congregation in Los Angeles. Original second-generation issues in this church date to the 1930s, and the experiences of the church in the post-1965 era are instructive in thinking about how change over time takes place.

Chapter Eight

Replanting Sacred Spaces

The Emergence of Second-Generation Korean American Churches

Sharon Kim

INTRODUCTION

The Korean church in Los Angeles is currently in a period of generational transition. There are nearly eight hundred Korean churches serving more than a quarter of a million Koreans residing in the Los Angeles area. However, with the increasing population of second-generation Korean Americans, the traditional Korean church that had served primarily the Korean-speaking immigrant population is now restructuring its organization in the hopes of retaining and attracting this newly emerging population. While there have been numerous studies on Korean immigrant churches, little has been written on the course of the second generation.[1] This essay analyzes the restructuring that is currently taking place within Korean churches by focusing on the inventive and improvisational manner in which second-generation Korean Americans are carving out new institutional niches to accommodate the intersection of race, generation, and ethnicity in the context of their Christian faith.[2]

The generational transition within Korean churches is sociologically important because it helps us to better understand two very important and related aspects in the Korean immigrant experience and the role that religion plays in the adaptation process. First, the social realities of Korean churches cannot be understood in the framework of immigration and assimilation that is applied to European immigrant churches. Nor can it be understood in the strict framework of pluralism, which stresses ethnic identity maintenance. Second-generation Korean Americans are neither assimilating into mainstream churches nor clinging onto the Korean ethnic churches of their immigrant parents. Rather, they are charting a third path by carving out entirely new ethnoreligious hybrid spaces. My research validates Stephen Warner's position that "if there was ever a linear process by which immigrants assimilated to American culture, it no longer exists."[3] The development and proliferation of second-generation churches provide a compelling case that long-standing theories in the social sciences on immigrant adaptation need to be replaced or modified to more accurately interpret the experiences of post-1965 immigrants.

Second, the rapid proliferation of new ministries and churches that target second-generation Koreans demonstrate that although second-generation Koreans demonstrate a high level of acculturation in English mastery, residential dispersion, educational achievements, and occupational mobility, they also exhibit a high level of ethnic identification through their involvement with these newly formed churches. In analyzing these improvisational sacred spaces, I focus on two questions: What are the forces, both internal and external, that motivate second-generation Korean Americans to construct and inhabit new ethnic churches? What do these new churches look like, and how do their multiple identities as children of immigrants, as racial minorities, as Protestants, and as Korean Americans shape their practice of religion?

METHODOLOGY

The analysis to be presented in this study is based on data obtained through participant observation, interviews, and reviews of relevant literature. A total of forty-six structured interviews were conducted with pastors, lay leaders, and members of fourteen different Korean American churches. Currently, there are primarily three different approaches to ministry for the English-speaking generation. The individuals interviewed represent the differing approaches. The first approach is to have a separate English ministry within an existing immigrant Korean church. The second approach is generally known as the townhouse model in which an independent English church is housed in the same building as the immigrant congregation. Both congregations are completely independent but coexist side by side in a mutually friendly relationship. The final type of Korean American church is the independent church that has no formal relationship with an immigrant congregation. There are currently thirty-four independent second-generation churches in the greater Los Angeles area.

In addition to personal interviews, this study incorporates data obtained through participant observation (during 1994–2000) at the following seven churches: Los Angeles Korean Church, Faith Church, Joyful Sound Church, Flowing Life Church, Resurrection Ministry, Family Church, and Fruitful Church.[4] Observations were made through attendance of worship services, small group Bible studies, prayer meetings, and events held at the seven churches.

RELIGIOUS INSTITUTIONS
AND SECOND-GENERATION ADAPTATION

For the first half of the twentieth century, the dominant interpretive framework for understanding immigrant adaptation was assimilation, or the melting pot theory. The assimilationist perspective contains the assumption that ethnic groups desire racial integration into the host society, and in order to do so they will put aside their ethnic allegiances, including involvement in ethnic institutions, and replace them with a singular identification with the host society. In past studies, ethnic institutions were established by the immigrant generation because of language and cultural constraints but eventually disappeared as the American-born generation assimilated into mainstream institutions. Assimilationist studies of ethnic churches adhere to a life-cycle framework of ethnic institutions.[5] During the first stage, ethnic churches are initially established to meet the needs of the immigrant generation, and hence the services and activities are conducted in the language of the old country. With the cultural assimilation of the later generations and the inevitable language shift, the ethnic churches enter their second stage, making organizational changes necessary in several areas. Bilingual religious leaders must be recruited, additional English-language services must be implemented, and the materials used in religious services must be made available in both languages. Structural assimilation, which involves large-scale entrance into the cliques, clubs, and institutions of the host society, brings ethnic churches to the third stage of development. The appeal of ethnic churches tends to gradually diminish because social and religious needs can be met equally well within the organizations of the host society. Likewise, structural assimilation leads to increasing intermarriage among subsequent generations, contributing further to the decline of ethnic churches. For white Americans, one outcome of widespread social mobility and intermarriage in a span of three or more generations is that ethnic identity has become an optional and harmless form of symbolic ethnicity.

Race is a key variable in understanding why second-generation Korean Americans, unlike the second generation of other white ethnic groups, choose to develop their own ethnic religious institutions. According to Michael Omi and Howard Winant, "One of the first things we notice about people when we first meet them (along with their sex) is their race. We utilize race to provide clues about who a person is."[6] Because race forms an important part of the context against which individuals negotiate their affiliations and understandings, it strongly influences the formation of second-generation churches and the decisions that individuals make to join them. The second generation experiences a host of tensions that emerge from their status as racial minorities, including feelings of marginalization and not quite fitting in. They continue to be perceived by the mainstream society as different, foreign, and not authentically American.[7] Although the majority of them are highly acculturated, well educated, and upwardly mobile, due to their status as a racially and culturally defined group, differences continue to exist between them and other Americans. These perceived differences in values, life experiences, struggles, and worldviews prevent full identification with the mainstream society, but at the same time they also serve as the point of common identification, comfort, and connection that binds fellow Korean Americans together within this third space.

In addition to race, the second generation faces a host of tensions associated with their status as children of immigrants. As a generation, they are eager to differentiate themselves from their immigrant parents, and this process of differentiation and mediation is wrought with numerous tensions between the two generations. Generational conflicts are a normal and widely recognized part of the processes of individuation and maturity, irrespective of cultural context.[8] However, the processes of immigration and adaptation exacerbates and adds layers of complexity to generational conflicts. These tensions manifest themselves within the immigrant church, making it an uncomfortable and unappealing place for the younger generation to worship.

The third space is born as a response to the lived tensions associated with the sense of discomfort and not quite fitting in in either the immigrant or mainstream American religious institutions. These new churches serve as arenas where they seek to find comfort and meaningful resolutions to their conflicted sense of identity. However, the third space is not simply a retreat or refuge from marginalization. To characterize it as such would mask the more inventive and empowering facets of these newly developed churches. In addition to being a place of refuge, the third space is also a place of self-definition and empowerment.

According to Alejandro Portez and Ruben Rumbaut, assimilation has become segmented in that there is no longer just one "America" that newcomers enter or only one "American identity" that they may adopt.[9] Immigrants enter a pluralistic social context with diverse categories to which they may be assigned. Recent research has suggested that the incorporation of today's second generation is likely to be segmented and that different groups will take different pathways to adulthood, depending on a variety of conditions and contexts. The study of second-generation Korean American churches is an excellent case study of how religion and religious institutions serve as important vehicles for improvisational adaptation.

THE TRADITIONAL FUNCTIONS
OF THE IMMIGRANT CHURCH

The Korean church has been, from the very first wave of immigration to the United States, the central institution in the Korean community. Past research on Korean immigrant churches has identified four basic sociological functions of the ethnic Korean church. First, churches function as social service agencies, providing its members with programs such as health care, language and citizenship classes, and information about jobs, housing, and business.[10] Upon arrival to the United States, many Korean immigrants began attending ethnic churches, where their practical needs associated with immigrant adjustment were met. Second, the Korean churches provided important social occasions where people could meet and interact with each other. The church offers services and programs throughout the week, and immigrants can come together to fellowship and experience a sense of belonging. Third, the church confers social status and positions of leadership upon immigrant members. This is particularly important in compensating for the downward mobility that Korean immigrants experienced upon immigrating. The Korean immigrant church provides a hierarchical structure that can serve as a ladder of achievement for church members. Finally, at immigrant churches the Korean culture is preserved through the celebration of shared history as well as the instruction of the Korean language and Korean customs for second-generation Koreans.

THREE MODELS OF MINISTRY
TO THE SECOND-GENERATION

The majority of Koreans in Los Angeles are post-1965 immigrants, so for nearly two decades Korean churches did not face the challenge of providing religious services to an English-speaking population. However, beginning in the late 1980s, as the second-generation children started coming of age, their needs and demands could no longer be met within the existing immigrant church structure. At that time, many immigrant churches began to implement a variety of solutions. Among these solutions were the purchasing of simultaneous translation equipment, hiring non-Korean ministers, and replacing Sunday school classes with Korean-language classes in the hopes that their children would learn enough Korean to participate in the main worship service.

However, the efforts did not satisfy the second generation, and many were leaving the immigrant church to attend either a non-Korean church or no church at all. Recognizing this trend, 1.5-generation pastors[11] pressured first-generation church leadership to establish an official English ministry as opposed to just offering an English service. Many of the larger immigrant churches, wanting to retain their younger pastors as well as the younger generation, began to establish and fund English ministries within their own churches.

An English ministry has its own senior pastor as well as a degree of autonomy over decisions affecting its own style and future. It is seen as a separate department of the immigrant church. However, control over the English ministry still remains within the hands of the immigrant leadership. One of the primary disadvantages in this model is the inability to reach out to non-Koreans. According to one member, "I have all types of friends. Not all my friends are Korean. Even when I want to share my faith, I hesitate in doing so because I cannot bring them to my church. They wouldn't feel comfortable there because they are not Korean." When asked if his ministry would eventually become multiracial, the senior pastor of the English ministry replied, "We talked about us becoming more multiethnic, but as long as we stay within the perimeter of this church it will be nearly impossible to be multiethnic because as soon as you walk in, you smell Korea. You smell *gook bap* [Korean soup with rice] because we serve two thousand *gook baps* every Sunday. You smell *kimchee,* and all these signs on the walls are written in Korean. You also see thousands of Koreans walking around here every Sunday. It is difficult for non-Koreans to come in here and feel like they fit in."

Continuing immigration from Korea helps maintain the vitality of ethnic and immigrant congregations. At one large immigrant church, the first generation for years had envisioned that the second generation would take over the leadership and navigate the future of the church. However, in recent years, this view has changed in light of the continuing stream of immigrants from Korea. The immigrant leadership is no longer speaking of passing the church on to the second generation but rather passing it on to the younger first-generation population. According to one leader, "We're investing quite a lot on ministry to Korean-speaking young adults. They have two full-time pastors, and the church is continuing to make a huge investment in this particular group. Why are they making that kind of investment? Because they want the immigrant church to continue. They [the Korean-speaking young adults] are the heirs. We [the second-generation young adults] are not the heirs. They will be inheriting the church, not us." The continuous stream of immigration from Korea ensures that the church will continue to service primarily a Korean-speaking population.

The second model, what is generally referred to as the townhouse church, is an independent and autonomous English-speaking church that exists side by side in the same physical space as a Korean-speaking church. According to one of the pastors, "I think right now it's critical to preserve a model like ours because the first generation and second generation needs to coexist side by side. Immigration still continues, and there is still a whole population of first-generation families, and their children need a youth group where they can grow up. If English ministries become geographically separate from immigrant churches, then you are asking immigrant families to choose one or the other, or you're causing the family to split. Korean families are already segmented too much. Our model gives a nice solution where families can come together to worship at one church. I think there will be a need for this model for several more years to come." Townhouse churches offer elements from the traditional service alongside the more contemporary aspects. For example, Ascension Ministry offers both a traditional choir and a contemporary praise band at each Sunday worship service.

Finally, the third approach is the independent second-generation church, which is not affiliated with any immigrant congregation. Independent churches first began to emerge when 1.5-generation pastors felt that their demands for an adequate ministry to the second generation were not being met. Increasingly, the 1.5- and second-generation members voiced discontentment about what they perceived was unfair treatment as second-class citizens in a church that was controlled by the first generation.

A mixture of discontent and divine vision motivated the majority of second-generation pastors to leave immigrant congregations to establish their own autonomous churches. First, the majority of younger pastors believed that the immigrant churches were not doing an adequate job of ministering to the second generation and that the needs of the immigrant population were the first priority. Second, many of the pastors communicated that they sensed a divine directive to establish churches for the second generation. One pastor's decision to launch an independent church came as a response to an encounter that he had with God. "I was resting at a Holiday Inn in Irvine, and while I was there I heard a voice saying 'Psalm 40.' I heard this twice. I think I heard it twice because God knew I was from Dallas seminary. So I looked at my Bible to see what it was, and it read, 'he put a new song in my mouth, a hymn of praise to our God.' When I looked out my window, I saw Orange County and knew that this is where God was calling me to plant a new church." Another pastor started his church in response to a repeated series of dreams in which he saw large waves crashing onto a white sand beach. In the waves, he saw a multitude of Asian faces. He believed that God had given him the dreams to tell him that second-generation Korean Americans would play a significant role in ushering in a new era of spiritual revival in the United States.

The attitudes among the first generation toward independent churches have slowly changed in the past ten years. When independent churches first emerged, most opposed their development on the grounds that they would break the family unit and weaken cultural maintenance. The first generation suggested that an English-speaking Korean church is just one step toward the steady decline of ethnic identity for the subsequent generations. According to an elder at a first-generation church, "First they want an English-speaking Korean church, then I am sure other non-Koreans will start to attend the church. Eventually there will be no more Korean churches for the following generations. . . . And this will lead to interracial marriage, and then the Korean identity will completely disappear." There is a strong conviction among the first generation that the Korean church is the main institution responsible for the preservation of the Korean culture. For many immigrant parents, when they want to pass on their heritage, religion becomes their key to cultural reproduction. For this reason, the protest against the development of separate churches was emotionally heated. In recent years, the attitudes among the first generation have begun to change as they realize that the younger generation has their finger on the pulse of something with unlimited potential. They are poised to accomplish what the immigrant church could never do: namely, to reach out to a niche far beyond the Korean community. This attitude shift is reflected in the ways in which several first-generation pastors have taken the younger leaders under their wings with financial, spiritual, and emotional support.

SPIRITUAL LABORATORIES: CREATING A NEW HYBRID SECOND-GENERATION KOREAN AMERICAN CHURCH

Second-generation churches are arenas of change and experimentation, and as they emerge within congregational spaces and develop their own unique spiritual expressions and visions, they draw from a variety of cultural and spiritual resources. Within these newly developed churches, the ministers hope to create a hybrid second-generation spirituality by appropriating and fusing together elements of Confucianism, Korean immigrant Protestantism, and various expressions of American evangelicalism. In their quest to invent an independent second-generation spirituality, the leaders of these new churches aim to adopt what they perceive to be essential beliefs, symbols, and practices from diverse sources and to reanchor them in their newly formed churches.

In multiethnic Los Angeles, second-generation pastors exist on the margins of different cultures. Milton Gordon argues that "the marginal man is the person who stands on the borders or margins of two cultural worlds but is fully a member of neither."[12] In a similar vein, according to Sang Hyun Lee, Korean immigrants are not only "in between" or "on the boundary" but are also "outside," or at the periphery of the American society.[13] However, for second-generation Koreans, their exposure to different cultural expressions of Christianity enables them to incorporate positive aspects of each in forming their own unique religious expression. I found that existing on the boundaries is viewed, by the second generation, as an advantageous position that provides them with a greater pool of resources from which to draw. Religion is an important vehicle for cultural innovation, particularly in periods of change and transition. The current period of generational change and experimentation in churches among second-generation Korean Americans in Los Angeles is an excellent example of how religion becomes a vehicle for cultural innovation.

WORSHIP STYLES AND VALUES

Many of these churches consciously incorporate many elements of mainstream evangelical Christianity. In particular, the style and form of worship at second-generation Korean churches mirror many of the same characteristics that Don Miller identified in his study of "new paradigm churches."[14] At all the churches, a contemporary Vineyard style of worship is led by a band of musicians on electric guitars, drums, and synthesizers, with lyrics projected onto large overhead screens. At many of the churches, physical expressions such as dancing, clapping, and the lifting of hands are common at Sunday worship services.

Second-generation leaders reject sharp distinctions between clergy and laity and have made conscious efforts to blur these lines within their churches. Embracing the notion of the priesthood of all believers, at these new churches lay members are encouraged to serve the church body in practical ways by exercising their spiritual gifts. The churches place a high priority on its members discovering, developing, and deploying their spiritual gifts, with many of the churches offering special classes or seminars on the topic. To ensure that all members are actively engaged in some form of ministry, the churches offer a variety of ministries ranging from sports outreaches, women's ministries, and homeless ministries to drug rehabilitation ministries. Repeatedly from the pulpits, members are encouraged to be contributors to the church body and not just consumers. At a majority of these churches, close to 80 percent of the members are actively involved as volunteers in some form of church-sponsored ministry.

Alongside the main Sunday worship services, a variety of small midweek groups are implemented to address practical needs including premarital counseling, parenting instruction, discipleship, and personal accountability. At these small group meetings, members worship, study the Bible, pray, and socialize with one another. These weekly meetings provide the members with a sense of family and community that they would not gain from just Sunday worship services alone. Also, at Sunday worship services, clergy and congregants usually dress informally in casual wear, including t-shirts, jeans, and shorts. The preacher often speaks from the heart, relying heavily on illustrations, anecdotes, and personal testimonials to communicate his message.

Although worship styles and administrative structures may resemble mainstream or new paradigm churches, second-generation churches are not mirror copies of mainstream churches. Rather, pastors of these new churches are quick to reject certain aspects of mainstream evangelical Christianity, which they feel are not consistent with their God-given mission. For example, one minister reflected on the dangers of modeling second-generation churches after mainstream American churches. "American Christianity is a ghetto Christianity. The American church is not globally minded but is a comfort religion that is concerned primarily with the here and now. Today in American churches, most of the teaching is about marriage, healing, time management, budgeting. . . . I don't think this is pleasing to the Lord. The reference point is wrong. Second-generation Korean Americans need to be more globally minded. They need to be more militant. I don't want the second generation to drive to church in their Volvos with their 2.5 children all neat and comfortable. American churches are so nonthreatening. . . . I think it's sickening." He encourages his members to live sacrificially and be globally minded and radical in their commitment to God.

Second-generation churches have also made intentional efforts to adopt as well as reject certain aspects of Korean immigrant religion. The majority of younger pastors reject the traditional roles and expectations of the senior pastor that are held at immigrant churches. Senior pastors of immigrant churches are known for their strong work ethic and sacrificial lifestyle and are generally held up on a pedestal by their church members. They often place their ministry and congregation above themselves and their families. In contrast, second-generation ministers reject hierarchical notions of leadership and the rigid separation of clergy and laity. In immigrant churches, respect and honor are oftentimes given automatically to the senior pastor just by virtue of the title. However, for the second generation, titles do not necessarily ensure respect. Rather, pastors have to earn respect through spending time with church members and proving that they genuinely care about them. According to one member, "the pastor has to be real . . . a person you can trust. He has to get to know me and understand where I'm coming from." Respect is not something that is just handed out on the basis of a title at second-generation churches. In fact, at several churches, titles have been eliminated altogether, and parishioners address their pastors solely by their first names. This is in sharp contrast to immigrant churches, where titles matter to the extent that Korean churches that decide to affiliate with American Protestant denominations have encountered difficulty, because Korean pastors insist on maintaining leadership titles that do not exist in mainstream American congregations.[15]

There is also an intentional effort on the part of second-generation pastors to change their church members' value systems. Repeatedly in sermons, pastors emphasize to their members that their identities are not tied to their socioeconomic status and that they should not be living their lives solely for material success. The new churches are making an intentional attempt to encourage their members to not limit themselves to the traditional moneymaking career options. At Joyful Sound Church, there is an intentional emphasis on the development and expression of the performing and creative arts. The church has on staff a full-time pastor to oversee its large and growing celebration arts ministry. According to one pastor, "There are so many creative second-generation Koreans at our church, but their creativity is stifled because their parents want them to make money. They want them to be doctors and lawyers and do the music and art things as hobbies on the side. The bottom line is that they want their children to make money. . . . I have some people in my ministry who struggle because they want to go to Pasadena Art Center, but their parents are like, 'What you're going to be, a cartoonist? I came to America so that you can be a cartoonist?'"

For the immigrant generation, financial success is a tangible expression of success in America. Many first-generation parents experienced downward mobility upon immigrating to the United States. Although highly educated, because of language and structural barriers many first-generation immigrant Koreans took on low-skilled, low-paying jobs with the hopes that their children would be able to achieve the American Dream. Their dream of economic mobility was thus deferred to the next generation.[16] Nonetheless, second-generation ministers define success not as economic advancement but rather as obedience to God's call upon an individual's life.

There are many elements of immigrant spirituality that these new churches aim to preserve and practice. Most importantly, many believe that immigrant Koreans are more communally oriented and that they better understand the concept of sacrifice and servanthood. The influence of American individualism has been negative, for it has fostered a low level of commitment to the church and a self-centered consumer mentality. As one ministered stated, "I went to a youth conference in New York where six thousand high school students attended. I was asked to lead the prayer time and had to change the entire plan that was assigned to me. I didn't like their plan of first praying for the world, then their country, their city, then their family, then themselves. I said that every time you focus inward, you become so self-centered and individualistic. At the end of the prayer time, you are essentially praying about yourself. This should not be. You should pray for yourself briefly at first, and pray more for others."

At second-generation churches, there is a conscious effort to reclaim a Korean or Asian conception of community, family, and group. Individual goals, identity, and viewpoints are viewed as secondary to the group's goals, identity, and viewpoints.

REACHING OUT: ENGAGING THE BROADER SOCIETY

In the aftermath of the 1992 Los Angeles uprisings, second-generation ministers were inspired by the activities of black churches and pastors who served as vocal leaders and spokesmen for their community's social and political agendas. They realized that the Korean church could no longer remain silent and inactive politically. It was in the midst of the social upheaval that younger pastors began to emerge as viable representatives of the Korean American Christian community. From church pulpits, second-generation pastors preached on the historical experiences of African Americans, the injustices of American capitalism, and strategies toward more peaceful relations between blacks and Koreans in Los Angeles. They believe that the Christian faith with its message of forgiveness and grace is the only solution to America's racial tensions. They have been at the forefront in encouraging dialogue among the different races as well as forming coalitions with pastors of different racial communities. Whereas immigrant churches have been insular and disconnected from mainstream society, these new ethnic churches aim to mobilize Korean Americans in order to raise up an autonomous Korean institution that could empower and address the specific needs of Korean Americans as well as positively impact mainstream society.

The Los Angeles uprisings also influenced the way many second-generation Korean Americans viewed themselves and their position in American society. Due to the government's abandonment of the Korean community during and after the riots, the United States took on entirely new meanings for second-generation Korean Americans. The absence of police protection during the riots, the delayed appearance of the National Guard, and the insufficient, frustrating government relief programs communicated to the younger generation that Korean Americans are still a marginalized and discriminated minority group in this country. This heightened awareness of the subordinated position of Korean Americans in American society had an impact on Korean American churches. According to a second-generation male, "The riots made a big impact on how we [of the] second generation viewed ourselves and how we viewed our position in the American society. The lack of police protection in Koreatown proved that we are still discriminated against. There is a sense among the second-generation population that we must cling to our ethnic heritage and bind together to exert a unified voice and message to the mainstream institutions. There is no better place than the church to build a grassroots community of people who are ready and positioned to speak on behalf of the community."

Young ministers, in the aftermath of the riots, were determined to define the political role of the church and to involve the church in the various social and political issues that concern the Korean American community. Within these newly emerging churches, there is an increasing desire and commitment to engage in civic involvement, particularly through acts of volunteerism. Fear coupled with cultural and language barriers inhibited many immigrant churches from stepping out of their insular communities. The determination of second-generation churches to engage in broader issues and causes is a reflection of the younger generation's stance that their future lies in America, not Korea. Although they may belong to ethnic churches, they see themselves as full members of American society. Hence, they have a responsibility that is mandated by their Christian faith and by virtue of being American to reach out to neighboring communities, particularly the disadvantaged sectors, with compassion and generosity. At one level, these efforts to be a blessing can be seen as acts of obedience to God's call. At another level, they can also be seen as an attempt by the second generation to prove to themselves and to the larger society that despite their involvement with ethnic institutions, they truly are American, and they do care about the welfare of this country.

Resurrection Ministry has been involved in a variety of different projects including a care package drive for the North Korean famine relief, Habitat for Humanity, Revlon Run/Walk, a health fair, Meals on Wheels, and the Angel Tree Project. Social service has been a long-standing priority in the mission of the church, and about 25 percent of the congregation is actively involved in ongoing compassion ministries.

Fruitful Church has developed its own independent and innovative outreach ministries to disadvantaged urban communities. For example, its Living Hope ministry is a weekly tutorial and mentoring program for children and youths residing in the Nickerson Gardens Housing Project in Watts. Every week, two dozen church members, in particular UCLA students and certified teachers, volunteer their Saturdays to tutor, mentor, and feed the children who participate in the program. In addition, each year the church sponsors Camp Jubilee, a summer camp where more than sixty children from the Nickerson Housing Project are treated to a fun-filled week of camping, fishing, hiking, and learning in the San Bernardino Mountains. According to one of the pastors, "There is a great fervor among the people in our generation to give and serve. Our Living Hope and Camp Jubilee projects are two of the most popular ministries at the church. We are never short on volunteers or donations for these two projects. The people are very generous and enthusiastic about reaching out to underprivileged communities." Many second-generation ministers possess a strong passion for serving the disadvantaged and needy sectors of the community.

HUNGER FOR COMMUNITY AND BELONGING

There is a high level of church participation among second-generation Korean Americans. Sixty-one percent attend a Korean church at least once a week.[17] The primary reasons that second-generation Korean American choose to attend a Korean church revolves around the issues of acceptance, community, and comfort. There is something about the Korean church that calls the second generation back home. Many expressed that they felt a sense of homelessness and alienation until they found and settled in a Korean American church. The second generation, as children of immigrants, experienced a distinct cultural upbringing that connects them to one another. There is a common understanding among second-generation Koreans, and one woman expressed it this way: "I'm not the only one who knows what it feels like to have grown up with immigrant parents. My Korean friends also know. Among my non-Korean friends, I am always conscious of my Korean American identity. However, with my Korean friends, my Korean identity is more of an unspoken and unconscious identity." This commonality of experience provides the sense of community and belonging among second-generation Korean Americans at these churches. According to one minister who grew up in a white suburb in the Midwest, "There is also a distinct second-generation phenomenon. Regardless of whether you grew up in a white community or an ethnic community, you tend to polarize with people like yourself. . . . We have a need to identify with those who shared in the same experiences and life struggles. I've done a lot of preaching at revivals and retreats, and it's amazing. When you start talking about some of the struggles that you had growing up, immediately no matter what area of the country you may be [in], you just connect so quickly. Something clicks. On the basis of that commonality, they begin to open up, and this commonality becomes the bridge toward the faith."

The commonalities in values consist of a set of core traditional Korean Confucian values such as filial piety, respect for parents, family centeredness, and work ethic. They also share a unique set of experiences as second-generation Korean Americans, navigating through issues such as parental expectations, identity crises, racial discrimination, and Americanization. These commonalities in experiences and values shape the way that Christianity is practiced at these new churches, where people have the liberty to carve out unique spaces in which their ethnic and religious identities intersect. They do this by weaving Korean cultural values, practices, and sensibilities into their practice of Christianity. For example, one Korean woman who used to attend the Inter-Varsity Christian Fellowship before she joined a Korean ministry remarked about the differences she noticed between Koreans and Caucasians at Inter-Varsity. "White people pray differently. They are much more informal and chatty with God. It's probably because they speak with their own parents in that way. . . . [F]or example, they'd start their prayers with, 'Hi God, How ya doing? It's me Susie.' I felt really uncomfortable with this kind of praying. For some reason, it almost sounded blasphemous to me. Koreans are different. I was taught to respect authority figures. This carries over to my relationship with God. Sure, the Bible says he's my friend, but he's still an authority figure. I think that's why we Koreans pray differently."

One second-generation male shared how his cultural upbringing influences the ways in which he interacts with others. "I went to a drug rehab at Saddleback Community Church [a mainstream megachurch in Southern California]. I was the only Asian in the group. I realized there that it's difficult to find people who can relate to both your addiction and your cultural background. I was very shy in the group. A lot of Asians are quicker to not speak and to listen as opposed to just blurt[ing] out your two cents. People were sort of raising an eyebrow at me because I wasn't saying a thing. They were probably thinking, 'Why is that Asian guy sitting there being defiant?' . . . [B]ut it's not defiance, it's just the way I was raised." He currently attends Joyful Sound Church and has started up a drug rehabilitation ministry for Asian Americans. He hopes that his ministry will be a safe and healing place for Asian American recovering drug addicts. Second-generation Koreans are attracted to churches such as Joyful Sound because they offer ministries and an environment where their culture is understood and incorporated into their spirituality.

Another appeal of these new churches is that they are ideal places to find future mates. Many commented that most people are too embarrassed to admit this, but a large percentage of single young adults go to second-generation churches because of the opportunity to meet other singles. One single woman described the "mating scene" at a large second-generation ministry. "One of the things that troubled me about this place was that there is too much emphasis on looking for a mate. I remember once when I walked into the sanctuary during the middle of the pastor's sermon. Everyone just shifted in their seats because they heard the door opening, and everyone looked back to see who it was rather than focusing on the message. When the service was over, I was waiting in an extremely long line for the bathroom, and by the time I had gotten into the bathroom, I realized that no one was using the stalls. The ladies were just fixing their makeup. As the women filed out of the bathroom, there were large groups of single men waiting to check out the women. It felt more like a nightclub than a church service." Some of the churches that I visited discouraged their members from treating the church as a place to find marriage partners. Others, however, openly encouraged dating and marriage among church members and even gave practical tips on how to pursue the person you are interested in.

For second-generation Korean Americans, matters of faith and spirituality are very important, if not central, components of their involvement with ethnic churches. Past studies have, for the most part, neglected to include an analysis of the spiritual dimensions of church participation and have anchored their analysis on the social, economic, cultural, and psychological motivations for ethnic church involvement. This bias, particularly among sociologists and Asian American studies scholars, is due to the twin influences of secularization and Marxist theories. First, a number of social theorists writing at the turn of the century predicted that religion would disappear by the end of the twentieth century. They argued that the so-called irrationalities of religion could not survive in an age of reason. Recently, however, sociologists have concluded that the secularization thesis was simply wrong. Religion has not disappeared in modern societies. Rather, it is alive, robust, and growing in many places around the world, particularly in the United States.

Second, beginning with the Marxist premise that religion is a social construction intended to opiate the disadvantaged, marginalized, and oppressed segments of society, Asian American scholars have largely approached the study of Korean American churches with a bias toward highlighting the compensatory functions of the ethnic church. For instance, scholars have pointed to the fact that because Korean immigrants feel marginalized in American society, they have turned to religion and ethnic religious organizations to provide them with much-needed social and psychological relief. These studies, however, disregard the centrality of faith and spirituality among Korean Americans and privilege the researchers' Marxist leanings.

Certainly, second-generation Korean Americans attend these new ethnic churches because their social, cultural, and psychological needs are met. However, it would be an incomplete analysis to leave out their spiritual motivations for joining second-generation churches. The missions of these new churches are distinct from other institutions in the community. Although they may provide a strong sense of community and meet other practical needs, these churches are not merely social clubs, therapeutic groups, or entertainment centers. Their purpose is to provide individuals with a strong sense of personal meaning, a purpose for living, and a day-to-day connection with the sacred. Members of these churches expressed the crucial role that their faith played in their everyday lives, particularly in satiating their hunger for meaning. According to one member of Fruitful Church, "My goal in life has changed since I became a Christian. Now I know why I live and what will happen to me when I die. I used to really love myself, and it was difficult to give up the reins of my life to anyone. Now, my values have totally changed. Now, it doesn't even matter whether I become a professor or a small shop owner, or even a missionary." In his study of the growth of Vineyard, Calvary, and Hope Chapels, Don Miller concluded that "there seems to be something deep within the human spirit that seeks self-transcending experiences and an ultimate grounding for the meaning of life. When established religions do not serve these needs, religious innovation occurs."[18]

Spiritual hunger draws many individuals into these newly formed churches. For some, their college years were pivotal turning points spiritually, because when dabbling in worldly fun could not satisfy their deep longings for meaning or a sense of purpose in their lives, they would return to the church and realize for themselves that only God could fill their spiritual void. For others, it was some point of weakness, suffering, or struggle that revealed their state of helplessness and hopelessness without God. Others recounted stories of experiencing meaningful transcendent moments that made an indelible mark on their lives. For the majority of second-generation Christians, church is not merely a place where they can meet and socialize with other Korean Americans. Rather, the church is primarily a place for developing, experiencing, and growing in their relationship with God. The fact that these new ethnic churches offer spiritual nourishment in an environment where their ethnic, racial, and generational identities are understood and affirmed is what makes these new churches appealing places to worship for second-generation Korean Americans.

Korean churches provide for the English-speaking population, as it does for the immigrant generation, a sense of integrative community in which individuals who would otherwise be isolated in impersonal environments become part of a family network of brothers and sisters. However, due to language limitations, for the immigrant population a Korean church was the only available option. But for the second generation who are more acculturated, a mainstream Caucasian church is available to service their spiritual needs. Nonetheless, they continue to choose to remain with coethnics in their churches. The language of choice can often be misleading in that it suggests that the individual is basing his decisions on just personal preference alone. However, for second-generation Koreans, personal choice is shaped by two factors. Certainly, there is the desire to connect and worship with others who share a similar set of experiences as second-generation Korean Americans. However, their choice is also shaped by feelings of marginalization and the perception held by the mainstream that they are, because of their race, foreigners and not true Americans. According to one second-generation male, "After college, I attended a Caucasian church in Sacramento . . . and I felt really out of place. It was a different environment altogether. Maybe it was because the whole thing about churches has to do with the social situations and family and values. Part of a church is part of a culture, and so the American churches have their American culture built in. For example, when I went to a small group meeting in someone's home and we start[ed] talking about personal issues. Their issues were so different from mine. They did not grow up as a Korean American with immigrant parents. They were all my age, so it wasn't a generational issue but rather a distinctly cultural issue. I was uncomfortable talking about myself because it make[s] me so much more Asian. It would've put me in a situation where I was not one of them." There is still a sense among many Korean Americans that mainstream churches do not provide the closeness and community that a Korean church does.

Although second-generation Korean Americans demonstrate a high level of acculturation in English-language mastery and educational achievements, they are still perceived as foreigners and are marginalized in American society. One member recalls his frustration during his years practicing medicine in the U.S. Air Force in Mississippi. "When I practiced in Mississippi, a lot of my patients were retirees and predominately Caucasians. They'd come in and want to know whether I was Japanese or Chinese. After that they'd say, 'you know, I helped your people during the Korean War.' Here I am a member of the U.S. Air Force in uniform treating them, and they keep insisting that they helped my people. They saw me simply as a Korean—a foreigner." Race is a key variable in understanding why second-generation Korean Americans, unlike the second generation of other white ethnic groups, remain within the Korean church. According to Omi and Winant, "One of the first things we notice about people when we first meet them (along with their sex) is their race. We utilize race to provide clues about who a person is."[19] Because race forms an important part of the context against which individuals negotiate their affiliations and understandings, it strongly influences the formation of second-generation churches and the decisions that individuals make to join these churches. External pressures such as the sociocultural subordination and the view of Asian Americans as perpetual foreigners create an unequal and oftentimes hostile environment for Korean Americans in primary encounters with mainstream social organizations such as churches.

Mary Waters, in her study of white ethnics, argues that the ways in which ethnicity is flexible and symbolic and voluntary for white middle-class Americans are the very ways in which it is not so for nonwhite and Hispanic Americans.[20] The lives of racial minorities are strongly influenced by their race or national origin regardless of how much they may choose not to identify themselves in ethnic or racial terms. Korean churches alleviate marginality by allowing Korean Americans to develop their own institutions to meet their particular needs in the forms that they prescribe.

Nonetheless, Korean American pastors rejected the notion that a Korean church exists for the English-speaking generation merely because they feel unaccepted at mainstream churches. Nor do they believe that the existence of a second-generation Korean church is a barrier to full adaptation and incorporation into American society. Rather, they believe that God has a specific, tailor-made mission for English-speaking Koreans Americans. Their goal is to transform the Korean church from merely a compensatory institution to an empowering one. These churches aim to do this by offering Korean Americans who were either born here or who immigrated at a young age the context in which they can connect with and develop pride in their ethnic identity. One male student who grew up in a suburb of Orange County recalls his embarrassment over his ethnic identity during his high school years. "I used to be so ashamed whenever I heard a bunch of other Korean students at my school speaking Korean to each other. They looked so nerdy and out of place. I used to pretend that I couldn't understand them. . . . [A]ll of my friends during high school were white. I wanted to be popular, so I tried to make all white friends. I tried really hard to be as white as I could." After having joined a Korean church and making close Korean friends, he now feels proud of being Korean. Second-generation pastors believe that developing pride in your ethnic identity is the first step in fulfilling your God-given destiny.

CONCLUSION

Second-generation Korean Americans with an unparalleled entrepreneurial fervor are carving out new institutional niches to accommodate the intersection of race, generation, and ethnicity in the context of their Christian faith. The manner in which second-generation Korean Americans have constructed their own hybrid religious institutions reflect the complex and contradictory set of challenges and tensions that the group faces in the United States as a racial minority and as children of immigrants.

Since the enactment of the 1965 Immigration Act, which abolished the country-by-country quotas that had made it difficult for non-Europeans to immigrate, more than sixteen million immigrants entered the United States, largely from Asia and Latin America. In numerical volume, this rivals the great flood of European immigrants of the early 1900s. With the emergence of a post-1965 second generation, recent studies have compared and contrasted the adaptation patterns between today's second generation and the children of those who immigrated at the turn of the last century. The adaptation patterns are significantly different today because the new immigrants themselves are different and the society into which they are adapting is markedly different from what awaited the European immigrants at the turn of the century. It is important to acknowledge the crucial impact of the historical and situational context that would differentiate the experiences of each immigrant group. The increase of post-1965 Korean immigrants to the United States has taken place in a historical and social context that has included the restructuring of the U.S. economy, the legacies of the civil rights movement, globalization with the advent of technological advances in communication and travel, the increase in transnational identification, a decline in mainline denominations alongside a documented growth in new religious groups, and a reconfiguration of institutional expressions among Christian houses of worship.

The formation and growth of second-generation churches needs to be analyzed with respect to the changing definitions of what it means to be an American. Second-generation Korean Americans, by forming their own hybrid religious institutions, are saying that they can be fully American without having to denounce their ethnic identity and difference. They are asserting that the definition of American identity is not fixed but rather is fluid and has the capacity to be redefined and reshaped by minority groups. By neither assimilating into mainstream churches nor remaining in the ethnic churches of their immigrant parents, second-generation Korean Americans, by establishing their own independent religious institutions, are communicating the fact that in today's American society, there are hybrid third spaces to inhabit. In addition, the hybrid third space is not viewed by the majority of second-generation Korean Americans as an inferior space to inhabit. Rather, existing on the boundaries or margins, it is viewed as an advantageous position because it provides a unique vantage point from which to view, adopt, reject, and reinterpret cultural and spiritual resources from diverse communities.

NOTES

1. Pyong Gap Min, "The Structure and Social Functions of Korean Immigrant Churches in the United States," *International Migration Review* 26 (1992): 1370–94.

2. For this study, "second generation" is defined as those born in the United States or those born abroad but who immigrated at six years of age or younger.

3. Stephen Warner, ed., *Gatherings in Diaspora: Religious Communities and the New Immigration* (Philadelphia: Temple University Press, 1999), 18.

4. The names of the churches and respondents have been changed for the sake of anonymity.

5. Mark Mullins, "Life Cycle in Ethnic Churches in Sociological Perspective," *Japanese Journal of Religious Studies* 14(4) (1987): 321–34.

6. Michael Omi and Howard Winant, *Racial Formation in the United States: From the 1960s to the 1980s* (New York: Routledge & Kegan Paul, 1986), 62.

7. Yen Le Espiritu, *Asian American Panethnicity: Bridging Institutions and Identities* (Philadelphia: Temple University Press, 1992).

8. Erik Erickson, *Childhood and Society* (New York: Norton, 1963).

9. Alejandro Portes and Ruben G.Rumbaut, *Immigrant America: A Portrait,* 2nd ed. (Berkeley: University of California Press, 1995).

10. Won Moo Hurh and Kwang Chung Kim, "Religious Participation of Korean Immigrants in the United States," *Journal for the Scientific Study of Religion* 29(1) (1990): 19–34.

11. Although there is no definitive parameters to define "1.5 generation," for the purposes of this study, those who immigrated at seven years of age or older will be considered 1.5 generation.

12. Miton Gordon, *Assimilation in American Life: The Role of Race, Religion, and National Origins* (Oxford: Oxford University Press, 1964).

13. Sang Hyun Lee, "Korean American Presbyterians: A Need for Ethnic Particularity and the Challenge of Christian Pilgrimage," in J. Coalter, John M. Mulder, and Louis B. Weeks, eds., *In The Diversity of Discipleship: The Presbyterians and Twentieth Century Christian Witness* (Louisville, KY: Westminster John Knox, 1991), 3.

14. Donald Miller, *Reinventing American Protestantism: Christianity in the New Millenium* (Berkeley: University of California Press, 1991).

15. Karen Chai, "Competing for the Second Generation: English Language Ministry at a Korean Protestant Church," in R. Stephen Warner and Judith G. Wittner, eds., *Gatherings in Diaspora: Religious Communities and the New Immigration* (Philadelphia: Temple University Press, 1998), 295–331.

16. John Lie and Nancy Abelmann, *Blue Dreams: Korean Americans and the Los Angeles Riots* (Boston: Harvard University Press, 1997).

17. Sharon Park, "Generational Transition within Korean Churches in Los Angeles" (Master's thesis, University of California, Los Angeles, 1996).

18. Don Miller, *Reinventing American Protestantism,* 4.

19. Omi and Winant, *Racial Formation in the United States,* 62.

20. Mary Waters, *Ethnic Options: Choosing Identities in America* (Berkeley: University of California Press, 1990).

Chapter Nine

Second-Generation Korean American Evangelicals on the College Campus

Constructing Ethnic Boundaries

Rebecca Kim

INTRODUCTION

Ethnic religious organizations play a crucial role in immigrant adaptation. They help immigrants to establish their own community, reconstruct their identity, and make sense of a new and unfamiliar environment.[1] This is certainly the case with Korean immigrants in the United States. Since the early 1900s when the first wave of Korean immigrants settled in Hawaii, churches have served as the center of the Korean American community, playing a pivotal role in Korean immigrants' adaptation to American society.

Compared to first-generation immigrants who must adjust to a myriad of changes, second-generation Korean Americans (hereafter SGKAs) have better English-language proficiency and greater exposure to and familiarity with American culture and have access to broader opportunities in mainstream society. They are not as dependent as foreign-born immigrants on the assistance of ethnic institutions and can take part in mainstream religious, civic, and social organizations with greater ease. High levels of educational and occupational attainment as well as rising rates of intermarriage among SGKAs speak to their integration into mainstream America.[2] This is particularly evident in Korean Americans' level of college enrollment. In some of the Ivy League universities, Asian Americans (Korean Americans included) account for more than 20 percent of the undergraduate enrollment. In California public universities, Asian Americans, mostly Korean and Chinese students, currently make up more than 40 percent of the student population at the University of California at Berkeley and the University of California at Los Angeles and 50 percent of the student population at the University of California at Irvine.

If college attendance is used as a measure of successful incorporation into mainstream society, we would expect that college students would be less ethnically oriented than their immigrant counterparts. The pattern today, however, is that the rapid growth in the numbers of Korean American and other Asian American students in top colleges across America accompanies an unexpected, phenomenal growth of Asian American student associations and organizations. Among these, the emergence of ethnic and Pan-Asian Christian organizations on campuses among Korean Americans is particularly noticeable.

Much of our knowledge about the growth in the numbers of Asian American campus evangelical organizations remains anecdotal due to the recent nature of the phenomenon and the lack of systematic quantitative or qualitative research. However, the news media concurs with campus evangelical leaders that Asian Americans, namely Korean and Chinese Americans, predominate in the major campus evangelical organizations of many top colleges in America, particularly in the western and northeastern United States.[3] For example, about 80 percent of the members of more than fifty evangelical Christian groups at UC Berkeley and UCLA are now Asian American and consist mostly of Korean Americans and Chinese Americans.[4] Campus Crusade for Christ (CCC), one of the largest campus Christian organizations at Yale, was 100 percent white in the 1980s, but now the members are 90 percent Asian. At Stanford, InterVarsity Christian Fellowship (IVCF), another major campus Christian organization, has become almost entirely Asian American.[5]

As a result of the growth in the number of Asian American evangelicals, some of the major campus evangelical organizations have formed Asian American ministries.[6] CCC and IVCF even have separate organizations for Korean students on several campuses. Independent Korean American as well as Pan-Asian American Evangelical Christian organizations led by Korean Americans have also formed on college campuses. Virtually every top-ranking university and college across America has at least one Korean American campus fellowship.

Many U.S.-born Korean American college students come from middle-class families and grew up in white or racially mixed suburbs. They are familiar with mainstream culture and organizations and face few barriers to participating in non–Korean American campus organizations. Moreover, as evangelicals, Korean Americans follow the principles of evangelical Christianity, which emphasizes preaching, loving, and proselytizing all nations beyond ethnic and racial barriers. Leaders in the evangelical Christian community have also eagerly dubbed Asian Americans as the exemplars of evangelicalism. They are labeled as "God's new whiz kids" who excel not only in school but also in the faith.[7] As college students on a large diverse university campus, Korean Americans also have many contacts with those outside of their ethnic and racial group, making it easier for them to cross ethnic and racial boundaries and be more inclusive in their religious participation.[8] This essay thus examines why English-speaking SGKA college students choose to participate in ethnic-specific campus ministries over multiethnic or white majority evangelical campus ministries and explores why their organizations continue to remain ethnically and racially segregated despite opportunities to be more inclusive.

RELIGION, ETHNICITY, AND SECOND-GENERATION ASIAN AMERICANS

Studies about Asian Americans' religious participation remain relatively scarce, but there is an emerging literature on the topic that points to two main explanations for U.S.-born Asian ethnic groups' separate ethnic religious participation: racialization and ethnicization.

Racialization Perspectives

According to racialization perspectives, different Asian ethnic groups develop solidarity based on their dawning recognition that they are treated by others as distinct primarily because of their physical appearance.[9] Racialization theories stress experiences of marginalization and being marked as different, particularly by the majority or hegemonic group(s), as the basis of ethnic or pan-ethnic grouping.

For example, Anthony Alumkal argues that Asian Americans retreat into evangelical campus fellowships as an act of self-preservation in a racially hostile environment.[10] Observing the growing numbers of Asian Americans in evangelical campus fellowships, Rudy V. Busto similarly argues that Asian Americans "retreat into evangelicalism" on the "increasingly racialized college campus where Asian American students are imaged as competitive, overrepresented and culturally monolithic."[11] Examining the reorganization of Chinese and Japanese American congregations around a new pan-ethnic Asian American identity, Russell Jeung adds that Asian Americans can escape the undesirable aspects of their racial status by making Christianity, rather than race, the locus of their identity.[12] In other words, ethnic or racial distinctions are transcended through a relationship with God. Racialization theorists thus argue that Asian Americans turn to evangelical fellowships, including pan-ethnic evangelical fellowships, to escape a world where race continues to matter.

By making race the operative principle of social differentiation, racialization theorists suggest that SGKAs would be equally comfortable in Pan-Asian congregations where their fellow members are Chinese and Japanese Americans. This, however, is not the case. Few SGKAs participate in pan-ethnic Asian American campus ministries when given the choice to participate in their own separate ethnic campus ministries. Moreover, most of the large Asian American campus evangelical organizations tend to be dominated by Chinese or Korean Americans. Pan-ethnic campus ministries (as well as pan-ethnic churches) with a sizable mix of the different Asian ethnic groups are hard to find.

Ethnicization Perspectives

Ethnicization perspectives acknowledge the significance of racial ascriptions and conflicts but tend to stress cultural distinctiveness as the primary source of ethnic religious group boundaries. According to the ethnicization perspectives, individuals are attracted to separate ethnic congregations because they share common cultural experiences that make them distinct from others.[13] For example, Karen Chai finds that the chance to be with those who share similar cultural background and experiences is one of SGKAs' main motives for attending the separate SGKA English-language ministries. "The most consistently cited reason was the opportunity to be with people who share their cultural background. . . . They are able to form close relationships with others who have been shaped by the same Korean cultural forces."[14]

Kelly Chong goes further and finds that participating in ethnic churches reinforces a distinct Korean ethnic identity for SGKAs. The Christian faith in the Korean American evangelical Protestant community is said to support the construction of a strong ethnic identity among SGKAs. Chong argues that the ethnic church ideologically defends and legitimates a "set of core traditional Korean values and forms of social relationships" and serves "as an institutional vehicle for the cultural reproduction and socialization of the second-generation into Korean culture." Thus, according to Chong, the essence of SGKAs' ethnicity is their parents' Korean culture.[15]

However, this kind of primordial ethnic retention argument clashes with findings that show that SGKAs' religious services are in many ways distinct from the first generation. Studies show that SGKA and other Asian American evangelicals' religious services are modeled after mainstream evangelical services, not their parents' churches.[16] SGKAs are also said to place their Christian identity above their ethnic identity, and for some SGKAs, a Christian identity overtakes their ethnic identity. As David Kyuman Kim finds, SGKA Christians "are becoming grounded, particularly those who have taken on an Evangelical form of faith, in religion that replaces a core 'Korean' identity."[17] Additionally, studies show that many SGKAs are alienated from the first-generation church and are leaving them, a movement dubbed, the "silent exodus."[18] More than 80 percent of SGKAs are said to leave their parents' ethnic church.[19] Moreover, SGKAs commonly complain that their parents' immigrant church is more of an ethnic institution rather than an authentically religious institution.[20] This leads to the questions of just how much of first-generations' traditional cultures and values constitute SGKAs' own ethnic religious organizations and why and how specific ethnic group boundaries are drawn within a diverse religious context.[21]

HISTORICAL BACKGROUND

Campus Evangelicalism

Many universities and colleges in the United States were originally formed with the intent of developing future Christian leaders and were often linked to particular Protestant denominations. Harvard University was formed by the Congregationalists in 1636 as the first higher institution of learning in the United States. Yale (in 1701) and Dartmouth (in 1769) were also formed by the Congregationalists. Columbia was formed by Episcopalians in 1754, Rutgers by members of the Dutch Reformed Church in 1766, Brown by Baptists in 1772, and Princeton by Presbyterians in 1776.[22] Higher education in the United States was established following the religious conviction that the future of society was dependent on having an educated clergy and that the Christian faith should be propagated.[23]

Over the years, however, numerous American colleges and universities have secularized and severed their ties with Christianity.[24] "Countless colleges and universities in the history of the United States were founded under some sort of Christian patronage, but many which still survive do not claim any relationship with a church or denomination."[25] Despite the official separation from Christian churches, independent Christian organizations on college campuses have nevertheless persisted. At a time when many colleges and universities were officially breaking their religious affiliations following World War II, parachurch evangelical organizations such as the CCC, the IVCF, and Navigators began to emerge and helped to fill the spiritual vacuums that were left after the cultural upheavals of the 1960s.

The growth of campus evangelical organizations is due in large part to the resurgence of evangelicalism. With a long history and numerous traditions as a religious and social movement in the United States,[26] evangelicalism is currently one of the fastest-growing of such movements. Although figures may vary depending on the sources and definition of evangelicalism, evangelical Protestants now comprise more than 20 percent of the U.S. population.[27]

As part of the larger evangelical movement, parachurch campus evangelical organizations tend to preach a literal scriptural interpretation of the Bible, emphasize personal faith and commitment to Jesus Christ for the forgiveness of sins, and stress the need to proselytize.[28] In terms of their organizational structure, campus evangelical organizations commonly have regional directors, local staff members, and a chief executive officer or president who is often the founder of the organization. Funds for the organizations are raised through the financial support of churches, groups, and individuals. Campus evangelical organizations are present on both public and private campuses and often have other noncampus-related programs.[29]

Many of the independently run parachurch campus ministries such as the CCC and the IVCF along with various denomination-supported evangelical campus ministries have witnessed a growth in the number of Asian American college students in and outside of their organizations. This change has largely been brought on by the rising number of Asian American college students who began matriculating into college and university campuses, particularly in the 1990s.[30]

Post-1965 Immigration, the Korean Church, and SGKA Evangelicals

Influenced mainly by the passage of the 1965 Hart Cellar Act,[31] the share of Asian immigrants grew from 5 percent in the 1950s to 35 percent in the 1980s as a proportion of the total admissions of immigrants in the United States.[32] Korea is one of the major immigrant-sending countries to the United States and has been on the list of top ten immigrant-sending countries since the 1980s.[33] With a 2000 census count of about 1.1 million, Koreans are the fifth-largest Asian group behind the Chinese, Filipinos, Japanese, and South Asians. Corresponding with their population growth since the 1970s, Asian Americans' (Korean Americans') college enrollment dramatically increased.[34] The number of Asian American undergraduates on college campuses almost tripled between 1976 and 1986 (from 150,000 to 488,000).[35]

The rapid growth in the number of Asian Americans on college campuses accompanied an increase in Asian Americans' involvement in ethnic and Pan-Asian Christian campus organizations, particularly among Korean and Chinese American students.[36] In the IVCF, the percentage of Asian American members in some of the West Coast, Northeast, and Midwest colleges can be as high as 80 percent.[37] At a triennial conference on missions organized by the IVCF in 2000, Asian Americans, many of them Korean Americans, represented more than a quarter of the participants. Agreement among campus evangelical organization leaders indicates that Korean Americans make up the majority of Asian Americans in mainstream evangelical organizations as well as in separate ethnic and Pan-Asian evangelical organizations.

The growth in the number of Korean American campus evangelicals is due in part to the increasing number of Korean American Christians in general. As of the year 2000, more than 30 percent of the Korean population in South Korea identified themselves as Christians. Meanwhile, the majority of the Korean population in the United States, more than 70 percent, identified themselves as Christians.[38] In some cities, the numbers are higher. A 1997–1998 survey conducted by Pyong Gap Min reports that 79 percent of Korean immigrants in Queens, New York, identified themselves as Christians, and 83 percent of them reported that they attend an (ethnic) church once a week or more often.[39]

METHODS

My data consists of participant observation, personal interviews, and the use of archival and organizational documents. I first visited thirty Christian campus ministries that ranged in ethnic diversity on a large university campus that has witnessed a significant growth in Asian American evangelical organizations, which I refer to as West University (WU). Afterward, I conducted in-depth participant observation in five evangelical campus ministries at WU.[40]

I compared two Korean American campus ministries for SGKAs,[41] which I refer to as the Korean American Mission for Christ (KAMC) and the Christian Student Fellowship (CSF), to the following campus ministries: an Asian American campus ministry, Asian American Christian Fellowship (AACF); a multiracial campus ministry, a chapter of the IVCF; and a predominately white campus ministry, a chapter of the CCC. With chapters on several other college campuses in Southern California, the KAMC and the CSF are two of the largest SGKA campus ministries at WU, with about sixty to one hundred weekly attendants. With seventeen chapters, the AACF is an Asian American campus ministry with about 100 regular attendants, most of whom are second- and later-generation Chinese Americans. As a chapter of one of the largest campus evangelical organization in America, the IVCF at WU is a multiracial campus ministry with about one hundred regular attendants and membership that reflects the ethnic diversity at WU. In contrast, more than 90 percent of the WU CCC's fifty or so members are white.[42]

In addition to participant observation, I conducted one hundred personal interviews[43] with the students as well as directors, staff, and pastors involved in campus evangelical organizations. Among the one hundred interviews,[44] fifty interviews were conducted with the leaders and members of Korean American campus ministries. The other fifty interviews were conducted with the leaders and members of other Asian American, multiracial, or white-majority campus ministries at or near WU.

WHY CHOOSE TO ATTEND KOREAN AMERICAN CAMPUS EVANGELICAL ORGANIZATIONS?

> I am troubled when [Korean] students come into my office and want to set up yet another Korean Bible study group. . . . [W]hy can't they join the number of Christian fellowships that are already on campus?
>
> University Campus Religious Organization Coordinator

One of the coordinators for campus religious organizations shared in an interview that she was concerned about the growth of separate ethnic-specific Christian organizations on campus, particularly among Korean American students. She said that she understood why international students who are more comfortable speaking Korean might want to worship separately for "language reasons" but could not understand why Korean Americans who spoke English fluently wanted to attend separate ethnic Christian campus organizations. So why do they want to set up yet another Korean American Christian fellowship? Why do SGKAs choose to attend Korean American campus evangelical organizations over multiethnic or white majority campus evangelical organizations?

The most common answer was "because it is just more comfortable." In one way or another, all of the SGKA students who were asked why they chose to attend a Korean American ministry over all of the other campus ministries gave this response. What, then, constitutes this comfort that contributes to SGKAs' separate ethnic religious group formation? I find that comfort is the result of three interactive processes involving both individual micro- and macrostructural factors.

SEARCH FOR COMMUNITY AND CHANGES IN ETHNIC DENSITY AND DIVERSITY

"I don't know about you, but I don't want to be just another nine-digit number walking around campus, just another person lost in the crowd." This statement was made at an evangelical rally set up by the IVCF where a former college student talked about how she found her identity and community through "Jesus Christ" and the "fellowship" offered by the IVCF. She began her talk by noting that she wanted community and wanted to be more than "just another nine-digit number walking around campus" and ended it by sharing that she found herself and was "saved" when she "met Jesus" and became part of "the [IVCF] family." Rallies such as this, which can be found at many of the other campus ministries, are organized around the premise that students are seeking community, a place where they can be known and connected.

A senior reflects on what it was like for him to start college: "You are thrown into this new situation, which you have never been in before, which is really exciting but also pretty scary; so you are looking for community, that family away from family." Another student comments on why campus ministries are so popular: "Why are they so popular? It is a place to meet people, where you can expect to be treated with respect; it gives you a sense of family and belonging."[45]

For many Christian students, a search for community also includes a search for fellow believers who can foster and sustain their religious faith in an otherwise secular university setting. As a student notes, "College is when you can break your faith, get lost in the crowd in all the craziness, so you have to meet good [Christian] friends." Another student explains further: "In campus ministries, you get to meet fellow brothers that understand the same morals that you have. So when others say, 'Hey, let's go drinking and stuff,' your Christian brother or sister will be like, 'Are you OK? Are you keeping up with your walk [with Jesus]?' and keep you in check."

Twenty to thirty years ago, an SGKA seeking religious community had few options; most of the campus ministries were white. Changes in ethnic density and diversity in recent years, however, make this no longer the case. When asked why there are so many Asian American evangelical organizations on the WU campus, one Chinese American student responds tersely, "Why? . . . because there are just so many of us!" Indeed, nearly 40 percent of WU is Asian American (most of them are Chinese Americans and Korean Americans). This kind of ethnic density simply offers Korean Americans and other Asian Americans seeking community more opportunities to congregate along ethnic lines.

Related to the change in ethnic density is the change in the ethnic milieu of college campuses. The birth of ethnic student movements and ethnic studies programs inspired by the civil rights and Black Power movements in the 1960s helped to lay the groundwork that changed higher education to be more multicultural and sensitive to ethnic diversity.[46] The pull of white assimilation declined, and the West European knowledge base of American higher education was challenged, and multiculturalism, a tolerance for ethnic and racial diversity, became more widely accepted.

Linked to changes in ethnic density and diversity is the vibrancy of the campus religious marketplace. While passing through the central walkway at WU, you can see and hear various campus ministries offering promises of salvation and genuine community. Particularly during the first few weeks of school, campus ministries set up their tables with bright signs on each side of this walkway, trying to grab the attention of the thousands of students who pass through. Signing up as early as 7:00 a.m. to get the best location on the walkway, campus ministries actively work to recruit new members. Some stand right in the middle of the walkway passing out flyers and stopping to speak to students walking by. One flyer for a campus ministry read, "Come and enjoy the great food and fellowship!" A Korean American campus ministry passes out its information on a miniature Chinese takeout box with their contact information written on the outside of the box. Inside the box, there is some candy and a heart-shaped eraser with a Bible verse attached to it. When students approach one of the tables set up by the campus ministries, they are greeted with smiles and a flyer and are asked to fill out a contact information sheet so that someone from the ministry can contact them later regarding its activities. Some campus ministries provide special gift packages for those who sign up and provide their contact information. They offer free candy, CDs, and drinks and are eager to tell students about their upcoming barbecues and other social gatherings. Meanwhile, someone shouts through the crowd, "Hey, stop by, you might even find your future wife here!" One of the campus ministry representatives comments, looking at the walkway, that it is like "a busy market except that all of the vendors are campus ministries."

In this vibrant and open religious marketplace, there are a number of pan-ethnic, multiracial, and predominately white campus ministries. But there are also more than four campus ministries that specifically target SGKAs.[47] Thus, an SGKA seeking religious community practically has the opportunity to participate in separate ethnic campus ministries; desire for community interacts with changes in ethnic density and diversity to make separate ethnic associations simply more possible.

Homophily and Ethnic and Racial Categorizations

"In the Christian community we call it the 'homogenous principle' . . . [whereby] people want to worship with people who are like them." As this Korean American pastor notes, individuals want to worship and gather with those who are most like themselves. Sociologists refer to this as the homophily principle: the idea that "similarity breeds connection," that ties between similar individuals are more binding.[48] I find the same homophilic forces at work in the campus evangelical community. Given the opportunity to participate in a variety of campus ministries, students choose a campus ministry where they can be with those who are most familiar and similar to them. For

SGKAs, this means that they will associate with those who are most likely to share the experience of growing up and having intergenerational and intercultural conflicts with first-generation immigrants in the United States.

When asked why they choose ethnic-specific Korean American campus ministries over others, SGKAs consistently answer that doing so is more or most comfortable. When asked what exactly makes it more comfortable for them, SGKAs point to the shared experience of straddling two cultures: growing up in America and having intergenerational and intercultural conflicts with the first generation. As one SGKA explains, "Most of us have first-generation parents. We know what goes on in a Korean house . . . parents' pressure, study study study, marry a Korean, don't talk back. So it is easier to get closer with other Koreans. They know where you are coming from."

Among the shared experiences that Korean American students mention, pressures to excel in school are the most common, as an SGKA explains: "Korean parents are like you have to do this this this to be successful . . . you have to go to medical school or law school and study study study. They think the best colleges are Harvard, Yale, Princeton. I am not saying white people don't stress education, but Koreans, they take it to another level." Another SGKA accounts how his mother even wrote his personal essay and filled out a college application for Harvard University even though he specifically told her that he did not want to apply. "My mom applied for me. She wrote my essays and everything . . . all grammatically incorrect. I even had to go to an interview. It lasted five minutes. I told her I didn't want to go there or apply, but she just wouldn't listen."

Many other SGKAs share stories about the pressures to please their parents by succeeding educationally and professionally while also trying to develop their own independent identity. They relay that their parents consider a college degree in the social sciences as a waste of time and money because they feel that such majors will not lead to financially lucrative careers. They pressure their children to major in the hard sciences such as medicine or law, fields that they believe will lead to a more financially successful and secure future. One SGKA even shares how his brother severed his ties with his parents because they adamantly opposed his decision to be a cartoonist after graduating from Princeton. Thus, what constitutes SGKAs' homophily is really the experience of growing up in America and having intergenerational and intercultural tensions with the first generation.

Although their worship services are largely indistinguishable from other evangelical campus ministries, the SGKA campus ministries note that they recognize that these tensions exist and try to be sensitive to them. For example, an SGKA pastor states that white evangelical organizations tend to focus on personal piety and offer a more individualistic form of Christianity and therefore cannot appreciate the social cultural background of SGKAs. He talks about how a white evangelical campus ministry would not easily understand the tensions that SGKA students might experience when they want to "make a greater spiritual commitment" yet hesitate because they fear their parents' disapproval. Another leader of an SGKA campus ministry adds, "If a Korean American student had trouble making a decision to go to summer missions because her parents disapproved, we are likely to be more understanding and supportive of that compared to, say, a white campus ministry. They would not understand her struggle as much." Thus, SGKA campus ministries say that they can best understand SGKAs' bicultural background and struggles with the first generation and thereby provide them a more desirable religious setting.

The basis of SGKAs' ethnic homophily, however, is not unique to SGKAs. Others, such as second-generation Chinese Americans, also grew up in immigrant parent homes straddling two cultures and share intergenerational and intercultural tensions. But what is essential is the extent to which SGKAs share similarities with another ethnic group. Both SGKAs and second-generation Chinese Americans have bicultural and intergenerational tensions growing up in immigrant parent homes, but SGKAs straddle Korean and American culture, not Chinese and American cultures. An SGKA makes this point by noting that while "all Asians eat rice, not all rice is the same." Korean rice is said to be "moist and stuck together," while Chinese rice is "separated and flaky." Thus, given the choice, SGKAs will participate in separate ethnic versus panethnic, multiracial, or predominately white campus ministries and associate themselves with those with whom they are most familiar and similar. This tendency, however, interacts with imposed ethnic and racial categorizations: "[When I was in junior high school], I was with my girlfriends at a party at my friend's house, and some of the guys were calling us, asking us who was at the party. . . . [A]nd my friend, Cathy, who was hosting the party, started naming off people. . . . [W]hen she got to my name I guess the guy on the other phone didn't know who I was, so in response Cathy said 'Oh, you know, the Chinese girl.' "

As the experience of the SGKA in the above quote expresses, individuals' desire for what is familiar and similar interacts with ethnic as well as racial categorizations used in the larger society. Even if an SGKA believes that he or she has the most in common with other whites or any other ethnic group, categorizations by others make it difficult for him or her to be viewed as such. An adopted Korean American woman explains: "There are times when [my adopted white family] would be sitting at a restaurant or something and people would just stare. . . . [O]ne time this kid at a restaurant stood up in the middle of dinner, pointed at me, and said . . . 'Look Mom, a Chinese girl.' I can think that I am like my [white] sisters all I want, but I won't be viewed that way." Another

Korean American woman similarly reflects on her experience of being racialized. "Growing up, I never thought that I was that different. But I remember kids telling me, because they tend to be very honest and direct, they would ask, 'Why is your face so flat? How can you see from your eyes?' " Thus, even if one thinks that he or she is similar to another ethnic group, ethnic and racial categorizations used by others will make it difficult for him or her to continuously be viewed as such. This is evident in the evangelical campus community.

An SGKA who went to the CCC weekly worship gathering recalls that "when I got there this guy told me, 'We are starting an Asian thing that you can go to.' " Even though he had come to take part in the white CCC, this student was encouraged to go to an Asian American CCC simply because he looked Asian. Similarly, response cards[49] from students with Asian-sounding names are turned over to the leaders of the Asian American CCC by the leaders of the predominantly white CCC. By the same token, when SGKAs pass out flyers to invite students to their campus ministry, they pass out the flyers to those who look Asian, a practice shared by many other Asian American campus ministries.

Thus, the desire for homophily interacts with ethnic and racial categorizations used in the broader society to strengthen ethnic and pan-ethnic identities and make separate ethnic religious associations more likely.

Desire for Majority Status and Marginalization

> I am tired of being apologetic. . . . I mean I am at a top university, I am going to make over 100 Gs [$100,000 a year], [I have] a hot car, a hot girlfriend. . . . [W]hy should I be the minority . . . pander to whites? . . . So I was like screw this, I am just going to do my own thing with my Korean crew.

As college students at top university campuses, SGKAs feel entitled to some benefits. They have gained access to major universities, are socioeconomically mobile, and seem to be reviving and leading the campus evangelical community. They thus want to be treated like the majority, not the minority. They find, however, that they are not only categorized as being ethnically or racially distinct; they are also marginalized as relatively inferior and find limited opportunities for mobility within a diverse or white-dominant setting. A Korean American pastor comments: "When I went to the headquarters [of one of the largest campus ministries in the United States], do you know? It is still all white, no blacks at the top. It is still white at the top. . . . So if Asians want to move up in power, they can't do it over there."

As the above comment suggests, having separate ethnic campus ministries is desirable because such ministries provide SGKAs more opportunities to extend themselves and take on leadership positions. As another Korean American staff explains, "We are separate because whites welcome Asians, but not into leadership positions, and they don't realize that by being status quo, they discriminate and make it hard for Asians to move up. . . . [T]hey are used to having leadership. . . . [S]o if Asians start their own separate organizations, they are more able to take on leadership positions." Thus, being in an ethnically homogenous religious setting means that SGKAs will have more opportunities for power and leadership than in a pan-ethnic, multiracial, or predominately white religious setting. This is something that the older leaders and staff stress, but marginalization is in the minds of the SGKA students as well.

To SGKA students, being part of a separate ethnic campus ministry means that they can escape any marginalization that they may experience in the broader society as Korean Americans or Asian Americans. As one SGKA student recounts, being in an ethnically homogenous Korean American campus ministry means that "you have the privilege of not thinking about the minority experience . . . never feeling that you are marginalized." Another SGKA made this comment by recalling his experience in Korea: "What I liked best about visiting Korea was that I felt this big burden, weight, lifted off my shoulders because I did not have to think about race, being Korean. You just felt lighter. In America, a significant part of your energy in everyday life is exerted thinking about race. You don't have to deal with that if you are just with Koreans." As another student explains further, "If you are with other Korean Americans, you are not going to be faulted for being Korean or looking Asian. You don't have to hear people say, 'Do you speak ching chong?' 'Do you guys eat dog?' 'Why are your eyes so small?'" Thus, SGKAs do not have to deal with the negative stereotypes, prejudice, and even simple misunderstandings that other ethnic and racial groups in the broader society might have about Koreans or those who look Asian if they are with other Korean Americans.

In this way, the desire for majority status and power interacts with the continuing marginalization in the broader society to make separate ethnic associations more desirable.

DISCUSSION

In examining why SGKA evangelicals continue to draw separate ethnic religious group boundaries, we found three interactive processes at work. First, the desire for community interacts with changes in ethnic density and diversity. An SGKA evangelical seeking religious community simply has more opportunity to participate in separate ethnic religious organizations in an ethnically dense and diverse structural setting. Second, the desire for what is most familiar and similar—homophily—interacts with imposed ethnic and racial categorizations. Given the choice to participate in a variety of ethnically diverse campus ministries, an SGKA will choose to associate with those who are most familiar and similar to him or herself: other SGKAs. This tendency, however, interacts with imposed ethnic and racial ascriptions in the larger society to make separate ethnic associations more likely. Even if an SGKA may think that he or she has more in common with another ethnic group, ethnic and racial ascriptions used by others make it more difficult to continue to view him or herself as such. Third, the desire for power and majority group status interacts with continued ethnic and racial marginalization. Having made inroads into mainstream institutions and organizations, SGKAs want the benefits and privileges that the white majority enjoys. They find, however, that they are continuously marginalized as an ethnic or racial minority and lack relative power. This interactive process is what constitutes the comfort that makes separate ethnic campus ministries more desirable, making it more likely that SGKAs form and participate in separate ethnic religious organizations of their own.[50]

My interactive model of ethnic religious group formation contributes to the literature on the religious participation of today's children of immigrants in three main ways. First, I find overall support for both racialization and ethnicization perspectives in explaining SGKAs' ethnic religious group formation. But I find that what is essential is the extent to which individuals can have homophily and unquestioned majority group status in a competitive religious marketplace and structural context where ethnic and racial ascriptions and marginalization continue to exist. Thus, the answer is not race versus culture or one explanation being more important than the other. Instead, what matters is the degree to which SGKAs can escape marginalization and have homophily in their own ethnic religious organization rather than in other pan-ethnic, multiracial, or predominately white religious organizations. Second, beyond racialization and ethnicization explanations, my interactive model of ethnic religious group formation articulates the preconditions—individuals' desires for community interacting with changes in ethnic density and milieu—that make separate ethnic associations more likely. Individuals seeking religious communities practically have more opportunities to participate in ethnically homogenous congregations within an ethnically dense context where diversity and explorations and expressions of ethnicity are encouraged. Third, in contrast to ethnicization arguments that emphasize cultures inherited from the first generation as the basis of SGKAs' homophily, I find that the culture that SGKAs share is an emergent one, an improvisation that is "made in the U.S.A." What constitutes a distinct SGKA ethnicity and the basis of their homophily is the experience of growing up in immigrant families and having intergenerational and intercultural strife with the first generation in America, which is essentially an American experience.

Given my finding that what really captures the SGKA experience is the intergenerational and cultural conflicts that they have with the first generation, further studies should be conducted on how successive generations will forge their sense of groupness. In other words, how will the third and fourth generations construct their emergent ethnicities if they do not have this intergenerational and intercultural tension to fuel a sense of ethnic groupness? Without such conflict, it may be argued that pan-ethnic religious group formation or even multiracial religious group formation will characterize later generations' religious participation. While this may be possible, we should not underestimate the ways that individuals can improvise and constantly create and re-create ethnic group differences. This is especially the case in today's technologically advanced global information society where individuals have the symbolic and practical competence to forge ethnic cultures and develop a renewed sense of groupness. This and continuing ethnic and racial ascription and adversity may continuously contribute to the construction of ethnic religious group boundaries for later generations. With this in mind, future research should be conducted on the coming third generation and how it may (or may not) construct an emergent ethnic identity: a basis of homophily and separate ethnic religious group formation.

NOTES

1. Jay P. Dolan, *The Immigrant Church* (Baltimore: Johns Hopkins University Press, 1975); Andrew M. Greely, *The Denominational Society* (Glenview, IL: Scott, Foresman, 1972); Will Herberg, *Protestant, Catholic, Jew* (Garden City, NY: Doubleday, 1955); Pyong Gap Min, "The Structure and Social Functions of Korean Immigrant Churches in the United States," in Min Zhou and James V. Gatewood, eds., *Contemporary Asian America* (New York: New York University Press, 1999), 372–91; Timothy L. Smith, "Religion and Ethnicity in America," *American Historical Review* 83 (December 1978): 1155–85; and Min Zhou, Carl L. Bankston III, and Rebecca Kim, "Rebuilding Spiritual Lives in the New Land: Religious Practices among Southeast Asian Refugees in the United States," in Pyong Gap Min and Jung Ha Kim, eds., *Religions in Asian America: Building Faith Communities* (Walnut Creek, CA: AltaMira, 2002).

2. High levels of educational and occupational attainment and rates of intermarriage have commonly been used to measure immigrants' and their descendants' successful integration (or assimilation) into mainstream American society. See Milton M. Gordon, *Assimilation in American Life* (New York: Oxford University Press, 1964); Jennifer Lee and Frank D. Bean, "Beyond Black and White: Remaking Race in

America," *Context* 2(3) (2003): 26–33; and Jennifer Lee and Frank Bean, "America's Changing Color Lines: Immigration, Race/Ethnicity, and Multiracial Identification," *Annual Review of Sociology* 30 (2004): 221–42.

3. Rudy V. Busto, "The Gospel According to the Model Minority?" *Amerasia Journal* 22(1) (1996): 133–47; and Evelyn Ch'ien, "Spirituality: Evangels on Campus: Asian American College Students Are Making the Grade with God," *A. Magazine: Inside Asian America,* April/May 2000.

4. Busto, "The Gospel According to the Model Minority?"

5. Ch'ien, "Spirituality"; Hong, "The Changing Face of Higher Education."

6. Campus Crusade for Christ, Navigators, and InterVarsity Christian Fellowship.

7. Busto, "The Gospel According to the Model Minority?"; Russell Jeung, *Faithful Generations: Race and New Asian American Churches* (New Brunswick, NJ: Rutgers University Press, 2005).

8. Nazli Kibria, *Becoming Asian American: Second-Generation Chinese and Korean American Identities* (Baltimore: Johns Hopkins University Press, 2003).

9. Antony Alumkal, "Race in American Evangelicalism: A Racial Formation Analysis," Paper presented at the American Sociological Association, Chicago, August 18, 2002; Michael O. Emerson and Christian Smith, *Divided by Faith* (Oxford: Oxford University Press, 2000); Russell Jeung, "A New People Coming Together: Asian American Pan-Ethnic Congregations" (PhD diss., University of California, Berkeley, 2000); and Russell Jeung, "Asian American Pan-Ethnic Formation and Congregational Culture," in Min and Kim, *Religions in Asian America,* 215–44.

10. Alumkal, "Race in American Evangelicalism."

11. Busto, "The Gospel According to the Model Minority," 37.

12. Jeung, "A New People Coming Together."

13. Karen Chai, "Competing for the Second Generation: English-Language Ministry at a Korean Protestant Church," in R. Stephen Warner and Judith G. Wittner, eds., *Gatherings in Diaspora: Religious Communities and the New Immigration* (Philadelphia: Temple University Press, 1998), 295–331; Kelly Chong, "What It Means to Be Christian: The Role of Religion in the Construction of Ethnic Identity and Boundary among Second-Generation Korean Americans," *Sociology of Religion* 59 (1998): 259–86; R. D. Goette, "The Transformation of a First-Generation Church into a Bilingual Second-Generation Church," in Ho-Youn Kwon and Shim Kim, eds., *The Emerging Generation of Korean Americans* (Seoul: Kyung Hee University Press, 1993), 237–51; Emerson and Smith, *Divided by Faith,* 2000.

14. Chai, "Competing for the Second Generation," 311.

15. Chong, "What It Means to Be Christian," 262.

16. Jeung, "A New People Coming Together," 2002; and Rebecca Y. Kim, "Negotiating Ethnic and Religious Boundaries: Asian American Campus Evangelicals," in Tony Carnes and Fenggang Yang, eds., *Asian American Religions: The Making and Remaking of Borders and Boundaries* (New York: New York University Press, 2004), 141–59. "Second generation" is defined as those who are born and raised in the United States with at least one immigrant parent.

17. Kim, "Negotiating Ethnic and Religious Boundaries," 41.

18. Young Pai, Delores Pemberton, and John Worley, *Findings on Korean American Early Adolescents* (Kansas City: University of Missouri School of Education, 1987).

19. Kwang Chung Kim and Shin Kim, "Ethnic Meanings of Korean Immigrant Churches," Paper presented at the Sixty North Park College Korean Symposium, Chicago, October 12, 1996.

20. Kim, "Negotiating Ethnic and Religious Boundaries," 2004.

21. SGKAs are the focus of this study because they are at the juncture of separation versus integration. On the one hand, they come from an immigrant community where an estimated 70 percent of the population attends ethnic churches; on the other hand, many are alienated from the immigrant ethnic church, turning the church of family members into the church of parents. SGKA campus evangelicals are studied because (a) their ethnic religious organizations are concentrated on college campuses where their numbers are particularly high, (b) they have the opportunity to participate in ethnically diverse religious organizations of their own, and (c) college campuses are the locus of new trends, activism, and identity development.

22. James Tunstead Burtchaell, *The Dying of the Light: The Disengagement of Colleges and Universities from their Christian Churches* (Grand Rapids, MI: Wm. B. Erdmans, 1998); and R. Hofstadter and C. D. Hardy, *The Development and Scope of Higher Education in the United States* (New York: Columbia University Press, 1952).

23. Burtchaell, *The Dying of the Light*, 1998; and Hofstadter and Hardy, *The Development and Scope of Higher Education in the United States*, 1952.

24. Philip Gleason, *Contending with Modernity: Catholic Higher Education in the Twentieth Century* (New York: Oxford University Press, 1995); George M. Marsden, *The Soul of the American University: From Protestant Establishment to Established Nonbelief* (Oxford: Oxford University Press, 1994); and Douglas Sloan, *Faith and Knowledge: Mainline Protestantism and American Higher Education* (Louisville, KY: Westminister John Knox, 1994).

25. Burtchaell, *The Dying of the Light,* ix.

26. Busto, "The Gospel According to the Model Minority?"

27. Barry A. Kosmin and Seymour P. Lachman, *One Nation under God: Religion in Contemporary American Society* (New York: Harmony Books, 1993). Due to the diversity of evangelicalism and its long history, these figures may differ depending on the sources and definition of evangelicalism. Finding data on evangelicalism is also complicated by the fact that evangelicalism is more of a social movement than a religion and is not tied to a particular denomination.

28. Whereas the term "evangelicalism" is used in reference to a social or religious movement and tradition, the term "evangelical" is commonly used to describe those Christians who affirm several theological principles: (1) belief in the complete reliability and authority of the Bible; (2) belief in the divinity of Christ and the efficacy of His life, death, and physical resurrection for the salvation of the human soul; and (3) the importance of conversion or being born again, having personal faith, and proselytizing nonbelievers. James Hunter, *American Evangelicalism: Conservative Religion and the Quandary of Modernity* (New Brunswick, NJ: Rutgers University

Press, 1983); and Richard Quebedeaux, *The Young Evangelicals* (New York: Harper and Row, 1974).

29. The Campus Crusade for Christ, started by Bill Bright at UCLA in 1951, is an interdenominational ministry that is known for aggressive evangelism and has chapters on numerous college campuses in America and other countries, with more than forty thousand staff members and volunteers (1993 figure). As an outgrowth of an evangelical student movement in England, the InterVarsity Christian Fellowship in the United States was founded in 1938. Compared to the CCC, which is known for its aggressive evangelism and personal confrontations, the IVCF is known for using a less aggressive approach of fellowship, which emphasizes small group Bible studies and spiritually supports interested students through Christian friendship. Started by Dawson Trotman in the 1930s and incorporated in 1943, the Navigators are known for their intensive Bible studies, scripture memorization, and training to build disciples. These three campus evangelical organizations, along with others, have witnessed a growth in the number of Asian American college students in and outside of their ministries.

30. Busto, "The Gospel According to the Model Minority?"

31. The Hart Cellar Act abolished the national origins quota system and made way for family reunification and skilled labor to enter the United States.

32. Zhou and Gatewood, *Contemporary Asian America.*

33. U.S. Immigration and Naturalization Service, *Statistical Yearbook of the Immigration and Naturalization Service* (Washington, DC: U.S. Government Printing Office, 1997).

34. Figures on the percentage of Korean American students in colleges and universities are hard to come by because most if not all schools collect aggregate admissions data for Asian Americans and do not distinguish by Asian ethnicities.

35. Jayjia Hsia and Marsha Hirano-Nakanishi, "The Demographics of Diversity: Asian Americans and Higher Education," *Change: The Magazine of Higher Learning* (November/December 1989): 20.

36. Busto, "The Gospel According to the Model Minority?"

37. Ch'ien, "Spirituality."

38. Won Moo Hurh, and Kwang Chung Kim, *Korean Immigrants in America: A Structural Analysis of Ethnic Confinement and Adhesive Adaptation* (Madison, NJ: Fairleigh Dickenson University Press, 1984); and Carnes and Yang, *Asian American Religions,* 2004.

39. Pyong Gap Min, "Immigrants' Religion and Ethnicity: A Comparison of Korean Christian and Indian Hindu Immigrants" in Jane Iwamura and Paul Spickard, eds., *Revealing the Sacred in Asian and Pacific America* (New York: Routledge, 2003), 125–42.

40. I chose the WU campus because it has a sizable Asian American student population and a variety of campus evangelical organizations. With about thirty thousand students, the WU campus student population is 38 percent Asian American, 35 percent white, 15 percent Latin American, and 5 percent African American (Fall 1999). I also conducted participant observation in first-generation Korean American campus

ministries, namely Korea-Campus Crusade for Christ. The data from my work in first-generation Korean American campus ministries, however, is not included in this essay.

41. Roughly half of the Korean American undergraduate population at WU is involved in Korean American campus ministries (1999). I use pseudonyms for the two SGKA campus ministries where I conducted most of my interviews.

42. The average campus evangelical organization that I studied had about forty to fifty members; the size of the organizations that I visited ranged from six to almost two hundred members. Most of the organizations met on weeknights on campus, and the meetings generally lasted anywhere from one to four hours. Many of the groups had separate leadership meetings after the main meeting or other special gatherings (e.g., dinner at a local restaurant or at a student's apartment, bowling, and other social events). The larger organizations met in lecture halls that seat more than one hundred people, and the smaller organizations met in smaller classrooms that seat approximately thirty people.

43. I first gathered descriptive information about the interview subjects (e.g., place of birth, grade, past and present religious involvement). I then asked them why and how they decided to participate in their campus ministry. All of the interviews were tape-recorded and lasted between thirty minutes to two hours.

44. In the interviews with members or leaders of the campus evangelical organizations, I asked questions on how they got involved in the particular organization, their religious background, and their role in the organization. I asked them questions on why they thought a separate Korean or Pan-Asian ministry was necessary and why they chose to attend their ethnic organization over a more mainstream organization. I also asked them, particularly the directors and staff members, what makes their Korean or pan-ethnic Asian ministry distinct from other organizations and what were the major concerns of their ministry. Additionally, I asked them why they thought Korean and other Asian Christian campus organizations are growing in many of the top universities. Interviews with students were all conducted on campus, and interviews with the staff and directors of the organizations were conducted in their offices or on campus.

45. This search for community often includes the search for a significant other.

46. Shirley Hune, "Opening the American Mind and Body: The Role of Asian American Studies," *Change* (November/December 1989): 59.

47. It should also be stressed that most SGKAs involved in campus evangelical organizations come from Christian backgrounds and grew up attending Korean churches. This does not mean that they will then automatically turn to separate ethnic campus ministries. However, their connections to ethnic churches does mean that they have social ties and information on campus ministries that are likely to direct them to coethnic rather than to other Asian American, multiracial, or white campus ministries.

48. Miller McPherson, Lynn Smith-Lovin, and James M. Cook, "Birds of a Feather: Homophily in Social Networks," *Annual Review Sociology* 27 (2001): 415; Emerson and Smith, *Divided by Faith;* Marsden, *The Soul of the American University;* R. Stephen Warner, "Work in Progress towards a New Paradigm for the Sociological Study of Religion in the United States," *American Journal of Sociology* 98 (1993): 1044–93.

49. Response cards are personal contact information cards that the CCC hands out to students.

50. I should note that not all SGKAs are always so comfortable with their separate ethnic religious participation. Many wonder: "If heaven isn't segregated, why are we so segregated?" "If Jesus came down to break down all barriers, why are we putting them up?" "Jesus said that we should preach the Gospel to all nations, so why are we just hanging out with other SGKAs?" SGKAs are also concerned that they are in what one SGKA described as a "bubble within a bubble." SGKAs in separate ethnic campus ministries are not only clustered in a Christian bubble but are concentrated in an ethnic bubble, separated from the ethnic and religious diversity in the broader campus community. Many Korean American students comment that their contacts became narrower and more Korean and Christian once they committed to attending a Korean American campus ministry. For some, all close social contact has become limited to Korean American Christians. One student went so far as to say that he no longer knew how to start a conversation with non-Korean American Christians because he was so used to "hanging out" with Korean American Christians. Despite these concerns, the pull of separate ethnic ministries remains strong. Given the choice of campus ministries in a diverse and competitive religious marketplace, SGKAs will choose to separate rather than integrate.

Chapter Ten

A Usable Past?

Reflections on Generational Change in Korean American Protestantism

David K. Yoo

The scene is a Korean American Protestant church in a major metropolitan area in the United States. Resources are not plentiful in this largely immigrant congregation in which most of the members work long hours. The church has had to move locations several times in an effort to balance the needs of a growing congregation while struggling with the expenses that accompany such growth. An issue of increasing concern has been the second generation and how the church can address their needs. On occasion, European Americans have helped lead the largely English-speaking boys and girls as well as an emerging young adult contingent. Teachers, drawn largely from the second-generation members, are often only slightly older than their students. Efforts to develop an English-language program have been piecemeal and often chaotic as a congregation already stretched thin tries to adapt and minister to the multigenerational needs within its walls. It is with considerable pride that the first English-language service is held. Although it takes some time, English-language services become part of the regular structure of the church, and the church adds pastoral staff who can fully accommodate the language and sociocultural needs of the second generation.

Anyone familiar with contemporary Korean American Protestantism will easily recognize the scenario described above. What might come as a surprise is that the English-language service referred to took place in 1933 at the church now known as the Los Angeles Korean United Methodist Church (LAKUMC). This essay delves into the history of the LAKUMC as a case study to offer some reflections on generational change. The longevity of this congregation (1904–present) represents a usable past that can provide insights into contemporary Korean American Protestantism, even as the continuing presence and life of this congregation are very much a part of those current developments.[1]

The unifying thread for understanding generational change in the history of the LAKUMC is the critical role played by denomination networks and structures. Under the umbrella of Methodism, the LAKUMC has been able to negotiate its identity as a racial-ethnic congregation, from its missionary beginnings to more recent developments in the form of church mergers with European American and English-language Korean American churches. Denominationalism has provided the LAKUMC innovative and creative spaces in which to address generational concerns over its long history. In underscoring the role of denomination, the story of the LAKUMC runs counter to the recent trends in American Protestantism that point to a de-emphasis and decline of the so-called mainline denominations such as the United Methodist Church.

Although a single case, the LAKUMC suggests that denominationalism continues to have relevance and that it can span across generational lines. And yet, the story is not one of triumph as much as it is of survival, resistance, and adaptability in the face of marginalization within the larger church and within society. In that sense, the LAKUMC may be instructional for American mainline Protestantism as it faces a loss of members as well as influence in U.S. society and culture. The key to the future may rest in a reorientation in which marginal status can be the basis for developing a vision for how the mainline denominations can be of service to their communities and to the larger society and the world at large. That churches such as the LAKUMC are embedded within such denominations should be a source of hope and encouragement.

The tie to American denominations can be traced to Korea, where Presbyterian and Methodist missionaries were at the forefront of introducing Protestant Christianity to Korea in the late nineteenth century.[2] Mission efforts have influenced the growth and development of Korean Protestantism during the last century or so.[3] That legacy has been carried back to the United States through the various instances of Korean migration in which a related and yet distinct Korean American Protestantism has emerged.[4] The origins of the LAKUMC, for instance, can be traced to former Methodist missionaries in Korea and to the expansive and international network of Methodism. The complicated relationship between Korean Americans and these majority European American denominations has been marked by fellowship, cooperation, and partnership as well as inhospitality, racism, and paternalism.[5]

In the early years, local support from the First Methodist Episcopal Church of Los Angeles and broader denominational assistance enabled the establishment of mission work among Koreans in 1904. As the need arose for English-language programs in the LAKUMC, former missionaries and denominational representatives often served as guest preachers. Others stepped in to help support the education program for young people. The LAKUMC along with other Korean American congregations also nurtured the next generation to consider attending church-related colleges and seminaries and answering a call into the Christian ministry.

In the more recent past, generational change at the LAKUMC has come in the form of several key mergers. At critical junctures throughout its history, the church has been open to change and willing to take risks, hallmarks not often associated with religious institutions. The improvisation of the congregation was in part driven by practical needs such as more space, but these moves also entailed considerable soul-searching. How would the blending of European and Korean American congregations affect the processes of religious and racial identity formation for all of the generations involved? In the 1960s, the decision by the leadership of the LAKUMC to merge with a European American Methodist congregation resulted in the introduction of a regular English-language service and opened the congregation to significant cross-cultural relationships. Future mergers, with another European American church as well as the joining of two English-language 1.5- and second-generation Korean American ministries, have further signaled how denominationalism has been at work within the LAKUMC to place the church at the creative forefront of Korean American Protestantism.[6]

STUDYING THE SECOND GENERATION

This essay, devoted to the study of generational change among Korean American Protestants, joins a body of similar literature that includes the work of Rebecca Kim and Sharon Kim in this volume.[7] Assimilation (or lack thereof) into the larger culture and society of the United States has been a persistent theme in the study of the second generation. Historians and sociologists, among others, have chronicled and debated how various groups have negotiated and fared in the process of immigration to and settlement in the United States. Regardless of where on the spectrum one falls, most students of immigration agree that adjustment to life in the United States for the second generation has been a multilayered process influenced by the particularities of race, religion, gender, class, region, and a number of other factors.[8]

In terms of Korean Americans, Sharon Kim's essay makes a good case that standard models of assimilation used for European immigrants as well as a strict framework of pluralism are less helpful in understanding how second-generation Korean churches are creatively carving out hybrid spaces in which to work through issues of race, ethnicity, generation, and religion. Although the contexts may differ from that of their parents, many second-generation Korean Americans are turning to ethnic-specific and/or Pan-Asian American Christian campus ministries or churches. Clearly, negative experiences of racism and prejudice have been a factor in why people have gravitated to these settings, but others have been motivated by more positive forces in which such organizations provide spaces to develop significant relationships and to serve as sources of meaning. Many second-generation Korean Americans continue to wrestle with issues of identity formation and how the particular claims of their Korean Americanness relate to the broader claims of their religious traditions. Some church leaders have been concerned about a silent exodus from churches by the second generation, but there also seems to be evidence that the distinctive nature of English-language Korean American ministries is still appealing to many.[9]

Not surprisingly, the existing research suggests that there is considerable range when it comes to the experiences of second-generation Korean Americans. Indeed, internal diversity is one of the defining characteristics of post-1965 Asian America, of which Korean America is a part. Measures such as household income, educational attainment, and occupation suggest real variation, even as homogenous images of an Asian American model minority persist.[10] Moreover, the 1.5 and second generations make up the vast majority of Asian American youths, about 90 percent based upon the 1990 census versus 6 percent for African Americans, 5 percent for European Americans, and 15 percent for the United States overall.[11] As stated earlier, much of what we know about the 1.5 and second generations has only begun to unfold, and the vast majority of studies have focused on the post-1965 era.

The story of the LAKUMC takes us further back in time, serving as a reminder that generational change is not new for Korean Americans who have been in the United States for more than a century. A longer view provides a perspective that places contemporary events within a larger frame of reference. It is also worth noting that while generational change is a familiar theme within the religious history of the United States, it has hardly been a uniform process. For Korean Americans, issues of race have been enduring elements of religious identity formation that have not been typical of many other immigrant groups and their descendants. The LAKUMC, having recently celebrated its own centennial, provides an opportunity to reflect upon generational change.

A LONG VIEW

The role of denominationalism can be traced to the very founding of the LAKUMC on March 11, 1904, when Mrs. Florence Sherman, a former Methodist missionary to Korea, and Hugh Heungwu Cynn, a student and reformer, began a mission in the city to minister to foreign students and immigrants.[12] As might be expected, the mission struggled to survive, moving locations in

search of affordable rent while trying to minister to a small and often tran-
sient population of students, laborers, and some families. The history of the
congregation in many ways parallels the story of Koreans in Los Angeles,
as churches such as the LAKUMC served as central institutions within the
racial-ethnic community. Given the annexation of Korea by Japan in 1910
followed by the colonial period (1910–1945), Koreans in the United States
formed a community of both immigrants and exiles.

If Protestant churches formed the core of communities in Hawaii and on
the mainland, then the politics of the movement to free Korea animated the
thoughts and prayers of most Korean Americans. Korean immigrants faced
economic hardships exacerbated by the ways that race intertwined with politics and culture for certain communities of color such as Asians. In the midst
of these events, the LAKUMC served the needs of its members through a
cadre of pastors and lay leaders who steered the church through decades of
lean budgets and physical relocations. It would not be until World War II that
the church acquired its own property, and in the following decade, a long
tenure by the senior pastor would also be accompanied by some demographic
changes that prefigured the large influx of post-1965 Korean immigrants.

The issues of generational change and the shifting linguistic needs of members of the LAKUMC date back to the smaller first wave of second-generation
members. The English language became part of the Sunday school instruction
as early as the 1930s. Ralph Ahn, whose first memories of the church date to
1932–1933 and span to the early 1950s, recalled that several older second-
generation women such as Emma Lee and Janet Hwang served as superintendent's of the Sunday school program. Ahn noted that the Bible studies and
memory verses were in English. The group of students was fairly small, but
he remembered camaraderie among the young people, perhaps because of
their small numbers but also because they were conscious of their status as
racial-ethnic minorities. Ahn also recalled the central place that women occupied in the church, not only in the Sunday school but as the backbone of the
church. His mother, Helen Ahn, the wife of patriot Ahn Chang-ho, was a very
active member of the LAKUMC throughout her entire life in the southland.[13]
Another member of the Ahn clan, Philip, the noted Hollywood actor, often
hosted pool parties for members of the church at his home in the San Fernando
Valley. In the summer of 1961, he entertained the Wesley Club of about seventy young people.[14] Portia Choi, the second daughter of the Reverend Young
Yong Choi, remembered fondly those elegant swim parties in which people
sang together and enjoyed the fellowship of friends and family.[15]

Denominational mission connections also provided opportunities for English-
language ministry to take place in the church. Occasional youth worship

services often featured the district superintendent or former missionaries who had served in Korea and other parts of Asia. These networks also resulted in some longer-term relationships. The Reverend Victor Peters, for instance, served the pastor in charge of the church's education program during the World War II era. The Methodist conference assigned the Reverend Henry Kemp-Blair to lead the congregation in 1952.

The first English-language worship service at the LAKUMC took place in December 1933. It would not be surprising if this was the first such recorded event among Korean American Christians on the mainland.[16] English-language services directed to the young people in the congregation became part of the worship life of the church, although largely on an occasional basis. It was not until the arrival of the Reverend Key H. Chang in the early 1940s that English could be more integrated into the regular worship format of the church. Fully bilingual and very well educated, Chang often spoke to the English-language segment of his congregation in various settings such as graduation ceremonies and other events geared to young people. He also wrote in English for Korean American publications.[17]

Lila Chang, the widow of the Reverend Key H. Chang, grew up within the church and remembered that the congregation was more of a space for the adults. Chang recalls that her mother, Marie Lee, practically lived at the church and was devoted to the life of the congregation. Unfortunately, the youth programs were sporadic and often unpredictable. Much depended upon the volunteer efforts of the older women and men among the second generation who had to contend with their own schooling, employment, and pressures of everyday life. The arrival of Reverend Chang did signal a real shift. For the first time, the regular worship service included the English language. Sometimes, the sermon would be given in both languages. In other times, a full sermon in Korean might be followed by a summary or brief version in English. Financial pressures forced Chang to step down from his pastoral position at the church in 1947. He and Lila Chang continued to be associated with the church but in a less-prominent leadership role.[18]

The place of English-language ministry continued throughout the 1940s and 1950s. The long tenure of the Reverend Young Yong Choi beginning in 1953 included initial efforts to include the English language for the second-generation adults who had come of age within the congregation. Those efforts gave way to the growing prominence of the Korean language in the post–Korean War years and especially in the post-1965 period, when the demographics of the Korean American community underwent a major transformation. Some of the second-generation members during this period left the church to pursue careers and housing opportunities in other parts of Southern California.

POST-1965 DEVELOPMENTS

The denominational ties of the LAKUMC would factor into the changes that had begun to take place in the church in the 1950s and early 1960s through two major events. The first, a church move and merger, signaled a new era for the congregation and might be interpreted as a harbinger of change. Part of that change, unbeknownst to most, was the second major event: the passage of the 1965 Immigration Act. An unintended consequence of the act opened the door to large-scale migration from Korea (and other parts of Asia and Latin America) to the United States. The church was directly affected by the new arrivals, experiencing growth and the rise of a newer and much larger 1.5- and second-generation population.

The merger between the LAKUMC and the Robertson Community Methodist Church took place in 1968. The Korean Church had begun to experience growth and soon needed more space, while the Robertson church, primarily European American, had experienced decline. By the time of the merger, the Robertson church had only a handful of elderly members remaining. One of the conditions set by the denomination for the merger was the institution of an English-language service so that the members on the Robertson side would have access to worship services in a language they could understand.[19]

While church mergers are certainly not new to American religion, this occurrence was noteworthy in that an older European American congregation was being brought together with an immigrant Korean congregation that would effectively signal a sea change in terms of the identity of the congregation. More mergers of this kind have been taking place in the post-1965 era, indicating demographic shifts in places such as California in which Asians and Latinos have been changing the face of the church as well as the state and region. Such changes have not always come easily as European Americans face the growing realities of an aging of mainline denominations and overall membership decline. The Robertson merger in 1968 served as an early sign of things to come.

Ironically, in the post–World War II era, many mainline denominations made efforts to address the so-called problem of ethnic congregations by encouraging these groups to merge with European American churches. Japanese American Christians, for instance, surfacing from U.S. governmental incarceration during the war, encountered such overtures in order that they might become more fully Americanized during a Cold War period marked by suspicion of anything that might be interpreted as un-American. Such attempts, however, were largely unsuccessful for two basic reasons. First, Japanese American churches had been effective in their ministry to congregants partly because they represented sites of racial-ethnic solidarity. Japanese American leaders, clerical and lay, had formed important internal networks and thus were resistant to suggestions of merger. The second reason that the proposed mergers largely failed had to do with the fact that many European American congregations did not welcome the opportunity for such racial mixing.[20]

The fact that the Robertson merger took place during the tumultuous civil rights era suggests that people may have sensed that new possibilities existed. In any event, the Reverend Young Yong Choi initially presided over the English-language service, and over the years various assistant and associate pastors also contributed to this ministry. It is likely that not all of the members were receptive to the merger, but it is a testament to the congregation's vision that they moved forward. Such a move made sense to a certain extent because there was a small group of English-speaking Koreans adults who could benefit from the service. These children of the original immigrants had come of age. An interesting result of the merger was the creation of a multiracial congregation within a congregation.

So often in the life of an institution, difficult decisions open up new possibilities that were not previously considered. In the case of Fred Gong, a second-generation Chinese American, the decision to merge played a significant role for him and his elderly mother. For the church, Gong's presence created a link to a Pan-Asian presence in addition to the coexistence with European Americans. Living in West Los Angeles and working as a commercial artist, Gong found out about the LAKUMC from a colleague who had invited him to attend the church. During his first visit to the church in the early 1970s, he remembered attending the main service that was conducted almost entirely in Korean by Reverend Choi. Gong then learned about the English service that took place prior to the Korean-language service, and this began a journey that lasted until the mid-1990s.[21]

Gong remembers that the Reverend Choi eventually asked him to work with the young people. Gong was reluctant, having little experience, although he had before this attended the First Chinese Baptist Church in the Los Angeles Chinatown. "Every reason that I gave to Dr. Choi about why I could not do it, he had an answer for, and so I started," said Gong, "and part of the reason I agreed was that he assured me that I would be an assistant to a more experienced teacher." That part was true, but the teacher left after a few weeks. However, by that time Gong was hooked.[22]

For some two decades Gong worked with young people, but as someone in his fifties, to him many of the adults seemed young. He recalled his years at the Korean Methodist Church with great fondness and spoke with pride of how so many of those he taught have gone on to become leaders of the community. As a teacher and youth counselor for the church, he tried to advise people to follow their hearts, not just their minds. Looking back, Gong said, "That was the most important work that I have ever done."[23]

In the 1970s and 1980s, the English-language ministry of the LAKUMC extended the process by which the church simultaneously moved forward with its identity as a racial-ethnic immigrant congregation and as a church with an established English-language ministry that could serve the needs of the young as well as the elderly. The Reverend In Nak Kim, associate pastor, recalled that he had primary oversight of the English ministry during 1981–1987, when staff changes prompted a shift to a primarily Korean-language ministry.[24] He noted that the creation of the Council on English Ministry in 1985 greatly aided the development of a postcollege group and ministry among the English-speaking members of the congregation.[25] Other pastors such as the Reverend Daesung Chung and the Reverend Youngstone Jhun worked with the English ministry in the latter part of the 1980s, helping to build a foundation for future ministry.[26]

It was not until the full-time appointment of the Reverend K. Samuel Lee in 1990, however, that a pastor was wholly assigned to the English-language ministry for adults. Up to this point, many of the Korean-language staff also addressed the English-speaking section of the church as part of their work with the Korean congregation or as part of their work with the youths.[27] The fluid lines between these different segments of the congregation spoke to a number of issues. For one, the number of English-speaking adults was small, whether in the former Robertson church or in the LAKUMC. Those numbers diminished with time, moreover, since many of these folks were elderly. The growth of the Korean-language ministry among immigrants was accompanied by the presence of 1.5- and second-generation youths, many of whom were coming of age during the 1970s and 1980s. That process has continued into the present as immigration from Korea has continued.

The use of English across different age groups would become an enduring part of the ministry of the LAKUMC. The developmental growth of more and more college-age and postcollege young adults meant that the church needed to address a growing concern that affected a host of Korean American congregations. If the Sunday school program oversaw instruction of young people from prekindergarten through the senior year of high school, then what were college age and postcollege members to do in terms of their church participation? For many college-age students, the question was somewhat mitigated by their departure from the church to attend school. And yet, some observers have noted that there has been a steady "silent exodus" especially by the second generation, who upon graduation often find no place in the Korean immigrant church. Some may return to their home churches to take up positions in the Sunday school or work with youths, but many found little nurture for their faith as they moved more fully into adulthood.[28]

Korean American Christians in recent times have had multiple options in terms of models of ministry that churches have experimented with to address the concerns of the English-speaking adult population. The LAKUMC English Ministry represented the model of a ministry under the umbrella of an existing Korean immigrant and Korean-language–based church. Other models included English ministry under the guidance of a non-Korean church as well as independent 1.5- and second-generation churches.[29] Pan-Asian American, multiethnic, multiracial, and parachurch institutions have also provided alternatives.[30]

The model of an English-language ministry within an existing immigrant church tends to be the norm, in varied forms, among many Korean American churches. Like the LAKUMC, this kind of ministry generally evolves as the need arises to minister to the growing 1.5 and second generation. The hybrid and makeshift attempts to launch an English-language ministry reflect the fact that many churches struggle with a lack of resources and face multiple challenges in nurturing both the English- and Korean-speaking segments of their membership. In such situations, English-language instruction and ministry, regardless of members' ages, may be close to nonexistent. In congregations with more of an ability to tackle this issue, finding qualified and dynamic leadership poses another type of obstacle.

In New York City, for instance, the Korean Methodist Church and Institute faced a situation similar to that of the LAKUMC in needing a ministry to address the needs of an emerging English-speaking Korean American segment of the church community. According to a history of the first decade of its English-language ministry, the New York church encountered a number of challenges. The author commented on the fact that there were no models to follow and how experimentation and improvisation were the norm. Finding pastoral staff was part of the hurdle, but unclear lines of responsibility and expectation between the Korean- and English-speaking membership often led to miscommunication and burnout for the pastors and key lay leaders.[31]

In Los Angeles, the association of the Reverend K. Samuel Lee with the LAKUMC is instructive in the nature of many English ministries based in Korean American churches. A doctoral candidate in counseling psychology at Arizona State University, Lee had relocated to Southern California in 1989 to take part in an internship at the counseling center at the University of California, Irvine. He also took up a post as a part-time youth pastor at the LAKUMC and served in this capacity until the end of June 1990. At the end of his internship, he was able to accept a full-time appointment as the pastor of the English Ministry starting on July 1, 1990.[32]

Lee's appointment to oversee the English Ministry ushered in a new era of full-time dedicated staff to this segment of the church population. His leadership and the coming of age of 1.5- and second-generation Korean American enabled the English Ministry to thrive. Just as things began to take off, Lee was asked to serve as the head of both the Korean and English ministries. The senior pastor, Jeen-Shoung Park, had died of cancer in December of 1990. Lee had built ties with the LAKUMC, and his bilingual skills and counseling background enabled him to minister to the congregation during this difficult time. His double duty also allowed the church to set into motion the process by which to find a successor to Reverend Park. In hindsight, Lee realized that accepting the interim Korean position took a heavy toll on him physically and emotionally and diverted energy and momentum from the English Ministry at a critical point in its development.[33]

Amid this loss, the church embarked on a move after many years at the Robertson location in light of space concerns. Once again, denominational networks proved important, as the LAKUMC was able to find space to share with the La Tijera United Methodist Church near the Los Angeles International Airport (LAX). The LAKUMC would build a new sanctuary on the shared campus at its current location at 7400 Osage Avenue in West Los Angeles. The Reverend Lee helped the church make the transition to its new space while continuing to oversee the English-language ministry.

In its efforts to address 1.5- and second-generation needs, the LAKUMC was once again a pioneer, as few churches at this point were able to establish fully functioning English-language ministries. As such an anchor congregation among Korean Americans in Southern California, the LAKUMC was also able to draw on its deep connections within the community. Lee had already been at the church when he was appointed to the English Ministry, and this further aided the transition that the church was undergoing. Under the Reverend Youngstone Jhun, there had been about sixty members associated with the English Ministry, but many had been youths. With Lee's arrival, steady growth took place in which approximately 90–135 adults were worshiping at the English service.[34]

Tammy Chung Ryu, longtime member of the LAKUMC and a key leader in the English Ministry, commented that Lee had been able to forge close relationships with many of the church members and to minister to them as a caring pastor. Perhaps Lee's background in counseling enabled him to provide a therapeutic presence in the church.[35] That background may have enabled Lee to help church members to work through personal issues and through the upheaval of the Los Angeles riots of April 1992.

Lee recalled that while many of the church members were not directly affected in terms of their homes or businesses, there were networks and connections to others that left many people in a state of shock and sorrow. The LAKUMC as well as Reverend Lee took part in United Methodist–sponsored efforts to address the issues raised by the tumultuous events as well as those programs aimed at healing and fostering better understanding. Lee recalled serving on a task force for the Los Angeles District of the denominational conference and exchanges between the LAKUMC and African American churches in South Central Los Angeles. While much of the activity was short-lived, the events of April 1992 did open up some avenues of communication and community building.[36]

Lee was also able to reach beyond the church walls through a regular column in the *KoreAm Journal*. Started in 1990 by James "Bear" Ryu, another key member of the English Ministry at LAKUMC, *KoreAm Journal,* a struggling ethnic publication, has today become a major outlet for Korean America, reaching some thirty-six thousand subscribers and many others through its website.[37] Given Ryu's commitment to the church and community, it made sense to provide Lee with a venue with which to minister through the printed word. Lee's columns addressed a wide range of concerns, but many were aimed at a culturally sensitive understanding of the Gospel and its implications for Korean American young adults. For instance, Lee claimed to his readers that Jesus understood what it meant to be bicultural and bilingual. As a Jew in Roman-occupied Israel, Jesus would also understand the feelings of marginalization. Instead of seeing one's status as a Korean American in a potentially negative light, Jesus's example served as a reminder of how the state of being in-between opened one up to the fullness of life.[38]

In another column, Lee took up the issue of the pros and cons of English-only Korean American churches. Having seen the dynamics that take place in English ministries housed within immigrant church contexts, Lee had thought the 1.5 and second generations might be better off in independent church settings. Too often seen as children or perpetual youths, English ministries were treated as second-class citizens in Korean immigrant congregations. Whether in terms of staffing, budget, or space, English-language ministries often suffered from neglect, interference, or both.[39]

And yet, Lee's thinking, perhaps because of his experience at the LAKUMC, had changed. He realized that independent churches may have more freedom, but they lacked the full spectrum of life that would enable them to mature. Language, itself, did not necessarily justify a complete separation when creative coexistence could benefit all generations. Lee had noted that many English-speaking Korean Americans continued to embody Korean immigrant values and perspectives. Much like Korean American families, churches faced real hurdles in terms of intergenerational communication. The potential for positive change from working through those issues outweighed the option of the parting of ways.[40]

The idea of how to keep the generations together weighed on Lee's mind as he prepared for his departure from the church in 1995. Nearing the end of his doctoral studies, he knew in 1994 that he would pursue a career in higher education and possibly student affairs. His concern for what would happen to the English Ministry at the LAKUMC was fueled in part by his knowledge that there was a dearth of qualified and dynamic leadership available. His eventual appointment as associate dean of student affairs and professor of practical theology at Wesley Theological Seminary in Washington, D.C., meant that the issue of the future would be soon at hand.[41]

THE 1995 MERGER

The expansion and stabilization of the English-language ministry at the LAKUMC represented the congregation's efforts to respond to the growing needs of its next generation. As part of the United Methodist Church, the LAKUMC continued the tradition of finding support and space within the denomination, marked most recently by the change of campus and facility-sharing near LAX after a long stay at the Robertson location. These major themes of Methodism and merger would once again shape generational issues for the church. Unlike the situation in 1968 with the Robertson church, however, the merger that took place in 1995 involved two largely Korean American, English-speaking ministries: the existing program at the LAKUMC and the Ascension Ministry based at the Westwood United Methodist Church. Denominationalism, not surprisingly, factored into the merger and even prior to it, as the California-Pacific Conference helped the Reverend Tom Choi implement his vision for the second generation in what would become the Ascension Ministry. In terms of the merger of both ministries, Choi remembered Los Angeles District superintendent Robert Smith proposing the idea, while Lee recalled broaching the subject with Choi. Regardless of the exact sequence of events, Methodist networks came into play in the 1995 merger. Classmates at Yale Divinity School, Lee and Choi had been well aware of each other's ministries in Southern California under the Methodist umbrella.[42] Choi, a second-generation Korean American, had founded an independent English-language ministry in 1986.[43]

Also writing in the pages of *KoreAm Journal,* Choi penned numerous columns in the early years of the journal, including his take on the future of Korean American ministry. Drawing parallels between the Israelites of the Hebrew Bible with twentieth-century Koreans, Choi traced the journeys of immigrants to their descendants, the 1.5- and second-generation Korean Americans. For these folks, the church would need to generate a diversity of ministries since many 1.5- and second-generation Korean Americans found it difficult to feel at home in the immigrant church. Toward this end, Choi suggested that English ministries needed greater control over their own destiny. The hope was that these individuals would recognize the importance and value of church in their lives. Finally, Choi underscored the need for new biblical models such as the Corinthians and Galatians, who encountered a new faith in a pluralistic setting.[44]

Choi put his vision into practice with the Ascension Ministry, which started out with a small group of mostly second-generation Korean Americans. At first, about twenty to thirty people attended weekly worship and Bible study. Moving from a largely young adult singles congregation, Ascension experienced a watershed of sorts in 1990 when nine to ten members got married. Numbers increased, and a shift took place to a couples- and family-based ministry, although singles continued to be an important part of the church. In 1991, Ascension decided to move to a contemporary worship format with the help of professionally trained musicians within the church. These various factors along with a maturing of the ministry built a momentum. By 1993, there were around ninety adults worshiping at Ascension. Choi considered this to be the peak year of Ascension's independent years. A year later, some staffing changes took place that created an openness to the idea of merger when it arose.[45]

As he recalled, Choi was not interested in the possible merger unless there could be administrative, financial, and programmatic autonomy. These factors were, in many ways, the reason that Ascension was begun. When the congregation considered the move, Choi recounted that in the end a slight majority favored the idea. Many of the core members of the Ascension Ministry, as did Choi himself, had family ties to the LAKUMC. As might be expected, such ties held both pros and cons in terms of a merger. One concern that Choi had for his members was the fact that a quarter of the church was non-Korean with many couples in which one spouse was not Korean.[46]

On the LAKUMC side of the merger, a number of concerns emerged. Because many of the English Ministry members also staffed the youth program, would these folks now no longer be part of helping the joint efforts of the LAKUMC to minister to the youths? Tammy Chung Ryu recalled that it was a very stressful time for members of the LAKUMC, especially those within the English Ministry who wrestled with the issue of a major change with the knowledge that Reverend Lee would no longer be their pastor. Receiving the news of Lee's departure and the need to process a possible merger at the same time proved to be more than a handful for the members of the church.[47]

Leaders within the Korean congregation at the LAKUMC, who were largely supportive of the merger, were not necessarily supportive of the proposed autonomy of the English Ministry. Lee used the analogy of parents having a difficult time letting their children grow into adulthood to describe how some immigrants viewed the autonomy aspect of the merger. It should also be noted that considerable support for the merger among the immigrants had its basis among parents of adult children who were active members of the Ascension Ministry.[48] Although not without struggle and questions on both sides, the merger went through in the spring of 1995 to become effective July 1, 1995.

Choi recalled that as the process began to unfold and merger seemed more of a reality, a joint meeting was held to discuss how the process would unfold. Discussions about such topics as worship style surfaced, and a decision was made to go with the more contemporary format of Ascension since they had an established praise band. Dick Wells, who served as the worship leader of the premerger Ascension Ministry and of the merged Ascension/English Ministry of the LAKUMC (1991–1998), recalled the wonderful mix of choir and praise band in the postmerger era. Although there was a shift to the more band-centered contemporary format, the congregation benefited from the combined strengths of vocal and instrumental talent within the church. Wells, a professional vocalist in demand for session and studio work in the entertainment world of Southern California, had grown up in the church and had always seen involvement in church music as an integral part of his life. The desire for excellence, the high level of musicianship, and the willingness of busy professionals to give of their time and talents are some of the lasting impressions that Wells has of his time with the Ascension Ministry. He credited the Reverend Tom Choi and others in the church for their vision for musical theater and mentioned the staging of *Jesus Christ, Superstar.*[49]

Joint worship of the LAKUMC English Ministry and Ascension began prior to the official start date in July to help both groups transition. For a short while, Choi and Lee led worship services of the newly formed Ascension/English Ministry together. On July 23, 1995, three hundred persons attended a merger celebration. For some of the original Ascension Ministry members, the merger represented a homecoming of sorts, since they had grown up in the LAKUMC. This was especially the case for Choi, whose father, the Reverend Young Yong Choi, had been the senior pastor of the church for twenty-eight years (1953–1981). Tom Choi had been born into the church and had grown up within it. He recalled that the merger had special meaning for him since he, at age thirty-seven, began his duties at the LAKUMC at the same age as his father had many years earlier.[50]

As has been so characteristic of the LAKUMC throughout its history, the merger was a historic event in which two models of English-language ministry came together. As one journalist noted, the merger represented a unique moment within the Korean American community. While so many immigrant churches had a history of internal dissension and splits, the merger represented a coming together. Moreover, because of the multiethnic, multi-racial composition of the original Ascension Ministry, the merger would also suggest the ways in which Korean American–based ministries of the future would need to address issues of identity and community against the incredibly diverse backdrop of Southern California.[51]

As might be expected, the blending together of two separate ministries took some time to work out. Part of the effort to build a sense of community came through various ministries of the church such as small groups. Judy Chung, former associate pastor and coordinator of the Ascension/English Ministry community life, spent much of her tenure at the church (1997–2002) nurturing and overseeing the expansion of small groups. Bible study and fellowship groups have historically played a critical role in the life of the congregation.[52] Like many Methodist churches, the Wesley Group, geared for college-age individuals, provided another important entry point into the life of the church.[53]

In addition to the specific ministries of the LAKUMC, denominational connections contributed to the nurturing of generational change and to the development of future leadership. Writing in the church newsletter in 2000, Chung spoke about her recent participation in the 19th Methodist Transgeneration (TG) Convocation in Atlanta, Georgia. The long-standing annual gathering of Korean American-based ministries within the United Methodist Church helped Chung to ponder both the hopes and the challenges and responsibilities of the Ascension Ministry of the LAKUMC. She noted that despite its struggles, the Ascension Ministry was at the threshold of a revival and new growth. A foundation had been set for the church to experience great things. Because so many English-speaking Korean American congregations within the Methodist fold lacked pastoral leadership, congregations such as the Ascension Ministry had a greater responsibility to utilize the talented people within its midst to help train future leaders for the church as a whole. Chung hoped that Ascension could host a TG intern on an annual basis so that the wider church could benefit from the exciting things taking place.[54]

In fact, Judy Chung had gotten her start at the LAKUMC as a TG summer intern in 1997. That experience confirmed the tug she had been feeling to leave the business world for ministry. Her internship began the start of a five-year stay at the church that included positions on staff as a ministry intern while in seminary. After her graduation, Chung became a full-time member of the staff, leaving the church in 2002 to take a position with the Los Angeles District Office of the California-Pacific Conference of the United Methodist Church. As it has been for many others, the TG Ministry internships and annual convocations have been a critical base for English-language ministry for Korean Americans within and outside of the denomination.[55]

A RECENT CHAPTER

Since 2002, the Reverend Timothy Ellington has been the pastor of the Ascension Ministry of the LAKUMC. His appointment marks another turning point in which a non-Korean is leading a ministry composed of largely Korean Americans. The fact that Ascension is part of the LAKUMC complex that also hosts a Korean immigrant congregation makes the situation an even more interesting one. Of course, non-Korean staff members have been serving in Korean immigrant church contexts for some time, but usually as part of the youth or college-age ministries.

Ellington was in some ways surprised at his appointment to Ascension, since he was unclear what direction he might take after being on an academic fellowship the year after his graduation from Fuller Seminary in Pasadena, California. Prior to seminary, he had worked on staff with a parachurch organization and for a while as a computer technical support person with a bank. He had a field placement experience with a Korean immigrant church, something he explored since his wife, Cindy, is a Korean American. Little did they know at the time that Tim would one day be the pastor for an English-language ministry within a Korean American context. Ellington has adopted a stance of listening and learning from his congregation. He inherits a leadership mantle for a church with good financial resources, a committed core of lay leaders, and a stable membership base that has remained at around one hundred adults for some time now.[56]

Questions remain about what direction the Ascension Ministry might take. Almost every person interviewed has mentioned the challenges of being a commuter congregation and how this fact works as a real barrier to building community among members and being a presence in the neighborhood. Given the very busy lives of so many of the members, Sundays tend to be the primary day of activity for most of the people. Programs on other days of the week have been sparsely attended. Bear Ryu mentioned that the United Methodist structure or system of pastoral appointments has diverted much energy into leadership transitions and adjustments. None of the recent English-language pastors has served for more than five years. While each pastor has brought gifts to the post, the church has had to address leadership changes and differences in vision and style on a repeated basis over the past dozen or so years.[57] In contrast, the rapidly growing English-based ministries among Korean or Asian Americans have often consisted of more stable leadership that has worked with lay members to implement a long-term vision for a given congregation.

David Chun, an active lay leader, echoed what many others have noted. There is a generational layering in the church in which the core and long-term lay leaders are largely those who are in their late thirties and their forties with children. These baby-boomer folks are accompanied by a younger group of those who might be termed Generation Xers. The older group tends to be more 1.5 generation in orientation with deeper ties to the Korean congregation, as many of them either grew up in the church or have had over the years more of a sustained relationship with the immigrant generation. The Generation Xers have fewer such ties to the Korean immigrant side of the LAKUMC.[58]

While categories are often more a shorthand than they are fully accurate, it seems that the future of the congregation will depend in part on how both generational groups of lay leaders and members (and possibly other group-ings) work through guidance and direction of the church. As an autonomous English ministry sharing physical space with a Korean immigrant congrega-tion and the largely European American La Tijera United Methodist Church, the Ascension Ministry points to the creative dimensions of English-language Korean American ministries. Financially secure and with a stable cohort of committed lay leaders of long tenure, the congregation has some good resources at its disposal.

CONCLUSION

From the very beginnings as a Methodist mission in 1904, the LAKUMC has been influenced by denominational structure. While the church was character-ized by a strong sense of Korean American–led clergy and lay leadership, the Methodist ties provided important resources and networks. The merger with the Robertson church enabled the LAKUMC to access much-needed space for growth but also to begin a formal English-language ministry in 1968 that would lay a foundation for the future. The Ascension Ministry, an indepen-dent ministry vision, benefited directly from denominational support, even though the Reverend Tom Choi and other key members had deep roots in the LAKUMC. The later merger, in 1995, between the English-language ministry already located at the LAKUMC with Ascension took place under the Meth-odist umbrella. The current campus of the LAKUMC, the Ascension Ministry, and the La Tijera United Methodist Church in West Los Angeles further testi-fies to the ongoing role of denominationalism for Korean American Protes-tantism.

Historian Timothy Tseng has suggested that Chinese American Protestant-ism experienced a major shift in the post–World War II era from mainline denominations to independent evangelicalism.[59] The argument could be made that Korean American Protestantism has certainly diversified in the post-1965 era, but it is still the case that the two largest denominational connections to

Presbyterians and Methodists remain strong. At the same time, however, the nature of those relations is marked by a certain ambivalence within many congregations, at least in relation to the European American hierarchy that exists. Differences in leadership style and theological orientations, for instance, can create circumstances in which connections among Korean American congregations and leadership exert more influence than the denomination per se. How the second generation will fare in these denominational relations will be something to monitor.

The LAKUMC has dealt with generational change by taking risks in a spirit of intentional experimentation. The English language, of course, has been part of the LAKUMC from the beginning, when there was a mix of Korean and English in the earliest days of mission work with Hugh Cynn and Florence Sherman. That legacy has extended into the very present, as those languages continue to mix and coexist. More than language, however, the creativity that has marked the LAKUMC and generational change suggests the ways in which religious life among Korean American Protestants defies any easy categorization. The variety of ways in which generational change is taking form in leadership, worship styles, congregational structure, and engagement with the world all point to a vitality that is still evolving and that will become markers of this generation. The particular path of the LAKUMC is one example of what can take place, but many other versions are under construction.

The place of denominations and innovation, of course, are not unique to Korean American Protestantism, as variations of these themes have been part of religion in the United States throughout its history. If the case study presented here serves as a reference point to generational change within Korean American Protestantism, then we might ask how it might speak to other related issues. Embedded in the discussion, for instance, is the issue of demographics. The LAKUMC reminds us that the major changes ushered in since 1965 represent not a sea change but rather an extension of racial dynamics in which Asians and Latinos have played and will continue to play a major role both inside and outside the churches. Another issue to ponder is how the presence of groups such as Korean Americans will influence the shape of long-standing denominations, especially as generational change has brought with it a new wave of independent congregations seeking to meet the needs of 1.5- and second-generation men and women who are coming of age.

Answers to these questions remain to be seen, of course, but understanding the past can be an important part of navigating the future. The rich history of the LAKUMC with regard to generational change suggests that denominationalism and a willingness to adapt will be important elements of ministries with a significant Korean American constituency.

NOTES

1. This chapter draws upon a history of the church that I coauthored: David K. Yoo and Hyung-ju Ahn, *Faithful Witness: A Centennial History of the Los Angeles Korean United Methodist Church, 1904–2004* (Seoul: Doosan, 2004).

2. L. George Paik, *The History of Protestant Missions in Korea, 1832–1910* (Pyongyang, Korea: Union Christian College Press, 1929).

3. Allen D. Clark, *A History of the Church in Korea* (Seoul: Christian Literature Society of Korea, 1971); Donald N. Clark, *Christianity in Modern Korea* (Lanham, MD: University Press of America, 1986); Kenneth M. Wells, *New God, New Nation: Protestants and Self-Reconstruction Nationalism in Korea, 1896–1937* (Honolulu: University of Hawaii Press, 1990); Wi Jo Kang, *Christ and Caesar in Modern Korea: A History of Christianity and Politics* (Albany: State University of New York Press, 1997); Chung-Shin Park, *Protestantism and Politics in Korea* (Seattle: University of Washington Press, 2003); James Huntley Grayson, *Korea: A Religious History* (London: Routledge Curzon, 2002), 155.

4. Ho-Youn Kwon, Kwang Chung Kim, and R. Stephen Warner, eds., *Korean Americans and Their Religions: Pilgrims and Missionaries from a Different Shore* (University Park: Pennsylvania State University Press, 2001).

5. I found the following article helpful in thinking through the mission legacy of Korean American Protestantism: Randi Jones Walker, "Lessons for a New America: An Anglo American Reflection on Korean American Church History," in Fumitaka Matsuoka and Eleazar S. Fernandez, eds., *Realizing the America of Our Hearts: Theological Voices of Asian Americans* (St. Louis: Chalice, 2003), 180–99.

6. Typically, "first generation" refers to immigrants, while "second generation" is the term given to the children of immigrants and born in the United States. The category "1.5 generation" (and its many variations on a sliding scale from 1.0 to 2.0) has been used to describe those who were born in Korea but who have experienced significant socialization in the United States. For more on the 1.5 generation, see Won Moo Hurh, "The 1.5 Generation Phenomenon: A Paragon of Korean American Pluralism," *Korean Culture* 14 (1993): 17–27; Kyeyoung Park, "'I Really Do Feel I'm 1.5': The Construction of Self and Community by Young Korean Americans," *Amerasia Journal* 25(1) (Spring 1999): 139–63.

7. A recent book by Antony W. Alumkal, *Asian American Evangelical Churches: Race, Ethnicity, and Assimilation in the Second Generation* (New York: LFB Scholarly Publishing, 2003), provides a helpful review of the existing literature, especially in chapters 1 and 2. Alumkal has published a number of essays on second-generation Asian American Christians, but his book brings much of this work together.

8. To name only two among many texts, see Nancy Foner, Ruben G. Rumbaut, and Steven J. Gold, eds., *Immigration Research for a New Century: Multidisciplinary Perspectives* (New York: Russell Sage, 2000); Jon Gjerde, *Major Problems in American Immigration and Ethnic History* (Boston: Houghton Mifflin, 1998).

9. By no means comprehensive, other studies include Sang Hyun Lee with Ron Chu and Marion Park, "Second Generation Ministry: Models of Mission," in Sang Hyun Lee

and John V. Moore, eds., *Korean American Ministry,* expanded English ed. (Louisville, KY: Presbyterian Church, USA, 1993), 233–55; Kelly Chong, "What It Means to Be a Christian: The Role of Religion in the Construction of Ethnic Identity and Boundary among Second-Generation Korean Americans," *Sociology of Religion* 59(3) (Fall 1998): 259–86; Karen J. Chai, "Competing for the Second Generation: English-Language Ministry at a Korean Protestant Church," in R. Stephen Warner and Judith G. Wittner, eds., *Gatherings in Diaspora: Religious Communities and the New Immigration* (Philadelphia: Temple University Press, 1998): 295–331; Sharon Kim, "Creating Campus Communities: Second-Generation Korean American Ministries at UCLA," in Richard W. Flory and Donald E. Miller, eds., *Gen X Religion* (New York: Routledge, 2000), 92–112; several articles in Ho-Youn Kwon, Kwang Chung Kim, and R. Stephen Warner, eds., *Korean Americans and Their Religions: Pilgrims and Missionaries from a Different Shore* (University Park: Pennsylvania State University Press, 2001) such as Peter Cha, "Ethnic Identity Formation and Participation in Immigrant Churches: Second Generation Korean American Experiences," 141–56, and Karen J. Chai, "Beyond 'Strictness' to Distinctiveness: Generational Transition in Korean Protestant Churches," 157–80; Soyoung Park, "'Korean American Evangelical': A Resolution of Sociological Ambivalence among Korean American College Students," in Tony Carnes and Fenggang Yang, eds., *Asian American Religions: The Making and Re-Making of Borders and Boundaries* (New York: New York University Press, 2004), 182–204; Elaine Howard Ecklund, "Models of Civic Responsibility: Korean Americans in Congregations with Different Ethnic Compositions," *Journal for the Scientific Study of Religion* 44 (2005): 15–28.

10. See Nazli Kibria, *Becoming Asian American: Second Generation Chinese and Korean American Identities* (Baltimore: Johns Hopkins University Press, 2002).

11. Min Zhou, "Coming of Age: The Current Situation of Asian American Children," *Amerasia Journal* 25(1) (Spring 1999): 1–27.

12. For a fuller history of the LAKUMC, see Yoo and Ahn, *Faithful Witness.* For general histories of Korean Americans, see Won Moo Hurh, *Korean Americans* (New York: Greenwood, 1998); Bong-youn Choy, *Koreans in America* (Chicago: Nelson-Hall, 1979); Wayne Patterson, *The Korean Frontier in America: Immigration to Hawaii, 1896–1910* (Honolulu: University of Hawaii Press, 1988); Wayne Patterson, *The Ilse: First Generation Korean Immigrants in Hawaii, 1903–1973* (Honolulu: University of Hawaii Press, 2000).

13. David Yoo interview with Ralph Ahn, June 10, 2003, Los Angeles.

14. *Korean Methodist Church Bulletin,* August 27 and September 10, 1961.

15. Portia Sungsook Choi, "Remembrance by a Minister's Daughter," unpublished manuscript in possession of author.

16. See Yoo and Ahn, *Faithful Witness,* chap. 3.

17. See ibid., chap. 4.

18. David Yoo phone interview with Mrs. Lila Chang, July 14, 2003.

19. See Yoo and Ahn, *Faithful Witness,* chap. 5.

20. I discuss these mergers in David K. Yoo, *Growing Up Nisei: Race, Generation, and Culture among Japanese Americans of California, 1924–1949* (Urbana: University of Illinois Press, 2000), 119–21.

21. David Yoo phone interview with Mr. Fred Gong, July 18, 2003.

22. Ibid.

23. Ibid. Gong's remarkable story, however, also includes a decorated career with the U.S. Air Force as a bombardier during World War II. He was awarded the Distinguished Flying Cross for the thirty-five bombing missions he flew on. Part of his story appears in "Soul Food," *KoreAm Journal* 5 (August 1995): 21. Perhaps even more noteworthy for the members of the LAKUMC, Gong thought, was the fact that he had become caretaker of his ailing mother, who had started to lose her sight and hearing in her thirties. After the death of his father, Gong moved back to Los Angeles from New York to become his mother's full-time caretaker, taking commercial art jobs when he could in order to pay the rent. When Gong's mother died many years later, the then sixty-year-old Gong, who had never married, felt that he wanted some time to himself. Gong left the LAKUMC in the mid-1990s, when age and his deep involvement in community affairs drew him into the heart of the Los Angeles Chinatown. At eighty, Gong is a well-known and loved volunteer who continues to work with people of all ages at the Chinatown Public Library.

24. Annual Charge Conference Report, Robertson Korean United Methodist Church (hereafter cited as Charge Conference), December 1987. Reports located in the files of the church. Thanks to Elder Stuart Ahn and the Reverend Timothy Ellington for making these reports available to us.

25. Charge Conference, 1985 and 1986.

26. Charge Conference, 1987 and 1989.

27. David Yoo interview with Tammy Chung Ryu in Los Angeles, July 13, 2003.

28. Peter T. Cha, "Ethnic Identity Formation and Participation in Immigrant Churches: Second-Generation Korean American Experiences, in Youn-ho Kwon, Kwang Chun Kim, and R. Stephen Warner, eds., *Korean Americans and Their Religions: Pilgrims and Missionaries from a Different Shore* (University Park: Pennsylvania State University Press, 2001), 141–56.

29. For discussions about various models, see Lee, Chu, and Park, "Second Generation Ministry"; Robert D. Goette, "The Transformation of the First-Generation Church into a Bi-Lingual Second-Generation Church," in Kwon et al., eds., *Korean Americans and Their Religions,* 125–40.

30. See Ken Uyeda Fong, *Pursuing the Pearl: A Comprehensive Resource for Multi-Asian Ministry* (Valley Forge, PA: Judson Press, 1999); Paul Tokunaga, *Invitation to Lead: Guidance for Emerging Asian American Leaders* (Downers Grove, IL: InterVarsity Press, 2003).

31. Ellen Lee, *The Planted Seed: History of the English Language Ministry of the Korean Methodist Church and Institute* (New York: Korean Methodist Church and Institute, 1995), 28, 36.

32. David Yoo phone interview with the Reverend Dr. K. Samuel Lee, July 10, 2003.

33. Ibid.

34. Hyung-ju Ahn interview with the Reverend Dr. K. Samuel Lee, Glendale, California, March 3, 2003.

35. Tammy Chung Ryu interview.

36. David Yoo phone interview with Reverend K. Samuel Lee, August 14, 2003. See also Ignacio Castuera, ed., *Dreams on Fire, Embers of Hope: From the Pulpits of Los Angeles after the Riots* (St. Louis: Chalice, 1992); Nancy Abelmann and John Lie, *Blue Dreams: Korean Americans and the Los Angeles Riots* (Cambridge: Harvard University Press, 1995); Robert Gooding-Williams, ed., *Reading Rodney King, Reading Urban Uprising* (New York: Routledge, 1993).

37. http://www.koreamjournal.com/about_us.php. Bear and Tammy Ryu are husband and wife.

38. Rev. Samuel Lee, "Korean American Christians in a Secular American Society," *KoreAm Journal* 5 (July 1990): 28.

39. K. Samuel Lee, "Pros and Cons of English-only Korean American Churches," *KoreAm Journal* 5 (December 1990): 36.

40. Ibid.

41. David Yoo interview with the Reverend Dr. K. Samuel Lee.

42. Ibid.

43. David Yoo phone interview with the Reverend Tom Choi, July 10, 2003. Choi coined the term "Ascension Ministry" as a symbolic reference to not only the resurrection of Jesus Christ but also the rise of the second-generation of Korean Americans.

44. Rev. Tom Choi, "First Generation Koreans Are the New Israelites," *KoreAm Journal* 5 (May 1990): 36.

45. Ibid.

46. Ibid.

47. Tammy Chung Ryu interview.

48. Reverend Dr. K. Samuel Lee interview.

49. David Yoo phone interview with Dick Wells, August 8, 2003.

50. Ibid.

51. Jennifer Jeyoung Jung, "A Different Sort of Church Wedding," *KoreAm Journal* 10 (June 1995): 21.

52. David Yoo phone interview with Reverend Judy Chung, August 12, 2003.

53. Charge Conference, 2001.

54. "A Report from Pastor Judy Chung," *iAM update* 14(9) (September 2000).

55. Chung just ended her term as president of the TG Ministry. For more information, visit their website: www.tgministry.org.

56. David Yoo interview with Reverend Timothy Ellington, Los Angeles, July 23, 2003.

57. David Yoo interview with James "Bear" Ryu, Los Angeles, July 13, 2003.

58. David Yoo interview with David Chun, Los Angeles, August 10, 2003.

59. Timothy Tseng, "Transpacific Transpositions: Continuities and Discontinuities in Chinese North American Protestantism since 1965," in Jane Iwamura and Paul Spickard, eds., *Revealing the Sacred in Asian Pacific America* (New York: Routledge, 2003), 241–71.

Selected Bibliography

Abelmann, Nancy, and John Lie. *Blue Dreams: Korean Americans and the Los Angeles Riots.* Cambridge: Harvard University Press, 1995.

Adams, David Wallace. *Education for Extinction: American Indians and the Boarding School Experience, 1875–1928.* Lawrence: University of Kansas Press, 1995.

Alexander, Bobby C. *Victor Turner Revisited: Ritual As Social Change.* Atlanta: Scholars Press, 1991.

All God's Children International. "Adoption and Relief Services." http://www.allgods children.org/.

Almaguer, Tomas. *Racial Fault Lines: The Historical Origins of White Supremacy in California.* Berkeley: University of California Press, 1994.

Alstein, Howard, and Rita Simon. *Transracial Adoptees and Their Families: A Study of Identity and Commitment.* New York: Praeger, 1987.

Altorki, S., and Fawsi El-Solh, C. *Arab Women in the Field: Studying Your Own Society.* New York: Syracuse University Press, 1988.

Alumkal, Antony W. *Asian American Evangelical Churches: Race, Ethnicity, and Assimilation in the Second Generation.* New York: LFB Scholarly Publishing, 2003.

———. "Race in American Evangelicalism: A Racial Formation Analysis." Paper presented at the American Sociological Association, Chicago, August 18, 2002.

Baden, Amanda L., and Robbie J. Stewart. "The Cultural-Racial Identity Model: Understanding the Racial Identity and Cultural Identity Development of Transracial Adoptees." Unpublished manuscript, 1996, http://www.transracialadoption.net.

Bednarowski, Mary Farrell. *Religious Imagination of American Women.* Bloomington: Indiana University Press, 1999.

Bellah, R. N., R. Madsen, M. W. Sullivan, A. Swidler, and S. M. Tipton. *Habits of the Heart: Individualism and Commitment in American Life.* New York: Harper & Row, 1985.

Berry, Kate A., and Martha Henderson, eds. *Geographical Identities in Ethnic America: Race, Space, and Place.* Reno: University of Nevada Press, 2002.

Bishoff, Tonya, and Jo Rankin, eds. *Seeds From a Silent Tree: An Anthology by Korean Adoptees.* Glendale, WI: Pandal, 1997.

Booth, A., D. R. Johnson, A. Branaman, and A. Sica. "Belief and Behavior: Does Religion Matter in Today's Marriage?" *Journal of Marriage and the Family* 57 (1995): 661–71.

Borshay, Deann. *First Person Plural,* 2000. http://www.pbs.org/pov/pov2000/firstper sonplural/.

Braziel, Jana Evans, and Anita Mannur, eds. *Theorizing Diaspora: A Reader.* Oxford, UK: Blackwell, 2003.

Breton, Raymond. "Institutional Completeness of Ethnic Communities and Personal Relations of Immigrants." *American Journal of Sociology* 70(2) (1964): 193–205.

Brevli, Fara Sultana. "News of the Weird: Specious Normativity and the Problem of the Cultural Defense." *Columbia Human Rights Law Review* 28(3) (1997): 657–83.

Burchinal, L. F. "Marital Satisfaction and Religious Behavior." *American Sociological Review* 22 (1957): 306–10.

Burt, Alfred. "Some Children See Him." Lyrics by Wihla Hutson. New York: Hollis Music, 1951.

Burtchaell, James Tunstead. *The Dying of the Light: The Disengagement of Colleges and Universities from Their Christian Churches.* Grand Rapids, MI: Eerdmans, 1998.

Busto, Rudy V. "The Gospel According to the Model Minority?" *Amerasia Journal* 22(1) (1996): 133–47.

Call, V. R., and T. B. Heaton. "Religious Influence on Marital Stability." *Journal for the Scientific Study of Religion* 36 (1997): 382–92.

Carnes, Tony, and Fenggang Yang, eds. *Asian American Religions: The Making and Remaking of Borders and Boundaries.* New York: New York University Press, 2004.

Carson, Timothy L. *Liminal Reality and Transformational Power.* Lanham, MD: University Press of America, 1977.

Castuera, Ignacio, ed. *Dreams on Fire, Embers of Hope: From the Pulpits of Los Angeles after the Riots.* St. Louis: Chalice, 1992.

Chai, Karen. "Competing for the Second Generation: English Language Ministry at a Korean Protestant Church." In R. S. Warner and J. Wittner, eds. *Gatherings in Diaspora: Religious Communities and the New Immigration,* 295–332. Philadelphia: Temple University Press, 1998.

Chang, Carrie. "Amen. Pass the Kimchee: Why Are Asian Americans on College Converting to Christianity in Droves?" *Monolid: An Asian American Magazine for Those Who Aren't Blinking* 1(1) (2000): 1–9.

Chidester, David, and Edward T. Linenthal, ed. *American Sacred Space.* Bloomington: Indiana University Press, 1995.

Ch'ien, Evelyn. "Spirituality: Evangels on Campus; Asian American College Students Are Making the Grade with God." *A.Magazine: Inside Asian America,* April/May 2000.

Cho, Myung Ji, Jung Ha Kim, Unzu Lee, and Su Yon Park. *Singing the Lord's Song in a New Land: Korean American Practices of Faith.* Louisville, KY: Westminster John Knox, 2005.

Choi, Sook-kyung. "Formation of Women's Movements in Korea: From the Enlightenment Period to 1910." In Sei-wha Chung, ed., *Challenges for Women: Women's Studies in Korea,* 103–26. Seoul: Ewha Women's University Press, 1986.

Chong, Kelly. "What It means to Be Christian: The Role of Religion in the Construction of Ethnic Identity and Boundary among Second-Generation Korean Americans." *Sociology of Religion* 59 (1998): 259–86.

Chong-bae, Mok. "Korean Buddhist Sects and Temple Operations." *Korea Journal* 23(9) (1983): 19–27.

Choy, Bong-Young. *Koreans in America.* Chicago: Nelson Hall, 1979.

Christian World Adoption, Inc. "A Christian International Adoption Agency." http://www.cwa.org/.

Chuh, Kandice, and Karen Shimakawa, eds. *Orientations: Mapping Studies in the Asian Diaspora.* Durham, NC: Duke University Press, 2001.

Chung, Jaesun, and Changmun Kim, eds. *Catholic Korea: Yesterday and Today.* Seoul: Catholic Korea Publishing Co., 1964.

Clark, Allen D. *A History of the Church in Korea.* Seoul: Christian Literature Society of Korea, 1971.

Clark, Donald N. *Christianity in Modern Korea.* Lanham, MD: University Press of America, 1986.

Cohen, Robin. *Global Diasporas: An Introduction.* Seattle: University of Washington Press, 1997.

Collins, Shelia. "Theology in the Politics of Appalachian Woman." In Carol Christ and Judith Plaskow, eds. *Womenspirit Rising,* 152–53, 157. New York: Harper & Row, 1979.

Conway, Jill Ker. *When Memory Speaks: Reflections on Autobiography.* New York: Knopf, 1998.

Cox, Susan Soon-Keum, ed. *Voices from Another Place.* St. Paul, MN: Yeong & Yeong, 1999.

Cummings, Bruce. *Korea's Place in the Sun: A Modern History.* New York: Norton, 1997.

Danico, Mary Yu. *The 1.5 Generation: Becoming Korean American in Hawaii.* Honolulu: University of Hawaii Press, 2004.

D'Antonio, V., W. N. Newman, and S. A. Wright. "Religion and Family Life: How Social Scientists View the Relationship." *Journal for the Scientific Study of Religion* 21 (1982): 218–25.

Das, Veena. *Critical Events: An Anthropological Perspective on Contemporary India.* Delhi: Oxford University Press, 1995.

Dear, Michael J., and Steven Flusty, eds. *The Spaces of Postmodernity: Readings in Human Geography.* Oxford, UK: Blackwell, 2002.

Dearman, Marion. "Structure and Function of Religion in the Los Angeles Korean Community: Some Aspects." In Eui Young Yu, Earl H. Phillips, and Eun Sik Yang, eds. *Koreans in Los Angeles: Prospects and Promises,* 165–83. Los Angeles: Center for Korean-American and Korean Studies, California State University, Los Angeles, 1982.

Deitcher, Eileen. "A Daughter of the Commandment: One Mother's Bat Mitzvah Reflections." *Korean Quarterly* 4(3) (2001): 19.

Deloria, Vine, Jr., and Clifford M. Lytle. *American Indians, American Justice.* Austin: University of Texas Press, 1983.

Dickie-Clark, H. F. *The Marginal Situation: A Sociological Study of a Coloured Group.* London: Routledge & Kegan Paul, 1966.

Dolan, Jay P. *The Immigrant Church.* Baltimore: Johns Hopkins University Press, 1975.

Dorsey, Peter A. *Sacred Estrangement: The Rhetoric of Conversion in Modern American Autobiography.* University Park: Pennsylvania State University, 1993.

Driver, Tom. *The Magic of Ritual: Our Need for Liberating Rites That Transform Our Lives and Our Communities.* San Francisco: Harper San Francisco, 1991.

Ebaugh, Helen Rose, and Janet Salzman Chafetz, eds. *Religion and the New Immigrants: Continuities and Adaptations in Immigrant Congregations.* Walnut Creek, CA: AltaMira, 2000.

Ebaugh, Helen Rose, and Fenggang Yang. "Religion and Ethnicity among New Immigrants: The Impact of Majority/Minority Status in Home and Host Countries." *Journal for the Scientific Study of Religion* 40(3) (2001): 367–78.

Emerson, Michael O., and Christian Smith. *Divided by Faith.* Oxford: Oxford University Press, 2000.

Erickson, Eric. *Childhood and Society* New York: Norton, 1963.

Espiritu, Yen Le. *Asian American Panethnicity: Bridging Institutions and Identities.* Philadelphia: Temple University Press, 1992.

Essed, Philomena, and David Theo Goldberg, eds. *Race Critical Theories,* Oxford, UK: Blackwell, 2002.

Eui Young Yu, Earl H. Phillips, and Eun Sik Yang, eds. *Koreans in Los Angeles: Prospects and Promises.* Los Angeles: Koryo Research Institute, Center for Korean-American and Korean Studies, California State University Press, 1982.

Feagin, Joe R. *Racial and Ethnic Relations.* Englewood Cliffs, NJ: Prentice-Hall, 1989.

Filsinger, E. E., and M. R. Wilson. "Religiosity, Socioeconomic Rewards, and Family Development: Predictors of Family Adjustment." *Journal of Marriage and the Family* 46 (1984): 663–70.

Foner, Nancy, R. G. Rumbaut, and S. J. Gold, eds. *Immigration Research for a New Century: Multidisciplinary Perspectives.* New York: Russell Sage, 2000.

Fong, Ken Uyeda. *Pursuing the Pearl: A Comprehensive Resource for Multi-Asian Ministry.* Valley Forge, PA: Judson, 1999.

Fugita, Stephen S., and Marilyn Fernandez. "Religion and Japanese Americans' Views of Their World War II Internment." Paper presented at the 1999 Association for Asian American Studies Conference, 1999.

Fugita, Stephen S., and David J. O'Brien. *Japanese American Ethnicity: The Persistence of Community.* Seattle: University of Washington Press, 1991.

Gans, Herbert. "Symbolic Ethnicity and Symbolic Religiosity: Towards a Comparison of Ethnic and Religious Acculturation." *Ethnic and Racial Studies* 17(4) (1994): 577–92.

Gerstle, Gary. *The American Crucible: Race and Nation in the Twentieth Century.* Princeton, NJ: Princeton University Press, 2001.

Gjerde, Jon. *Major Problems in American Immigration and Ethnic History.* Boston: Houghton Mifflin, 1998.

Glazer, Nathan. *Affirmative Discrimination: Ethnic Inequality and Public Policy.* Cambridge: Harvard University Press, 1975.

Gleason, Philip. *Contending with Modernity: Catholic Higher Education in the Twentieth Century.* New York: Oxford University Press, 1995.

Glenn, N. D., and M. Supancic. "The Social and Demographic Correlates of Divorce and Separation in the United States: An Update and Reconsideration." *Journal of Marriage and the Family* 46 (1984): 563–75.

Glenn, N. D., and C. N. Weaver. "A Multivariate, Multisurvey of Marital Happiness." *Journal of Marriage and the Family* 40 (1978): 269–82.

Goette, R. D. "The Transformation of a First-Generation Church into a Bilingual Second-Generation Church." In Ho-Youn Kwon and Shim Kim, eds., *The Emerging Generation of Korean Americans,* 237–51. Seoul: Kyung Hee University Press, 1993.

Goldscheider, Frances. "Recent Changes in the U.S. Young Adults Living Arrangements in Comparative Perspective." *Journal of Family Issues* 18 (1997): 708–24.

Gooding-Williams, Robert, ed. *Reading Rodney King, Reading Urban Uprising.* New York: Routledge, 1993.

Gordon, Milton. *Assimilation in American Life: The Role of Race, Religion, and National Origins.* Oxford: Oxford University Press, 1964.

Grayson, James Huntley. *Early Buddhism and Christianity in Korea: A Study in the Explanation of Religion.* Leiden, Netherlands: Brill, 1985.

———. *Korea: A Religious History.* New York: Routledge Curzon, 2002.

Greeley, Andrew M. *The Denominational Society: A Sociological Approach to Religion in America.* Glenview, IL: Scott, Foresman, 1972.

Greer, Anne Wenh-in. "The Asian North American Community at Worship: Issues of Indigenization and Contextualization." In David Ng, ed., *People on the Way: Asian North American Discovering Christ, Culture, and Community,* 147–75. Valley Forge, PA: Judson, 1996.

Hall, David D., ed. *Lived Religion in America: Toward a History of Practice.* Princeton, NJ: Princeton University Press, 1997.

Handlin, Oscar. *The Uprooted.* Boston: Little, Brown, 1951.

Harris, Scott Collins. "Korean Church Growth in America, 1903–1990: History and Analysis." PhD dissertation, South Western Baptist Theological Seminary, 1990.

Hatch, R. C., D. E. James, and W. R. Schumm. "Spiritual Intimacy and Marital Satisfaction." *Family Relations* 35 (1986): 539–45.

Hayashi, Brian Masaru. *"For the Sake of Our Japanese Brethren": Assimilation, Nationalism, and Protestantism among the Japanese of Los Angeles, 1895–1942.* Stanford, CA: Stanford University Press, 1995.

Heaton, T. B. "Religious Homogamy and Marital Satisfaction Reconsidered." *Journal of Marriage and the Family* 46 (1984): 729–33.

Heilbrun, Carolyn G. *The Last Gift of Time: Life beyond Sixty.* New York: Ballantine, 1997.

Herberg, Will. *Protestant, Catholic, Jew.* Garden City, NY: Doubleday, 1955.

———. *Protestant, Catholic, Jew: An Essay in American Religious Sociology.* Chicago: University of Chicago Press, 1983.

Herman, Ellen. "Harry Holt's Dear Friends Letter, 1955." The Adoption History Project, June 22, 2005, http://darkwing.uoregon.edu/~adoption/archive/HoltDear Friendsltr.htm.

Hertig, Young Lee. *Cultural Tug of War: The Korean Immigrant Family and Church in Transition.* Nashville: Abingdon, 2001.

Hill, Peter C., and Ralph W. Hood, eds. *Measures of Religiosity.* Birmingham, AL: Religious Education Press, 1999.

Hofstadter, R., and C. D. Hardy. *The Development and Scope of Higher Education in the United States.* New York: Columbia University Press, 1952.

Holt, Bertha. *The Seed from the East.* Los Angeles: Oxford University Press, 1956.

Holt International Children's Services. "Introduction to Holt." http://www.holtintl .org/intro.shtml.

Hong, S., B. S. Kim, and S. P. Kim. "Adoption of Korean Children by New York Couples: A Preliminary Study." *Child Welfare* 58 (1979): 419–27.

Hsia, Jayjia, and Marsha Hirano-Nakanishi. "The Demographics of Diversity: Asian Americans and Higher Education." *Change: The Magazine of Higher Learning* (November/December 1989): 20.

Hune, Shirley. "Opening the American Mind and Body: The Role of Asian American Studies." *Change* (November/December 1989): 59.

Hunt, R. A., and M. B. King. "Religiosity and Marriage." *Journal for the Scientific Study of Religion* 17 (1978): 399–406.

Hurh, Won Moo. "Comparative Study of Korean Immigrants in the U.S.: A Typological Study." In B. S. Kim et al., eds., *Koreans in America,* 60–99. Montclair, NJ: Association of Korean Christian Scholars in North America, 1977.

———. *Korean Americans.* New York: Greenwood, 1998.

———. "The 1.5 Generation Phenomenon: A Paragon of Korean American Pluralism." *Korean Culture* 14 (1993): 17–27.

———. "Toward a New Community and Identity: The Korean American Ethnicity." In B. S. Kim and S. H. Lee, eds., *The Korean Immigrant in America,* 1–36. Montclair, NJ: Association of Korean Christian Scholars in North America, 1980.

Hurh, Won Moo, and Kwang Chung Kim. "Religious Participation of Korean Immigrants in the United States." *Journal for the Scientific Study of Religion* 29(1) (1990): 19–34.

Iannaccone, Lawrence R. "Risk, Rationality, and Religious Portfolios." *Economic Inquiry* 33(2) (1995): 285–95.

Iwamura, Jane N., and Paul Spickard, eds. *Revealing the Sacred in Asian Pacific America.* New York: Routledge, 2003.

Jacobsen, Matthew Frye. *Whiteness of a Different Color*. Cambridge: Harvard University Press, 1998.

Jeung, Russell. "Asian American Pan-Ethnic Formation and Congregational Culture." In Pyong Gap Min and Jung Ha Kim, eds. *Religions in Asian America: Building Faith Communities,* 215–24. Walnut Creek, CA: AltaMira, 2002.

———. *Faithful Generations: Race and New Asian American Churches*. New Brunswick, NJ: Rutgers University Press, 2005.

———. "A New People Coming Together: Asian American Pan-Ethnic Congregations." PhD diss., University of California, Berkeley, 2000.

Joselit, Jenna Weissman. *Immigration and American Religion*. New York: Oxford University Press, 2001.

Joyce, Patrick D. *No Fire Next Time: Black-Korean Conflicts and the Future of America's Cities*. Ithaca, NY: Cornell University Press, 2003.

Kang, Wi Jo. *Christ and Caesar in Modern Korea: A History of Christianity and Politics*. Albany: State University of New York Press, 1997.

Kemp, Jamie. "Abandoning Disgrace." *Korean Quarterly* 4(2) (2000/2001): 21.

Kerchkoff, Alan, and Thomas McCormick. "Marginal Status and Marginal Personality." *Social Forces* 34 (October 1977): 48–55.

Kibria, Nazli. *Becoming Asian American: Second-Generation Chinese and Korean American Identities*. Baltimore: John Hopkins University Press, 2003.

Kim, Andrew E. "Korean Religious Culture and Its Affinity to Christianity: The Rise of Protestant Christianity in South Korea." *Sociology of Religion* 61(2) (2000): 117–33.

Kim, Claire Jean. *Bitter Fruit: The Politics of Black-Korean Conflict in New York City*. New Haven, CT: Yale University Press, 2000.

Kim, David Kyuman. "Enchanting Diasporas, Asian Americans, and the Passionate Attachment of Race." In Jane N. Iwamura and Paul Spickard, eds., *Revealing the Sacred in Asian Pacific America,* 334–37. New York: Routledge, 2003.

Kim, Eleana, ed. *Guide to Korea for Overseas Adopted Koreans*. Seoul: Overseas Koreans Foundation, 2004.

Kim, Elaine H. "Men's Talk: A Korean American View of South Korean Constructions of Women, Gender, and Masculinity." *Dangerous Women: Gender and Korean Nationalism,* 67–118. New York: Routledge, 1998.

Kim, Elizabeth. *Ten Thousand Sorrows: The Extraordinary Journey of a Korean War Orphan*. New York: Doubleday, 2000.

Kim, Hyung-Chan. *The Korean Diaspora: Historical and Sociological Studies of Korean Immigration and Assimilation to North America*. Santa Barbara, CA: ABC-CLIO, 1997.

Kim, Ilsoo. *New Urban Immigrants: The Korean Community in New York*. Princeton, NJ: Princeton University Press, 1981.

Kim, Jin S. "Jesus the Adoptee: A Contextual Theology of Liberation for the Adoptive Community." *Church of All Nations Discipling for Outreach,* January 16, 2003, http://www.cando.org/resources/sermon.asp?contentid=61.

Kim, Jung Ha. *Bridge-makers and Cross-bearers: Korean-American Women and the Church*. Atlanta: Scholars Press, 1997.

————. "Korean American Protestant Faith Communities in the United States." In Pyong Gap Min and Jung Ha Kim, eds., *Religions in Asian America: Building Faith Communities,* 194. Walnut Creek, CA: AltaMira, 2002.

Kim, Kwang Chung, ed. *Koreans in the Hood: Conflict with African Americans.* Baltimore: Johns Hopkins University Press, 1999.

Kim, Kwang Chung, and Shin Kim. "Ethnic Meanings of Korean Immigrant Churches." Paper presented at Sixty North Park College Korean Symposium, Chicago, October 12, 1996.

Kim, Kwang Chung, Ho-Youn Kwon, and R. Stephen Warner, eds. *Korean Americans and Their Religions: Pilgrims and Missionaries from a Different Shore.* University Park: Pennsylvania State University Press, 2001.

Kim, Sharon. "Creating Campus Communities: Second-Generation Korean American Ministries at UCLA." In Richard W. Flory and Donald E. Miller, eds., *Gen X Religions,* 92–112. New York: Routledge, 2000.

Kim, Yong Choon. "The Nature and Destiny of Korean Churches in the United States." *Journal of Social Sciences and Humanities* 67 (1989): 33–47.

Kim, Rebecca Y. "Negotiating Ethnic and Religious Boundaries: Asian American Campus Evangelicals." In Tony Carnes and Fenggang Yang, eds., *Asian American Religions: The Making and Remaking of Borders and Boundaries,* 141–59. New York: New York University Press, 2004.

Kosmin, Barry A., and Seymour P. Lachman. *One Nation under God: Religion in Contemporary American Society.* New York: Harmony Books, 1993.

Korean Adoptees Ministry. "Welcome to Korean Adoptees Ministry." http://www .kam3000.org.

Korean Buddhist Chogye Order of America, Inc. *Twentieth Anniversary Almanac (1974–1993).* Los Angeles: Sa Chal Temple, 1994.

The Korean Catholic Directory, 1994. Seoul: Catholic Conference of Korea.

Korean Government, National Statistical Office. *Korean Statistical Yearbook,* 43rd ed. Seoul: Korean Government National Statistical Association, 1996.

Kwon, Okyun. *Buddhist and Protestant Korean Immigrants: Religious Beliefs and Socioeconomic Aspects of Life.* New York: LFB Scholarly Publishing, 2003.

————. "Religious Beliefs and Socioeconomic Aspects of Life of Buddhist and Protestant Korean Immigrants." PhD diss., City University of New York, 2000.

Kwon, Victoria H. *Entrepreneurship and Religion: Korean Immigrants in Houston, Texas.* New York: Garland, 1997.

Laid, Jon. "Women and Stories: Restorying Women's Self-Consciousness." In Monica McGoldrick, Carol Anderson, and Froma Walsh, eds., *Women in Families: A Framework for Family Therapy,* 425–50. New York: Norton, 1989.

Lancaster, Lewis R., and Richard K. Payne, eds. *Religion and Society in Contemporary Korea.* Berkeley: Institute of East Asian Studies, University of California, Berkeley, 1997.

Latourelle, Rene, ed. *Vatican II: Assessment and Perspectives,* 3 vols. Mahwah, NJ: Paulist Press, 1989.

Lee, Ellen. *The Planted Seed: History of the English Language Ministry of the Korean Methodist Church and Institute.* New York: Korean Methodist Church and Institute, 1995.

Lee, Jennifer, and Frank D. Bean. "Beyond Black and White: Remaking Race in America." *Context* (Summer 2003): 26–33.

Lee, Ki-baik. *A New History of Korea.* Translated by Edward W. Wagner. Cambridge: Harvard University Press, 1984.

Lee, Sang Hyun. "Called to Be Pilgrims." In S. H. Lee, ed., *Korean American Ministry: A Resourcebook,* 90–120. Louisville, KY: Presbyterian Church, 1987.

———. "Korean American Presbyterians: A Need for Ethnic Particularity and the Challenge of Christian Pilgrimage." In Milton J. Coalter, John M. Mulder, and Louis B. Weeks, eds., *In The Diversity of Discipleship: The Presbyterians and Twentieth Century Christian Witness,* 312–30. Louisville, KY: Westminster John Knox, 1991.

———. "Pilgrimage and Home in the Wilderness of Marginality: Symbols and Context in Asian American Theology." *Princeton Seminary Bulletin,* n.s., 16(1) (1995): 49–64.

Lee, Sang Hyun, Ron Chu, and Marion Park. "Second Generation Ministry: Models of Mission." In Sang Hyun Lee and John V. Moore, eds., *Korean American Ministry,* 233–55. Louiseville, KY: Presbyterian Church, 1993.

Lenski, Gerhard. *The Religious Factor: A Sociological Study of Religion's Impact on Politics, Economics, and Family Life.* Garden City, NY: Doubleday, 1961.

Lewis, I. M. *Ecstatic Religion: An Anthropological Study of Spirit Possession and Shamanism.* New York: Routledge, 2003.

Lien, Pei-te, and Tony Carnes. "The Religious Demography of Asian American Boundary Crossing." In Tony Carnes and Fenggang Yang, eds., *Asian American Religions: The Making and Remaking of Borders and Boundaries,* 38–51. New York: New York University Press, 2004.

Lincoln, C. Eric. *The Black Church in the African American Experience.* Durham, NC: Duke University Press, 1990.

Lipsitz, George. *The Possessive Investment in Whiteness: How White People Profit from Identity Politics.* Philadelphia: Temple University Press, 1998.

Livezey, Lowell W., ed. *Public Religion and Urban Transformation: Faith in the City.* New York: New York University Press, 2000.

Long, Judy. *Telling Women's Lives: Subject/Narrator/Reader/Text.* New York: New York University Press, 1999.

MacIntyre, Alasdair. "The Virtues, the Unity of a Human Life, and the Concept of a Tradition." In Lewis P. Hinchman and Sandra K. Hinchman, eds., *Memory, Identity, Community: The Idea of Narrative in the Human Science,* 241–63. Albany: State University of New York Press, 1997.

Marsden, George M. *The Soul of the American University: From Protestant Establishment to Established Nonbelief.* Oxford: Oxford University Press, 1994.

Matsuoka, Fumitaka, and E. S. Fernandez, eds. *Realizing the America of Our Heart: Theological Voices of Asian Americans.* St. Louis: Chalice, 2004.

McPherson, Miller, Lynn Smith-Lovin, and James M. Cook. "Birds of a Feather: Homophily in Social Networks." *Annual Review Sociology* 27 (2001): 415–44.

Miller, Donald. *Reinventing American Protestantism: Christianity in the New Millennium.* Berkeley: University of California Press, 1997.

Min, Anselm Kyongsuk. "From Autobiography to Fellowship of Others: Reflections on Doing Ethnic Theology Today." In Peter Phan, ed., *Journeys at the Margin,* 135–59. Collegeville, MN: Liturgical Press, 1999.

———. *The Korean Church 2000: Beyond Authoritarianism and Ecclesiocentrism.* Waeguan, Korea: Benedict Press, 2000.

———. "From Tribal Identity to Solidarity of Others: Theological Challenges of a Divided Korea." *Missiology* 27(3) (July 1999): 333–45.

———. "Solidarity of Others in the Body of Christ." *Toronto Journal of Theology* 12(2) (1998): 239–54.

———. *The Spiritual Ethos of Korean Catholicism.* Seoul: Sogang Jesuit University Social Research Institute, 1971.

Min, Anselm Kyongsuk, William E. Biernatzki, and Luke Jin-Chang Im. *Korean Catholicism in the 70's.* Maryknoll, NY: Orbis, 1975.

Min, Pyong Gap. *Caught in the Middle: Korean Merchants in America's Multiethnic Cities.* Berkeley: University of California Press, 1996.

———. "Immigrants' Religion and Ethnicity: A Comparison of Korean Christian and Indian Hindu Immigrants." In Jane Iwamura and Paul Spickard, eds., *Revealing the Sacred in Asian and Pacific America,* 124–42. New York: Routledge, 2003.

———. "The Structure and Social Functions of Korean Immigrant Churches in the United States." *International Migration Review* 26 (1992): 1370–94.

———. "The Structure and Social Functions of Korean Immigrant Churches in the United States." In Min Zhou and James V. Gatewood, eds., *Contemporary Asian America,* 372–91. New York: New York University Press, 1999.

Min, Pyong Gap, and Jung Ha Kim, eds. *Religions in Asian America: Building Faith Communities.* Walnut Creek, CA: AltaMira, 2002.

Mitchell, S., K. Newell, and W. Schumm. "Test-Retest Reliability of the Kansas Marital Satisfaction Scale." *Psychological Reports* 53 (1983): 545–46.

Moore, Barrington, Jr. *Moral Purity and Persecution in History.* Princeton, NJ: Princeton University Press, 2000.

Moore, Robert L. "Ministry, Sacred Space, and Theological Education: The Legacy of Victor Turner." *Chicago Theological Seminary Register* 75(3) (1985): 1–10.

Morrison, Stephen C. "Adoption . . . Isn't It Our Responsibility?" Mission to Promote Adoption in Korea (MPAK), http://www.mpak.com/HomeEnglish.htm.

Mullins, Mark. "Life Cycle in Ethnic Churches in Sociological Perspective." *Japanese Journal of Religious Studies* 14(4) (1987): 321–34.

National Indian Child Welfare Association. Testimony of the National Indian Child Welfare Association regarding proposed amendments to the Indian Child Welfare Act: S 569 and HR 1082, 1997, http://www.nicwa.org/policy/legislation/HR2750/index.asp.

Nichols, J. Randal. "Worship As Anti-Structure: The Contributions of Victor Turner." *Theology Today* 41(4) (1987): 45.

The Official Handbook of the Legion of Mary. Seoul: Catholic Press, 1987.

Official Report of the Nineteenth Annual Conference of Charities and Correction, 1892. Reprinted in Richard H. Pratt, "The Advantages of Mingling Indians with Whites," *Americanizing the American Indians: Writings by the "Friends of the Indian," 1880–1900.* Cambridge: Harvard University Press, 1973.

Okihiro, Gary Y. *Privileging Positions: The Sites of Asian American Studies.* Pullman: Washington States University Press, 1995.

Omi, Michael, and Howard Winant. *Racial Formation in the United States: From the 1960s to the 1980s.* New York: Routledge & Kegan Paul, 1986.

Oparah, Chinyere, Sun Yung Shin, and Jane Jeong Trenka, eds. *Outsiders Within: Racial Crossings and Adoption Politics.* Cambridge, MA: South End Press, 2006.

Oris, Robert A. "Introduction: Crossing the City Line." In Robert A. Oris, ed., *Gods of the City: Religion and the American Urban Landscape,* 1–78. Bloomington: Indiana University Press, 1999.

Pai, Young, Delores Pemberton, and John Worley. *Findings on Korean American Early Adolescents.* Kansas City: University of Missouri School of Education, 1987.

Paik, L. George. *The History of Protestant Missions in Korea, 1832–1910.* Pyongyang, Korea: Union Christian College Press, 1929.

Park, Andrew Sung. *The Wounded Heart of God: The Asian Concept of Han and the Christian Doctrine of Sin.* Nashville: Abingdon, 1993.

Park, Chung-Shin. *Protestantism and Politics in Korea.* Seattle: University of Washington Press, 2003.

Park, Hyung, and Eui Hang Shin. "An Analysis of Causes of Schisms in Ethnic Churches: The Case of Korean American Churches." *Sociological Analysis* 49 (1988): 234–48.

Park, Insook H., J. Fawcett, F. Arnold, and R. Gardner. *Korean Immigrants and U.S. Immigration Policy: A Pre-Departure Perspective.* East-West Population Institute Paper Series, No. 114. Honolulu: East-West Center, 1990.

Park, Kyeyoung. "I Really Do Feel I'm 1.5! The Construction of Self and Community by Young Korean Americans." *Amerasia Journal* 25(1) (1998): 139–63.

———. *The Korean American Dream: Immigrants and Small Business in New York City.* Ithaca, NY: Cornell University Press, 1997.

Park, Sharon. "Generational Transition Within Korean Churches in Los Angeles." Master's thesis, UCLA, 1996.

Park, Soyoung. "Korean American Evangelical: A Resolution of Sociological Ambivalence among Korean American College Students." In Tony Carnes and Fenggang Yang, eds., *Asian American Religions: The Making and RE-Making of Borders and Boundaries,* 184–204. New York: New York University Press, 2004.

Patterson, Wayne. *The Korean Frontier in America: Immigration to Hawaii, 1896–1910.* Honolulu: University of Hawaii Press, 1988.

———. *The Ilse: First Generation Korean Immigrants in Hawaii, 1903–1973.* Honolulu: University of Hawaii Press, 2000.

Portelli, Alessandro. *The Death of Luigi Trastulla and Other Stories: The Form and Meaning in Oral History.* Albany: State University of New York Press, 1991.

Portes, Alejandro, and Ruben G. Rumbaut. *Immigrant America: A Portrait,* 2nd ed. Berkeley and Los Angeles: University of California Press, 1996.

Portes, Alejandro, and Min Zhou. "The New Second Generation: Segmented Assimilation and Its Variants." *Annals of the American Academy of Political and Social Sciences* 530 (1993): 74–96.

Quebedeaux, Richard. *The Young Evangelicals.* New York: Harper and Row, 1974.

Reist, Benjamin. *Theology in Red, White and Black.* Philadelphia: Westminster Press, 1975.

Rhee, Siyon. "Separation and Divorce among Korean Immigrant Families." In Young I. Song and Ailee Moon, eds., *Korean American Women: From tradition to modern feminism,* 151–59. Westport, CT: Praeger, 1998.

Rho, Jung Ja, and Walter R. Schumm. "Components of Family Life Satisfaction in a Sample of 58 Korean/American Couples." *Psychological Reports* 65 (1989): 781–82.

Roberts, Keith A. *Religion in Sociological Perspective.* 3rd ed. Belmont, CA: Wadsworth, 1995.

Robinson, Katy. *A Single Square Picture: A Korean Adoptee's Search for Her Roots.* New York: Berkley Books, 2002.

Roediger, David. *The Wages of Whiteness: Race and the Making of the American Working Class.* London: Verso, 1991.

Rose, Peter I. *They and We: Racial and Ethnic Relations in the United States.* New York: McGraw-Hill, 1997.

Rothschild, Mathew. "Babies for Sale: South Koreans Make Them, Americans Buy Them." *Progressive* 52 (1) (1988), http://modelminority.com/modules.php?name=News&file=article&sid=478.

Saxton, Alexander. *The Rise and Fall of the White Republic: Class Politics and Mass Culture in Nineteenth-Century America.* New York: Verso, 1991.

Scott, James C. *Domination and the Arts of Resistance: Hidden Transcripts.* New Haven, CT: Yale University Press, 1990.

Shehan, C. L., E. W. Bock, and G. R. Lee. "Religious Heterogamy, Religiosity, and Marital Happiness: The Case of Catholics." *Journal of Marriage and the Family* 52 (1990): 73–79.

Shin, Eui Hang, and Hyung Park. "An Analysis of Causes of Schisms in Ethnic Churches: The Case of Korean American Churches." *Sociological Analysis* 49 (1988): 234–48.

Shrinavas, M. N. *Religion and Society among the Coorgs of South India.* New Delhi: Oxford University Press, 1952.

Sisters of St. Paul of Chartres. http://www.spctaegu.or.kr/eng/index.php.

Sloan, Douglas. *Faith and Knowledge: Mainline Protestantism and American Higher Education.* Louisville, KY: Westminister, 1994.

Smith, Andrea. "Soul Wound: The Legacy of Native American Schools." *Amnesty Magazine,* Amnesty International USA, http://www.amnestyusa.org/amnestynow/soulwound.html.

Smith, Timothy L. "Religion and Ethnicity in America." *American Historical Review* 83 (1987): 1155–85.

Sookhee Jung. "Thirty Years of Korean American Catholicism." *Hankook Ilbo* (Los Angeles edition), December 31, 1999, A13.

Spitze, G., and J. Logan. "Sons and Daughters, and Intergenerational Social Support." *Journal of Marriage and the Family* 52 (1990): 420–30.

Stanley, S. M., and H. J. Markman. "Assessing Commitment in Personal Relationships." *Journal of Marriage and the Family* 54 (1992): 595–608.

Stark, Rodney, and William S. Bainbridge. *A Theory of Religion.* New Brunswick, NJ: Rutgers University Press, 1996.

Stark, Rodney, and C. Y. Glock. *American Piety: The Nature of Religious Commitment.* Berkeley: University of California Press, 1968.

Stonequist, Everett V. *The Marginal Man: A Study in Personality and Culture Conflict.* New York: Russell & Russell, 1937.

Straker, James. "Abandonment and Adoption: How Understanding the Journey Is a Gift to the World." *Korean Quarterly* 4(2) (2000/2001): 16.

Sukhwan, Oh. *The Ministry of 2nd Generation in 21st Century: Korean Americans, Arise and Take the Land!* Bellflower, CA: Christian Han-Mi Association, 1999.

Takaki, Ronald. *Strangers from a Different Shore: A History of Asian Americans.* New York: Back Bay Books, 1998.

Tamao, Sharon M. "The Cultural Defense: Traditional or Formal?" *Georgetown Immigration Law Journal* 10(2) (1996): 241–56.

Taylor, Robert J., Jacqueline Mattis, and Linda M. Chatters. "Subjective Religiosity among African Americans: A Synthesis of Findings from Five National Samples." *Journal of Black Psychology* 25(4) (1999): 524–43.

Thomas, D. L., and M. Cornwall. "Religion and Family in the 1980s: Discovery and Development." *Journal of Marriage and the Family* 52 (1990): 983–92.

Thomas, D. L., and G. C. Henry. "The Religion and Family Connection: Increasing Dialogue in the Social Sciences." *Journal of Marriage and the Family* 47 (1985): 369–79.

Tokunaga, Paul. *Invitation to Lead: Guidance for Emerging Asian American Leaders.* Downers Grove, IL: InterVarsity Press, 2003.

Trenka, Jane Jeong. *The Language of Blood: A Memoir.* St. Paul, MN: Borealis, 2003.

Tseng, Timothy. "Transpacific Transpositions: Continuities and Discontinuities in Chinese North American Protestantism since 1965." In Jane Iwamura and Paul Spickard, eds., *Revealing the Sacred in Asian Pacific America,* 241–71. New York: Routledge, 2003.

Turner, Victor. *Dramas, Fields, and Metaphors: Symbolic Action in Human Society.* Ithaca, NY: Cornell University Press, 1974.

———. *The Forest of Symbols: Aspects of Ndembu Ritual.* Ithaca, NY: Cornell University Press, 1967.

———. *From Ritual to Theater: The Seriousness of Human Play.* New York: Performance Art Journal Publications, 1982.

———. "Passages, Margins, and Poverty: Religious Symbols of Communitas." *Worship* 46 (1972): 390–412, 482–94.

———. *Ritual Process: Structure and Anti-Structure.* New York: Aldine, 1969.

U.S. Senate, Special Committee on Aging. *Aging in America: Trends and Projections.* Washington, DC: U.S. Government Printing Office, 1988.

Walker, Randi Jones. "Lessons for a New America: An Anglo American Reflection on Korean American Church History." In Fumitaka Matsuoka and Eleazar S. Fernandez, eds., *Realizing the America of our Hearts: Theological Voices of Asian Americans,* 180–99. St Louis: Chalice, 2003.

Wallin, P. "Religiosity, Sexual Gratification, and Marital Satisfaction." *American Sociological Review* 22 (1957): 300–305.

Warner, Stephen. "Work in Progress toward a New Paradigm for the Sociological Study of Religion in the United States." *American Journal of Sociology* 98 (1993): 1044–93.

Warner, R. Stephen, and Judith G. Wittner, eds. *Gatherings in Diaspora: Religious Communities and the New Immigration.* Philadelphia: Temple University Press, 1998.

Waters, Mary. *Ethnic Options: Choosing Identities in America.* Berkeley: University of California Press, 1990.

Weber, Max. *The Protestant Ethic and the Spirit of Capitalism.* London: Hyman, 1930.

———. *The Sociology of Religion.* Translated by E. Fischoff. Boston: Beacon Press, 1993.

Wells, Kenneth M. *New God, New Nation: Protestants and Self-Reconstruction Nationalism in Korea, 1896–1937.* Honolulu: University of Hawaii Press, 1990.

Williams, Paul. *Mahayana Buddhism: The Doctrinal Foundations.* London and New York: Routledge, 1989.

Williams, Raymond Brady. *Religions of Immigrants from India and Pakistan.* Cambridge: Cambridge University Press, 1988.

Wilson, M. R., and E. E. Filsinger. "Religiosity and Marital Adjustment: Multidimensional Interrelationships." *Journal of Marriage and the Family* 48 (1986): 147–51.

Winant, Howard. *The World Is a Ghetto: Race and Democracy since World War II.* New York: Basic Books, 2001.

Woodrum, Eric. "Religion and Economics among Japanese Americans: A Weberian Study." *Social Force* 64 (1985): 191–204.

Wu, Frank H. *Yellow: Race in America beyond Black and White.* New York: Basic Books, 2002.

Yoo, David, ed. *New Spiritual Homes.* Honolulu: University of Hawaii Press, 1999.

Yoo, David K. *Growing Up Nisei: Race, Generation, and Culture among Japanese Americans of California, 1924–1949.* Urbana: University of Illinois Press, 2000.

Yoo, David K., and Hyung-ju Ahn. *Faithful Witness: A Centennial History of the Los Angeles Korean United Methodist Church, 1904–2004.* Seoul: Doosan, 2004.

Yoon, In-Jin. *On My Own: Korean Businesses and Race Relations in America.* Chicago: University of Chicago Press, 1997.

Yoon, Yi Heum, ed. *The Yearbook of Korean Religions.* Vol. 1. Seoul: Korea Research Institute for Religion and Society, 1993.

Yu, Eui-Young, ed. *Black-Korean Encounter: Toward Understanding and Alliance.* Los Angeles: Institute for Asian American and Pacific Asian Studies, California State University, Los Angeles, 1994.

Yuh, Ji-Yeon. *Beyond the Shadow of Camptown: Korean Military Brides in America.* New York: New York University Press, 2002.

Yung, Judy. *Unbound Voices: A Documentary History of Chinese Women in San Francisco.* Berkeley: University of California Press, 1999.

Zhou, Min. "Coming of Age: The Current Situation of Asian American Children." *Amerasia Journal* 25(1) (Spring 1999): 1–27.

Zhou, Min, and James V. Gatewood. *Contemporary Asian America: A Multidisciplinary Reader.* New York: New York University Press, 2000.

Zhou, Min, Carl L. Bankston III, and Rebecca Kim. "Rebuilding Spiritual Lives in the New Land: Religious Practices among Southeast Asian Refugees in the United States." In Pyong Gap Min and Juhg Ha Kim, eds., *Religions in Asian America: Building Faith Communities,* 37–70. Walnut Creek, CA: Altamira, 2002.

Zia, Helen. *Asian American Dreams.* New York: Farrar, Straus and Giroux, 2000.

Contributors

RUTH H. CHUNG is Associate Professor of Clinical Education and Counseling Psychology at the University of Southern California. She is the author of many journal articles, and her research interests include cross-cultural psychology, Asian American families, and issues of acculturation and identity formation in Asian American communities.

JAE RAN KIM is a writer, teacher, and social worker. She was born in 1968 somewhere around Taegu, South Korea, and was adopted to Minnesota in 1971. Her poems, essays, and articles have been published in the *Star Tribune,* the *Korean Quarterly,* the *Minnesota Monthly, KoreAm Journal,* and the *South End Press.* She currently works for a child welfare agency and is a community faculty instructor at Metropolitan State University.

JUNG HA KIM is Senior Lecturer in Sociology at Georgia State University. She is the author of *Bridge-Makers and Cross-Bearers: Korean American Women and the Church* (1996) and coeditor (with Rita Brock, Kwok Pui Lan, and Seung Ae Yang) of *Off the Menu: Asian American Women's Religion and Theology* (2007).

REBECCA KIM is Assistant Professor of Sociology at Pepperdine University. She is the author of *God's New Whiz Kids? Korean American Evangelicals on Campus* (2006).

SHARON KIM is Assistant Professor of Sociology at California State University, Fullerton. She has published a number of articles and book chapters dealing with her research interests in immigration, religion, and generational formation among Korean Americans.

OKYUN KWON is Social Science Research Analyst at the U.S. Department of Justice. He is the author of *Buddhist and Protestant Korean Immigrants: Religious Beliefs and Socioeconomic Aspects of Life* (2003). His research interests include immigration, religion, crime and deviance, and race and ethnicity.

SANG HYUN LEE is K. C. Han Professor of Systematic Theology and Director of the Asian American Program at Princeton Theological Seminary. He is the author of *The Philosophical Theology of Jonathan Edwards* (1988) and editor of *Writings on Trinity, Grace, and Faith (Works of Jonathan Edwards)* (2003).

ANSELM KYONGSUK MIN is Professor of Religion at Claremont Graduate University. He has most recently written *The Solidarity of Others in a Divided World: A Postmodern Theology after Postmodernism* (2004) and *Paths to the Triune God: An Encounter between Aquinas and Recent Theologies* (2005).

SHARON A. SUH is Associate Professor of World Religions at Seattle University. She is the author of *Being Buddhist in a Christian World: Gender and Community in a Korean American Temple* (2004).

SUNG HYUN UM is the founder of Family Building Ministries in Southern California. He received his PhD from Fuller Theological Seminary.

DAVID K. YOO is Associate Professor of History, Claremont McKenna College and Core Faculty, Intercollegiate Department of Asian American Studies, at the Claremont Colleges. He is the author of *Growing Up Nisei* (2000) and editor of *New Spiritual Homes* (1999).

Index

The University of Illinois Press
is a founding member of the
Association of American University Presses.

Composed in 10.5/13 Times Roman
with Palatino display
by BookComp, Inc.
for the University of Illinois Press
Manufactured by Cushing-Malloy, Inc.

University of Illinois Press
1325 South Oak Street
Champaign, IL 61820-6903
www.press.uillinois.edu